LOST TREASURE SHIPS

Lost Treasure Ships

OF THE NORTHERN SEAS

❧

A Guide and Gazetteer to 2000 Years of Shipwreck

Nigel Pickford

CHATHAM PUBLISHING
LONDON

MBI PUBLISHING COMPANY
MINNESOTA

First published in Great Britain in 2006 by
Chatham Publishing
Lionel Leventhal Ltd,
Park House, 1 Russell Gardens,
London NW11 9NN

Distributed in the United States of America by
MBI Publishing Company
Galtier Plaza, Suite 200, 380 Jackson Street,
St Paul, MN 55101-3885, USA

British Library Cataloguing in Publication Data
Pickford, Nigel
Lost treasure ships of the northern seas: a guide and gazetteer to 2000 years of shipwreck
1. Shipwrecks – North Atlantic Ocean
2. Scuba diving – North Atlantic Ocean – Guidebooks
3. Underwater archaeology – North Atlantic Ocean – Case studies
I. Title
910.9'1633

ISBN-13: 9781861762504
ISBN-10: 186176250X

ISBN 1 86176 250 X

Designed and Typeset by Roger Daniels
Printed and bound in China

Contents

Author's Acknowledgements

I would particularly like to thank Stuart Bacon, Lyle Craigie-Halkett, Bob Hickson, Herbert Linkesch, Aaron Playle and John Rose for their help with this book. I would also like to thank the staff at the many archives and libraries where I have worked for their invaluable assistance.

Picture Credits

National Maritime Museum, London: pages 10, 19, 27, 45, 47, 52, 57, 67, 69, 72, 87, 88, 89, 92, 102, 104, 125, 126, 137, 139, 143, 158, 172, colour plates GOLDEN LION and DUNWICH BANK WRECK

Bob Hickson: page 11

Whitstable Museum: page 15

British Museum: pages 18, 21, 28, 30, 31

Stuart Bacon: pages 37, 39, 41, 42, 44, 30 58, 60, 61

National Library of Scotland, Edinburgh: pages 49, 51

US Naval Academy Museum, Annapolis: pages 63, 93, 97, colour plate CARLISLE

Kalmar Lans Museum, Sweden: pages 76-7, 83, 84, colour plate KRONAN

Zeeuws Maritiem muZEEum, Vlissingen: pages 105, 107, 108 (bottom right), colour plate VLIEGEND HERT

John Rose: pages 108-9 (except 108 bottom right)

National Board of Antiquities, Finland: pages 113, 114, 115, 117, colour plate VROUW MARIA

Beverley R. Robinson Collection, Annapolis: page 119, colour plate BONHOMME RICHARD

Aaron Playle: pages 159, 170

David F. Krawczwyk: page 174

Martin Cahill: page 181

Other illustrations from author's collection and public-domain sources.

Introduction

T HE TERRITORIAL DEFINITION OF 'Northern Seas' used for this book comprises the waters which include the North Sea and the Baltic Sea but exclude the English Channel, the seas to the west of the Shetlands and those off the western coast of Norway. The selected region contains a number of particularly treacherous areas for shipping. The most notorious navigational hazard is probably the Goodwin Sands at the southern entrance, but the sandbanks off Yarmouth have claimed almost as many victims as the Goodwins, and the shifting sands off the coast of Holland, which stretch from the Terschelling southwards to Vlissingen, have proved equally voracious of human life, ships and cargoes. There are numerous other navigational difficulties, however, apart from those posed by the sandbanks. The Jutland coast of Denmark is particularly dangerous for ships caught on a lee shore during one of the fierce north-westerly gales that frequently blow there. The narrow waterway of the Kattegat makes entry into the Baltic difficult to negotiate. Bornholm Island, straddling the seaway between Germany and Sweden, has witnessed countless vessels pile up on its shores. The fogs that shroud the Orkneys and Shetlands have resulted in large numbers of ships striking the surrounding reefs. Even more bewildering to the seaman must be the myriad of tiny islands that fringe the south-west coast of Finland, a constant risk to shipping heading up the Baltic to Helsinki, Tallin or St Petersburg. In many places, such as through the Pentland Firth or off the estuary of the River Elbe, currents can run at a terrifying eight kilometres an hour playing havoc with a ship's positioning. In the northern parts of the region the waves, during the frequent winter gales that beset the area, can reach twenty-five to thirty metres in height. It was not for nothing that the Romans regarded the North Sea as the worst place in the world for storms.

For at least the last 2,000 years the North Sea and the Baltic have also comprised one of the busiest shipping highways of the world. Trade between the British Isles and the Continent, until the second half of the last century, was of necessity almost entirely conducted by water. But it was not just Britain's island status that made the North Sea such a vital conduit for trade. Before the advent of the railway opened up the hinterlands of central Europe it was the North Sea that provided part of the waterway between Southern and Northern European countries. Until the late nineteenth century overland travel was generally regarded as slower, more dangerous and more expensive than transport by sea. Even after the railway became dominant a nation such as Germany with its rapidly expanding shipping industry still needed to use the North Sea as its main exit to the Americas. In view of all this maritime activity it is hardly surprising that so many of Europe's largest ports such as London, Antwerp, Amsterdam, Harwich, Hamburg, Edinburgh, St Petersburg and Stockholm all face this larger North Sea area.

By far the greatest part of the trade that has flowed through the region has been in the form of bulk commodities such as wood from Scandinavia, coal from Britain, fish from the great herring fisheries off Scotland, wheat from the eastern Mediterranean, and today, of course, pre-eminently oil. There has, however, also, until very recently, been a small-in-volume, but high-in-value, movement of precious metals facilitating the much larger trade in goods. Much has been said and written about the transatlantic shipments of gold and silver from the Americas to Spain between the sixteenth and the nineteenth centuries. What is less well known is that much of the gold and silver

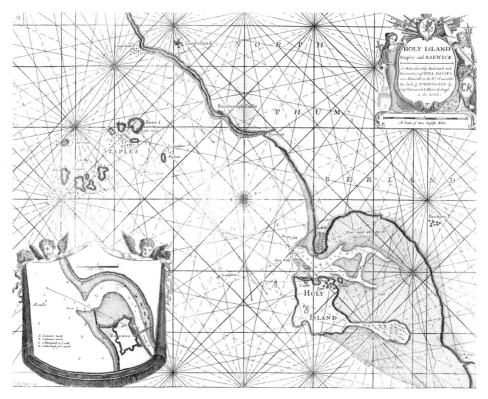

Historical charts help to establish old place names that might be mentioned in contemporary accounts of shipwrecks. This Greenville Collins chart was published in 1693 and shows the Northumberland coast around 'Barwick' (Berwick-on-Tweed). Note that the top of the chart is South.

that was imported into Spain during this period was later shipped from Cadiz and Lisbon on behalf of merchants based mainly in London, Hamburg, Antwerp and Amsterdam. Merchant ships of various national flags, although the majority were British or Dutch, were used to carry these precious cargoes northwards from the Iberian peninsular. During the eighteenth century in particular British warships were used to carry Spanish gold and silver across the Bay of Biscay and into northern Europe. A Law Report in *The Times* for 26 December 1787 carried the following throwaway remark, 'There is hardly a King's ship coming from Lisbon which does not carry bullion', which makes clear the wide extent of the practice. It was not strictly permitted for the captain of a Royal Navy ship to undertake these private shipments of bullion, but it was a valuable and much-coveted perk of the job, and one that the Admiralty was not really prepared to stamp out as it might have had repercussions on their ability to recruit.

In addition, particularly during the seventeenth century, there was a constant onward flow of Spanish silver and gold from the great maritime trading nations such as Britain and Holland to Russia, Sweden and the other smaller nations bordering the Baltic for the purchase of much needed raw materials such as wood, tar and iron. The shipment of precious metals was the most convenient way of balancing the books. There were also other subsidiary routes across the North Sea along which gold and silver regularly flowed. One of the most important was that between Holland and Britain. In the second half of the seventeenth century a regular and semi-official packet service was established between Harwich and Helvoet Sluice. The primary purpose of it was the carriage of post but it was often used also for the transmission of gold and other valuables. The ships employed were relatively small, about 120 tons burthen, and carried sixteen or eighteen light guns. A similar important packet route existed between London and Edinburgh, and again the ships used were lightly gunned and designed for speed rather than the carriage of bulk cargo. Inevitably, between two such important financial centres, gold and silver frequently formed part of the cargo carried.

Periods of war have always resulted in the urgent transportation of specie, either away from an enemy threat or towards an army that requires payment, and the North Sea and Baltic Sea down the centuries have witnessed their fair share of conflict. From the late sixteenth century to the mid-seventeenth century Spain was constantly shipping treasure to its army in the Spanish Netherlands which was engaged in war with the United Provinces of Holland. A number of these ships came to grief, in particular those caught up in the great armada of 1639. The Napoleonic Wars resulted in Britain making exceptional movements of bullion back and forth to the Continent in ships such as the *Lutine* and the *Guernsey Lily*, both of which were wrecked. During World War I an exceptional shipment of gold appears to have been made to Russia in the armoured cruiser *Hampshire* which was blown up off the Orkneys. In World War II the evacuation of gold out of Holland resulted in the loss of *Pilot Boat 19* (see the entry in the wreck listings at the end of the book). The list of wartime casualties is not exactly endless but it is certainly considerable.

Perhaps the most significant category of ship that can reasonably be classed as a treasure ship, large numbers of which transited the North Sea during the seventeenth and eighteenth centuries, is that of the East Indiamen. The majority of outward-bound East Indiamen carried bullion cargoes and many of the returning ships carried valuables such as porcelain and precious stones. The routes taken by these East Indiamen of all nations, with the exception of the French, involved entry and exit to and from the North Sea, both around the north of Scotland, as well as along the English Channel and through the southern entrance. Only the English East India Company used the southern entrance exclusively. Most of the Western European nations that border the North Sea have had their own East India fleets at one time or another. Pre-eminent in this sphere were the Dutch and the British, but the Swedish, Danish and Germans have also had significant East India fleets. The total number of losses of East India Company ships in the North Sea area alone is in the region of one hundred.

Another type of ship that has been accorded treasure-ship status in these pages is the warship that was known to be carrying 'brass' cannon. With individual ornately wrought guns fetching up

The biggest ships in most merchant marines were East Indiamen, long-distance traders with India and the Far East, which also tended to carry the most valuable cargoes. This is the British *Thames* of 1819, one of the largest at 1400 tons.

to £50,000 a piece it is evident that those wrecks that contain large quantities of such cannon represent considerable potential value. A significant number of ships furnished with brass armaments were lost in the North Sea during the three Anglo-Dutch wars of the seventeenth century and also in the Baltic as a result of the Swedish, Danish and Russian wars of the same period.

It should be emphasised at the outset that this book is not intended as an invitation to divers to set out in rubber dinghies, or more sophisticated vessels, and plunder the shipwrecks of the North and Baltic Seas. Not only are there clear issues of personal safety involved but all wrecks are covered by complex legislation. The legal framework differs from nation to nation and also depends on whether the wreck is found in national or international waters. In Britain, for instance, wrecks that lie within territorial waters are covered by The Merchant Shipping Act 1894 (amended 1994) which mainly concerns itself with salvage rights, the Protection of Wrecks Act 1973 designed to protect wrecks of historical importance, and the Protection of Military Remains Act 1986 which is primarily concerned with war graves. Wrecks that lie outside the twelve-mile territorial limit can still come under the British legal regime of the various acts if the people concerned in the salvage are British citizens or the objects recovered are brought onto British land. The recovery of objects from historic wrecks is not necessary illegal but it only should be carried out with official sanction, professional archaeological support and expert legal advice.

It is the intention of this book, however, that it should stimulate curiosity about a variety of historic periods that are encapsulated by particular shipwrecks. For that reason in the first part as wide a variety of shipwreck as possible has been selected. Part of the fascination of shipwrecks is that they are by their very nature extremely precise and finite events and yet they lead out into much wider areas of enquiry. On one level a shipwreck poses a set of detailed but limited questions. The

It is not often a wreck can be identified by such an incontrovertible piece of evidence as the ship's bell. This is from the steamer *Alster* sunk in a ramming accident off Great Yarmouth in June 1881.

most fundamental of these, and also often one of the most difficult to solve, is, where exactly did it sink? Clues can exist in a variety of sources. Sometimes the log book of the ship itself survives the sinking having been taken off by one of the surviving officers. There are also often extant log books of other ships that were sailing in company, or, if it was a war loss, then the log books of other ships involved in the same battle. There can be courts of enquiry and, where admiralty ships are concerned, courts martial. Sometimes passengers as well as officers provide useful reports that survive in letters, diaries, memoirs or in newspaper accounts. Contemporary weather and tidal reports are vital in establishing a ship's probable last movements. Historical charts help to establish old place names that might be mentioned in the various contemporary accounts. Modern-day information from fishermen on net snags in the likely area of sinking can also provide useful investigative information of a different kind. The number of potential sources is almost as great as the variety of forms of written and spoken discourse. But accurate positional information is far from being the only issue. There is also the question of what did the ship look like, what were its dimensions, how was it fitted out, what armaments did it carry. Sometimes original ships' plans still exist, but more usually it is a matter of working from contemporary paintings, drawings, photographs and all the miscellaneous technical data that survives in shipping company archives and public record offices. Without a good understanding of the construction of the ship it can be very difficult to identify the right wreck. The nature of the cargo carried and how and where it was stowed is another whole area of enquiry. Then there is the often elusive issue of what, if any, salvage may have taken place, both official and unofficial, in the intervening years between the original sinking and the latter-day rediscovery.

If a ship that is lost also happens to be a treasure ship then there is an added layer of mystery and obfuscation that requires unravelling and, for myself, this is what makes this category of shipwreck particularly fascinating. How much treasure, if any, was really on board? Was the sinking an insurance scam or possibly a fraud committed by unscrupulous salvors on gullible investors? Who owned the treasure, what was its purpose and where was it going? Where in the ship would it have been carried? Has some of it or all of it been recovered since the ship went down? Occasionally the answers to these questions are straightforward. Usually they are not.

These are all very precise and relatively technical problems. But the researching of a shipwreck is always much more than the assembling of a fact sheet. It is also the reconstruction of a human tragedy. A large part of the fascination of any shipwreck lies in trying to discover the stories of the people involved. What were they like, what kind of lives did they lead, what sort of world did they exist in, how did they connect to the larger political and social processes of their time.

The second half of the book provides brief details on a large number of ships that can reasonably be classified as treasure ships. It does not claim to be exhaustive or definitive. The number of potential sources for shipwreck information is virtually endless. Nor does it claim that all the facts presented are necessarily accurate, though reasonable care has been taken to try and ensure that as few mistakes as possible have crept in. One constant reason for possible error, that is difficult to eradicate, is that different authorities state different things. There is frequently no consensus about the truth. This is also, of course, part of what makes shipwreck research fascinating. It is constantly necessary to assess the likely validity of any particular source. It is hoped that this second half will be a useful starting point for the reader's own further research. It is far from being the last word on the matter.

1

The Secret of
Pudding Pan Shoal

ROUND THE BEGINNING OF THE 1770S there was great excitement among the learned antiquarians of England on the discovery that Roman earthenware dishes were regularly being dredged up from the mouth of the River Thames by the oyster fishermen of North Kent. This was an age when gentlemen of education liked to fill their collecting cabinets with relics of previous civilisations and for this purpose fine examples of Roman remains were particularly treasured items. In the summer of 1773 a certain Mr Boyce, who was working as a surgeon at Sandwich, showed his friend, John Pownall, who was employed by the Excise, some examples of the pottery that he had acquired from the local fisherfolk. What made the finds rather special was that they included many unbroken pieces. Boyce informed his friend that they had been taken up 'near the entrance of Whitstable Bay'.

The enterprising John Pownall promptly took himself off to Whitstable and in conversation with an old fisherman was told that large numbers of these Roman pots and pans had been discovered and were now in general domestic use by the locals. Most of them were reddish in colour but occasionally a black one was found made from a finer clay, but these were more likely to be in a broken condition. According to the fisherman all these finds came from one particular place which he described as being 'two or three leagues from the shore. . . and well known to the fishermen by the name of Pudding Pan Sand or Rock'. They had been picked up on various occasions but were particularly numerous after periods of 'tempestuous weather'.

The names Pan Sand, Pan Speck and Pan Shoal together with Pudding Pan Rock were soon laid down on the sea charts of the entrance to the Thames and have continued to

Most of the Roman finds off Whitstable have been randomly caught in the nets of oyster dredgers, making precise location of the source extremely difficult.

appear there, albeit somewhat sporadically, and in a variety of other locations, like the pots themselves, ever since. It seems highly probable that the use of the word 'pan' to describe these various seabed features was a direct result of the Roman pans that were being picked up in their vicinity. One of the best early charts first to show the shape and extent of these sands and shoals is that drawn in 1794 by James Grosvenor, a River Thames pilot, with the assistance of James Bean, master of the Nore Buoy yacht. Both men were well placed to know the exact location of Pudding Pan Rock.

John Pownall's curiosity was thoroughly aroused. He hired the old fisherman to take him to the exact spot where the pots were being dredged up and, in Pownall's own words, 'found it to lie at the entrance of a channel at the back of Margate Sand, now known by the name of Queen's Channel, and about two leagues from the coast'. He went on to add, 'the extent of the shoal I could not exactly judge of, but conceived by the soundings about it, that it was not much larger than the hulk of a moderate sized ship, having upon it about nine feet at low water, and about three fathom all around it.'

He was well rewarded for his day's work. They picked up three 'entire pans' of what was described as red-coloured Samian ware. They also found fragments of the darker, finer earthenware referred to as Tuscan Brown. In addition they pulled up a large concretion of stones weighing the best part of a hundredweight that Pownall thought to be an example of early Roman brickwork. This latter find was to give rise to much confusion and learned debate for the next hundred years and more.

It is obvious from John Pownall's description of the shoal from where the pots were picked up that he thought he was dealing with a shipwreck. He actually makes the connection between the shoal and 'the hulk of a moderate sized ship'. His brother, however, Thomas Pownall, a retired Governor of Massachusetts, was quick to elaborate his own theory on the source of the pots. He thought the 'Roman brickwork' that his brother had hauled up out of the sea was evidence of the remains of a pottery factory that the Romans had established in the Thames estuary at that point. He also suggested that the master of the factory had been a certain M. Atillianus because his was the name stamped on the base of the recovered pots. He went public with his theory in the pages of *Archaeologia* in 1778. *Archaeologia* was a newly established learned journal where these matters of ancient history were aired for the benefit of like-minded scholars.

The research and speculations of the Pownall brothers received short shrift from their fellow antiquarians in subsequent editions of *Archaeologia*. E. Jacob writing in the next edition published in 1782 took the Pownalls to task for failing to distinguish between Pudding Pan Rock and Pudding Pan Sand, 'distant from each other above three miles'. He went on to make the following all-important distinction. 'The Pan Sand is close to and forms the North side of the Queen's Channel, consists entirely of sand, becomes dry for some part of every tide, and is never dredged upon by our fishermen. Pan Pudding Rock is never dry, and is conjectured to be in length near half a mile and in width about thirty perches (165 yards). . . lies almost East West and is right in the passage from the Narrows or the Woolpack to the buoy of the Spaniards.' He added that it is 'well known to our fishermen as it affords plenty of oysters'. The implication of this was clear. John Pownall must have picked up his pottery pieces from the Rock, not the Sand. The Excise man was also, in Jacob's opinion, completely out in his measurements when he described the shoal as being about the size of the 'hulk of a moderate sized ship'. Jacob's greatest expressions of derision, however, were reserved for Governor Thomas Pownall's theories about there having once been a pottery works on the shoal. He found the idea preposterous that the Romans would ever have established a factory in such a remote and awkward place. He also claimed that he had pieces in his own collection that had been taken up from the sea as long ago as about 1720.

The arguments rumbled on down the centuries as such arguments often do. In 1861, for instance, a Mr J. Brent wrote a defence of Thomas Pownall's factory theory in the *Journal of the Proceedings of the Society of Antiquaries of London*. There was much discussion about whether or not the original coastline might not have been four or five miles further north than it was at present, placing the putative factory on the mainland rather than on a tiny island in the middle of the Thames Estuary. It was not until the archaeologist R. A. Smith carried out his exhaustive analysis of all the extant pieces of recovered pottery he could lay his hands on in the early years of the twentieth century that the debate was finally resolved. Smith listed over twenty different potter's names stamped on the base of the wares that had been recovered, thus disproving once and for all Thomas Pownall's theory that all the pots had been produced under the direction of a single master potter called Atillianus. Atillianus was actually responsible for only

The earthenware relics all date to the period 160-200 AD and originate from the Lezoux region of Central France. These examples are now in the Whitstable Museum.

eighteen of nearly 200 pots that Smith examined. More significantly all the potters on the list were known to have been based in the factories of the Lezoux region in central France. The knowledge that all the pots originated from the same small district in France, famous for its production of Roman earthenwares, made it indisputable that this was not a factory on Pudding Pan Rock but a shipwreck. The Lezoux potteries flourished between 50 and 260 AD but Smith was able to date the wreck as being most probably between 160 and 200 AD. The pots lack the floral decoration that was a common feature of the early period of Lezoux. It also seems probable that the Pudding Pan ship set out from the port of Boulogne as this was a common point of departure for ships coming from France to London at this period.

With the publication of Smith's findings interest in the Pudding Pan wreck was running high again and a number of local worthies got together to fund a new investigation to see whether or not the wreck could be located. A certificated diver by the name of Hugh Pollard was commissioned to undertake the work. His subsequent report is so lucid and practical that it is well worth quoting at length, as much for what it tells us about the difficulties of this kind of operation as it does about the seabed and the wreck itself.

On receiving your instructions I went down to Whitstable and commenced operations on Wednesday, 22nd April, having chartered the fishing smack *Grace Stuart*, 16 tons, Captain George Frend, and arranged for hire of diving-dress, air pumps, and all necessary gear previously. I chose Whitstable as a base for the following reasons: the local boatmen know the ground and bearings perfectly; suitable boats can be obtained there cheaply; and Herne Bay, though two miles nearer, would be less easy to start from, and prices would be almost double. Wednesday was quite fine, with very little breeze at flood tide, dropping to dead calm on the ebb. I took bearings from the chart and sounded for the actual rock. This (as charted) the Captain and crew declared was non existent, the lowest water at extreme low tides being 2.5 fathoms. After a prolonged search with different bearings, I was forced to admit that nowhere was there any variation in the bottom to the extent of two fathoms. I then inquired where the last pot was dredged up, and found that it was in a water lane in the direct line of the Girdler light on Reculver, about 1 mile North of the rock as charted. The bottom here, as elsewhere, was cement stone. This stone has nothing whatever to do with building material (as stated by previous explorers), and is merely the local name. I ordered the dredges out, and, working four dredges only, brought up stones, shells, etc. but there were no indications of building material or pottery. Thursday was fine, and coming nearer land I dredged, and went down in those places where the currents would be likely to deposit pots, but without success, the mud having been so stirred up that at two and a half to three fathoms nothing could be seen further than two feet away. Also the tide induces strong currents that are a great hindrance to any accurate investigation. Friday was too stormy, owing to North East winds and snow blizzard, for me to leave the roadstead. On Saturday I put out, but the sea was so rough that I was forced to return. Monday was moderately calm at high tide, and I managed to work two tides, being out from ten to seven o'clock. I dredged most of the time, the mud being still stirred up, and found at three widely distant sites one thick fragment of pottery (off Swalecliffe Chimney) and two small red fragments (about a mile apart, off the Pan Sands). Tuesday I put off, but

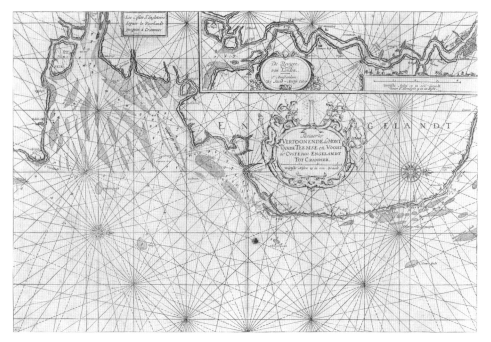

Dutch cartographers were the first to map in detail the sandbanks of the southern North Sea,
but this 1669 map of the Thames estuary does not show Pudding Pan.

was obliged to return owing to the rough weather. If tiles about 18 inches by 12 inches are
found (as they have been), I should think they would mark the site of the wreck, but the scour
of the tides rolls the pottery too far to make certain of its original position. If suitable
conditions prevailed it might be possible to locate the wreck, and a large amount of stuff
would probably remain, as it is only when the South wind prevails that the bottom is soft
enough for it to wash out. In North or East winds it sets hard like stiff sand. . .

Pollard's frustrations will be painfully familiar to most divers that have experience of looking for
wrecks in the North Sea area. It is a business beset by bad weather, poor visibility and charts that
do not seem to reflect accurately the topography of the seabed. All the same his explorations
were not without their achievement. The business of Roman brickwork having been pulled out
of the sea by John Pownall was finally laid to rest. The brickwork was almost certainly nothing more
than a conglomerated mass of naturally occurring stones cemented together by an equally natural
process of concretion. Other theories about Roman-built pottery factories, lighthouses or navigational marks all began to look rather fanciful. But as for pinpointing the wreck itself, which was
the real purpose of the expedition, the prospect for that seemed further away than ever. Not only

did Pollard find fragments of the pottery at some distance from the previously supposed wreck site of Pudding Pan Shoal, and at some distance from each other, but the shoal itself has disappeared. Charts from the late eighteenth century and right down throughout the entirety of the nineteenth century all show a shoal or rock very much where Jacob said it was in his article of 1782, that is in a direct line between the Woolpack Sand and the Spaniard Sand. The size of it as laid down was generally consistent with Jacob's measurements, that is half-a-mile by 165 yards, although the orientation tended to be north-south rather than east-west as described by Jacob. As far back as the late seventeenth century a Dutch chart uses the word 'Pan' to describe the presence of an obstruction in the same general area, incidentally casting doubt on J. Pownall's theory that the pans had only started turning up since 1755. By the beginning of the twentieth century, however, the obstruction appears to have disappeared entirely. It is significant that soon after Pollard's failure to locate the rock the shoal was dropped from the official admiralty charts, even though the name Pudding Pan Rock continues to be applied at the place where the shoal was once located. Clearly there never was a large single rock of the dimensions mentioned by Jacob. The most likely explanation is that there was a raised area of seabed, which included in its make-up a large number of cement boulders. It appears that since Pownall's original investigations this raised area has become erased by a build-up of surrounding sand, thus levelling out any sharp alteration of depth. It is interesting to note that despite Pollard's failure to find a distinct Pudding Pan Shoal as such, his

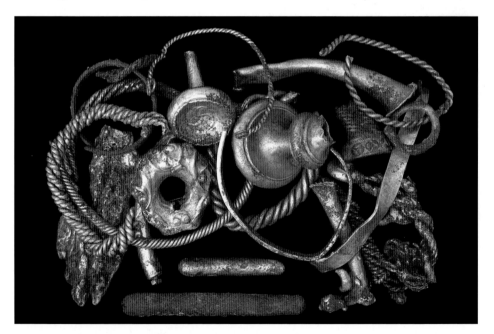

Part of a hoard of elaborate gold jewellery found at Snettisham in Norfolk and dating from the first century BC. Celtic gold objects were highly-prized and much traded, even before the Roman invasion of Britain.

Caesar's invasion of
Britain as envisaged by
the artist Harold Wyllie.

faith in the existence of the wreck was not diminished. He was also confident that if the wreck could be found it would probably still be largely intact and contain 'a large amount of stuff'. It remained a tantalising prospect.

The history of trade between the islands of Britain and the Continental mainland goes back more than a millennium before the birth of Christ. Shipwrecks in Langdon Bay (Kent) and Salcombe (Devon) testify to metal trading across the channel during the Middle Bronze Age (1200–1100 BC). It is hardly surprising then that from well before 100 BC Britain should be renowned as a potentially valuable source of raw materials and a desirable trading partner. The Roman geographer Strabo, writing at the end of the first century BC, details the attractions of trade with the island. Exports from Britain included grain, cattle, gold, silver, iron, hides, slaves and hunting dogs. Imports consisted of ivory chains and necklaces, amber gems, glass vessels and 'other pretty wares of that sort'. Pottery was soon to become one of the most prolific of those 'pretty wares'. It is odd that Strabo does not include tin in his list of desirable exports. The Phoenicians, of course, had famously fetched tin from Cornwall to the Mediterranean for several centuries before the Romans had ever arrived. That Strabo was well aware of this is evident from the fact that elsewhere in his work he describes how the Phoenician traders kept both the route and the source of this highly coveted metal a closely guarded secret. He tells the story of how one adventurous Roman sea captain who tried following the Phoenician fleet to discover the source of their riches was lured by the Phoenicians on to shoals and had his ship wrecked for his trouble. He was very probably an early victim of the dangerous rocks off the Scillies. By the time of Publius Crassus, however, governor of Spain from 96–93 BC, the great tin secret was out of the bag. Crassus voyaged from Spain to Britain and gave a detailed description of both the tin-mining process and the source.

In 55 BC Julius Caesar famously accomplished his first invasion of Britain, graphically described in his *Conquest of Gaul (De Bello Gallico)*. He mentions in passing that one of the attractions for him was the river pearls that could be obtained from the mussel beds, presumably those of the Thames estuary. It is difficult to believe, however, that he organised two major military expeditions simply to facilitate his pearl collection. He came with eighty ships and about 8,000 men and a further eighteen ships carrying a cavalry contingent. The latter were dispersed by a storm and never made it on to British shores but the foot soldiers landed in Kent, probably in the vicinity of Deal although the exact spot has been a fruitful subject for scholastic debate. The following year he returned with a fleet of 800 ships. Clearly he wanted to impress upon the natives the strength of the Roman military machine and the folly of lending support to any dissidents on the Continental mainland and in this he was largely successful. Britain was allowed to continue as an offshore backwater for the next hundred years provided it paid token tribute to the supremacy of the Roman Empire. It was not until the time of the Emperor Claudius in 43 AD that Britain was finally conquered and occupied by the Romans. By this time, again according to Strabo, there were four main trade routes from the Continent to Britain, 'from the Rhine, from the Seine, from the Loire and from the Garonne. . .'. He further explained that 'the crossing to Britain from the rivers of Gaul is 320 stades [about forty miles]. People setting sail on the ebb tide in the evening land on the island about the eighth hour on the following day.' One of the most important imports at this period and for the next several centuries was fine Italian wine. Strabo states that high-quality Italian wine arrived in amphorae in the Thames via the Rhône and the Rhine. Nor was it just wine that was arriving. A recent amphora find close to Pan Sand included 6,000 olive pips. A taste for Mediterranean-style food in Britain clearly dates back well before the advent of Elizabeth David.

By 100 AD ships carrying Roman goods would also have been a frequent presence on the North Sea, particularly voyaging southwards from the mouth of the Rhine, along the coasts of Holland and Belgium before striking out towards the Thames estuary or the important Roman ports of Richborough or Colchester. The northern Roman fleet was called the Classis Germanica. It was based at Alteburg, three kilometres to the south of Köln. Other important naval establishments were built along the lower Rhine at Novaesium (Neuss), Vetera (near Xanten), Noviomagus

(Nijmegen), Katwijk and at Aretsburg in Voorburg (part of The Hague). The last two ports played an important role in controlling the commerce between Germany and Britain as well as in subduing the pirates. The Classis Germanica was largely the creation of Drusus the Elder, who excavated a canal from the River Rhine to the Zuyder Zee to facilitate the fleet's access into the North Sea. Drusus was the first Roman general really to explore these Northern seas. By the second decade AD this northern fleet was a very formidable force. For the campaign of the years 15 to 16 Germanicus apparently built 1,000 ships at Insula Batavorum on the estuary of the Rhine. At the end of the campaign this fleet was struck by a storm while navigating along the Eastern shore of the North Sea and some of the vessels were blown as far afield as the coast of Britain where they were wrecked. Maritime disasters of one kind or another were not infrequent.

According to the annals of Tacitus in 61 AD Suetonius Paullinus lost several ships. In 68 to 69 AD the rebel leader Civilis destroyed a fleet of Roman ships at the eastern end of the Insula Batavorum. The following year the British Roman fleet that was transporting Legion XIV from Britain to Gaul was destroyed by Canninefates. Also around this time the fleet of General Cerialis was destroyed sailing down the Rhine from Novaesium.

One of the great anomalies of underwater archaeology to date is that while nearly 1,000 wrecks from the Roman period have been discovered in the waters of the Mediterranean, many still containing their original cargoes, very few have yet been found in the North Sea area, or any of the seas around Britain, and none with what might be described as a full cargo. A number of Roman-period ships have been found in the River Rhine, two in the Thames, one at Blackfriars and one at London's former County Hall, and some along the rivers of the south coast and one even as far away as Ireland. But all of these finds have been along an in-

A pottery jar with a lively depiction of a chariot race found at Colchester. This was made locally in East Anglia but is good enough to be traded overseas.

land waterway rather than in the open sea. The obvious explanation for the difference is that the Mediterranean was much busier than the North Sea during the Roman era. This is to some extent true but it conceals as much as it informs, for the North Sea was, in fact, also much traversed by merchants carrying Roman goods in the earlier centuries of the first millennium. The lack of cargoes coming to light probably has more to do with the sandy nature of the bottom of the North Sea compared with the clear rocky waters of the Mediterranean than the quantities of shipping involved. This is what makes the Pudding Pan Shoal wreck of particular interest and importance, for here we have a seagoing ship apparently lost with a full cargo in northern waters.

In 2001 the University of Southampton launched a major underwater project that was intended finally to solve the mystery of the elusive Pudding Pan wreck. A large area of seabed near where
the Pudding Pan Shoal was once thought to have existed was to be carefully monitored with the
assistance of a side-scan sonar. Such sophisticated detection equipment had not been available to
previous wreck hunters and so optimism was understandably high. This was a much more ambitious programme than that carried out by Thomas Pownall or Hugh Pollard. The total area covered was twenty-one square kilometres. This was building on a previous survey for the wreck carried
out in 1998 that had covered six-and-a-half square kilometres to the south of Pan Sand. In the
course of the survey 450 targets were identified and seventy-eight dives were carried out which
amounted to a total of twenty-five hours spent under water. Thirty-nine of the highest priority
anomalies were examined. The net result was the discovery of one small sherd of red-coloured
Samian ware.

It is not fair, however, to judge the success or otherwise of the project simply by tangible finds.
A large amount of valuable data was gathered on the topography of the seabed, tidal movements
and currents. Perhaps even more useful will be the follow-up project being carried out in conjunction with the local fishermen which collates and computerises all the ongoing finds of pottery, log-
ging the various tracks of the dredges at those times when finds are made. The archaeologists
involved remain confident that the wreck is still out there waiting to be discovered and, like Hugh
Pollard, they believe it will eventually be found largely intact. From the wear patterns on the pots
that have been recovered so far, it is believed that the bulk of the pottery pieces are most likely
still stacked one on top of the other in an inverted position on the seabed. Like Pollard one hundred years beforehand, the 2001 expedition has also concluded that 'the wreck clearly has not been
destroyed or seriously disturbed by modern fishing techniques.' It does, however, lie in 'deep sand
or silt'.

Recently there was a further development in tracking down the whereabouts of the Pudding Pan
wreck that seriously complicated the whole business. As mentioned above, an amphora complete
with 6,000 olive pips was found 500 metres to the north of Pan Sand by the fisherman Brian
Tyrrell. As all the previous finds of Roman pottery appeared to relate to the south of the Pan Sand
this was either a whole new angle on the sinking or the presence of a second Roman wreck in close
proximity to the first. The theory of a separate and distinct wreck is supported by the University
of Southampton team because the amphora is thought to date from between 50 and 150 AD,
while the pots are considered to be from a period 160 to 200 AD. However, the potential for over-
lap here is so close that it is obviously not entirely out of the question that amphora and pots all
come from the same vessel. This is particularly true as the amphora is of a rare kind, which makes
exact dating difficult. The physical distance between an amphora 500 metres to the north of Pan
Sand and pots scattered over a wide area several miles to the south also does not necessarily imply

the presence of more than one wreck. It is not difficult to conceive of a scenario in which the Roman ship was already in difficulties as it approached Pan Sand from the north. Cargo may well have been jettisoned at this point to try and lighten the ship and the amphora full of olives may have been among such items. The ship then beat over Pan Sand spilling cargo as it went and finally foundered somewhere in the area of Pudding Pan Rock as originally charted. However, until the wreck is finally found such theories must remain pure speculation.

The question naturally arises as to whether there might exist procedures for locating a wreck like the one on Pudding Pan Shoal that have not yet been tried. So far as I am aware the key area has not yet been searched using a magnetometer or a sub-bottom profiler. The objection may well be raised that there would not be sufficient ironwork in a ship of this period to obtain a magnetometer reading. But magnetometers are continually improving both in sensitivity and discrimination and it might be an approach that is just possibly worthwhile.

That there is a high probability of the presence of some ironwork is evident from the description of Veneti shipping by Julius Caesar who had a sharp eye for all technical matters that might have military implications.

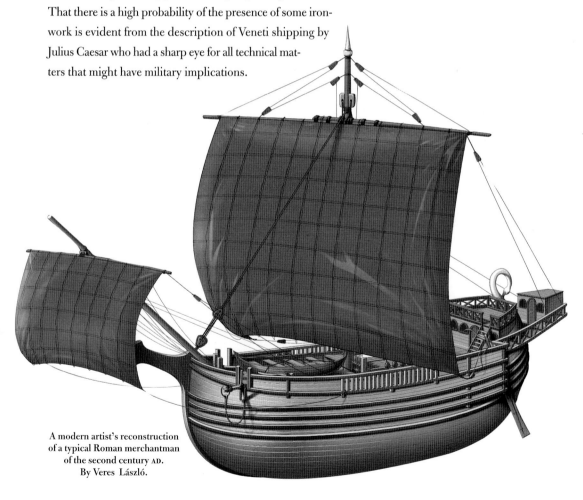

A modern artist's reconstruction
of a typical Roman merchantman
of the second century AD.
By Veres László.

The Gauls' own ships were built and rigged in a different manner from ours. They were made with much flatter bottoms, to help them ride shallow water caused by shoals or ebb- tides. Exceptionally high bows and sterns fitted them for use in high seas and violent gales, and the hulls were made entirely of oak, to enable them to stand any amount of shocks or rough usage. The cross-timbers, which consisted of beams a foot wide, were fastened with iron bolts as thick as a man's thumb. The anchors were secured with iron chains instead of ropes. They used sails made of raw hides or thin leather, either because they had no flax and were ignorant of its use, or more probably because they thought that ordinary sails would not stand the violent storms and squalls of the Atlantic and were not suitable for such heavy vessels. In meeting them the only advantage that our ships possessed was that they were faster and could be propelled by oars; in other respects the enemy's were much better adapted for sailing such treacherous and stormy waters. We could not injure them by ramming because they were so solidly built, and their height made it difficult to reach them with missiles or board them with grappling irons. Moreover, when it began to blow hard and they were running before the wind, they weathered the storm more easily; they could bring to in shallow water with greater safety, and when left aground by the tide had nothing to fear from reefs or pointed rocks – whereas to our ships all these risks were formidable.' Caesar, *De Bello Gallico*, as translated by S. A. Handford.

The Pudding Pan ship was most probably built some 200 years after this was written but it is unlikely that the basic structural design of such vessels had altered that much in the interim. The Roman-period wreck found in Guernsey and excavated by Margaret Rule dates to the late third century, some hundred years after the Pudding Pan wreck, and yet according to Ms Rule, 'the similarity between the Venetic ships of 56 BC (as described by Caesar) and the Guernsey ship is startling.' The Guernsey ship has been estimated as being twenty-five metres in length with a six-metre beam. It was built entirely of oak with a flat bottom. It was carvel built, that is the side-planking butted end-on-end rather than overlapping. It had a single mast and probably carried a single square-shaped sail. The construction also included a considerable amount of ironwork.

Meanwhile, the Pudding Pan wreck remains one of those tantalising maritime mysteries still waiting to be solved.

2

Viking Treasure

NUMBER OF VIKING SHIPS have been excavated in western European waters during the last century. Those at Gokstad, Oseberg and Skuldelev are probably the most famous. Relics have mainly been found in burial mounds or as a result of river dredging. Very few have been discovered on the open seabed in a situation that might suggest that their remains are where they are as a direct result of shipwreck. The reason for this is fairly obvious. Most Viking ships were of a relatively small size and fragile structure using planks of wood only one or two inches thick, without massive posts, cross timbers or keel. Added to this, they did not carry cannon or any other significant weighty metal objects. These two factors combined mean that they are unlikely to leave much behind in the way of surviving evidence when they are wrecked, unless the circumstances for preservation are particularly propitious.

Then there is the further problem in the lack of written historical records. From the sixteenth century onwards there is still surviving a surprisingly large quantity of written material relating to shipping losses, in the form of court records, letters, log books, diaries, memoirs, charts, account books, company

A Viking longship of about 800 AD; a modern artist's reconstruction by Veres László. The shallow draft of such vessels enabled them frequently to beach with relative safety when driven ashore by adverse weather.

ledgers, contemporary histories and so on. Obviously for some shipwrecks there are great lacunae in the information. There is often that key piece of the puzzle that is irritatingly absent. But even for some relatively early shipping losses the wealth of detail that can be discovered is surprisingly large. I once carried out research for a salvage company on a Portuguese ship captained by Vincent Sodre, Vasca da Gama's uncle. The ship was wrecked on the Curia Muria Islands in the Indian Ocean in 1503. The archival material available was both voluminous and of such pinpoint accuracy that the remains of the wreck were rediscovered on the first day of the search. The wreck had lain there untouched for nearly 500 years. Unfortunately, this kind of archival accuracy is the exception even for post-1500 wrecks. When it comes to losses in the Viking era the historical record is extremely thin and what there is often unreliable.

Despite the inherent difficulties, in 1972 a group of archaeologists and approximately one hundred amateur volunteers were involved in a highly ambitious search for the remains of two Viking ships called the *Hjalp* (the *Help*) and the *Fifa* (the *Arrow*) that were rumoured to have wrecked in the Shetlands in the year 1148. These two wrecks were selected because the information about their loss in the *Orkneyinga Saga* is relatively precise enabling a theoretical reconstruction of their final voyage.

The Shetland Islands are today administratively part of Scotland and the British Isles, but their cultural and historical links with Scandinavia have always been extremely close. A lot of Nordic words survive in the local dialect. Place names frequently have Nordic associations. The local style of boat building even has a clear physical resemblance to the old Viking longboats with their slender fine lines, high stern and stem posts and low freeboard. None of this is very surprising. Lerwick, the capital of the Shetlands, is as near to Bergen as it is to Aberdeen and for several centuries the islands were part of the larger Norwegian-Danish empire. It was only in 1469 that Christian I of Norway transferred the islands to King James III of Scotland as part of his daughter's marriage dowry.

In 1148, or thereabouts, Rognvald, Earl of Orkney, was invited by King Ingi of Norway to visit him in Bergen. Ingi was a young and inexperienced ruler having only recently come to the throne on the death of his father Harald Gilli. His position was insecure, particularly as he had an elder bastard brother called Eystein who might easily be tempted into acting as a focus for the opposition. In these precarious circumstances Ingi's closest counsellors, two brothers called Ogmund and Erling, thought it advisable for Ingi to form an alliance with the strong man across the water, Rognvald. These were violent and brutal times. Rognvald himself had only taken possession of the Orkneys after arranging with his accomplice, Sweyn Asleif, to have the previous earl, called Paul, done away with in mysterious circumstances. It was shortly after this that Rognvald's father, Kol, suggested to his son that he build a great cathedral at Kirkwall. The size of it was clearly meant to impress the local populace and perhaps by this means secure their allegiance. Perhaps it was also

St Magnus church on
Orkney. It was founded by
Rognvald, Earl of Orkney,
possibly to atone for the
recent murder of
Earl Paul.

intended as an act of atonement for Earl Paul's murder. The enormous stone cathedral was dedicated to St Magnus. Rognvald's mother, Gunhild, was Magnus's sister. The cathedral is still standing today and recent excavations of the site claim to have unearthed relics of both St Magnus and Rognvald.

By 1148 Rognvald obviously felt secure enough in his own power base to accept King Ingi's invitation to travel to Norway. He took with him his own son, Earl Harald, aged fourteen. Harald, according to the sagas, was tall and strong-limbed but somewhat on the ugly side. The outward voyage was uneventful. In Bergen there followed the usual diplomatic formalities of present giving and feasting. The main topic of conversation was the crusades. One of the guests called Eindridi was just back from the Holy Land. It was agreed between Eindridi and Rognvald that they would both take part in a new crusade that was being planned. From the diplomatic point of view the visit seems to have been a big success. When it came to Rognvald's departure Ingi presented him with two beautiful finely carved longships, the *Hjalp* and the *Fifa*. The exact proportions of these boats are not known but they would most probably have been about eighty feet long and about ten to fifteen feet in the beam with spaces for twenty to thirty rowers. In style it would have been similar to the Gokstad ship found in a burial mound in Norway and now beautifully conserved in the Oslo Viking Museum. They were elegant, speedy, highly manoeuvrable and seaworthy ships that would have made a most impressive sight skimming the grey waves of the northern seas. They would have carried a single mast, which could be lowered at will, and which would have been set with rectangular brilliantly coloured sails in stripes or chequers. As royal gifts the prow and stern were doubtlessly ornately worked in gold and there would have been one of those elaborately gilded and intricately designed weather vanes of the kind for which Viking ships were to become famous. The workmanship and woodcarving would have been of particularly high quality. Like the Gokstad ship they would have had rows of highly coloured and patterned shields decorating both flanks. The rudders would have been retractable enabling them to negotiate shallow waters. On departure the *Hjalp* and the *Fifa* were loaded with chests containing other smaller presents such as chess sets, jewellery and delicately crafted weapons. These chests may have doubled as seats for the rowers thus saving space and unnecessary weight.

The small fleet set out from Bergen on a Tuesday evening with a favourable easterly wind. The Vikings were skilled meteorologists and would have paid great attention to the weather omens before determining a day and time of departure. Much emphasis was put on not making certain long voyages during the wrong season. Bergen to the Orkneys, however, would normally have taken only two or three days, so it would not have been considered a long voyage. For almost half the distance it would also be possible to see certain prominent mountain tops, provided the weather was clear.

The first night all went well. With a following wind Viking longboats could travel at up to twelve knots. But on the Wednesday Rognvald and Harald ran into unpredicted storms. By this time they would have been fifty or more miles out to sea. Although the shape and design of the longboats makes them look extremely fragile and easily vulnerable to heavy weather, they are in fact noted for their remarkable sailing qualities. In 1895 M. Andersen sailed a replica of the Gokstad boat from Norway to America and particularly commented on the boat's weatherliness. The longboats were

The *Hjalp* wreck site may have contained pieces of jewellery similar to this beautiful example of a Viking trefoil brooch.

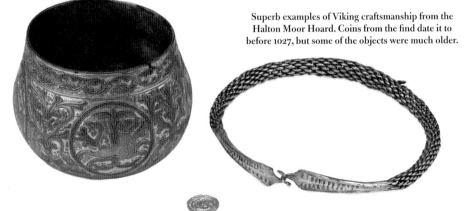

Superb examples of Viking craftsmanship from the Halton Moor Hoard. Coins from the find date it to before 1027, but some of the objects were much older.

constructed in such a way that made them very supple so that they yielded to heavy seas rather than simply resisting them. This was partly due to the thinness of the wood used and partly because the lower strakes were lashed to the ribs with cords made from such items as walrus tendons, which had far greater qualities of elasticity than an iron nail. The entire construction was shell-built and clinker-fastened, with the ribs being fitted afterwards, which again made it less rigid. It seems likely that when the storm broke the small fleet lowered sails, shipped the masts and lay to, just using the oars and the rudder to stop the boats from broaching to in a trough of the waves. The importance of keeping the boat head on to the seas is described in a short passage from the Gudmundar saga: 'Then they drifted once more at the mercy of the gale, and during the night the men who were awake keeping watch heard loud and terrible crashes, and saw a huge wave which they thought would be their destruction if it struck the ship broadside on.' Lamps were lit and the boats managed to stay together. It is possible that special weatherboards were erected along the boats' sides to try and limit the ingress of the seawater. Pumps were not to be used on Viking ships for another hundred years but bailing would no doubt have been continuous. It is not known whether any great damage was done but they would normally have carried supplies of a material called wadmal for mending any torn sails, together with the inevitable needles, thread and cord. For repairs to the hull they would have had available nails, spikes, rivets and a full set of carpenter's tools. By Thursday the storm had subsided. The problem was that Rognvald no longer knew where he was. He had fallen into a condition frequently referred to in the sagas as *hafvilla*, which was essentially 'the state of being lost'. The Vikings had no compass to navigate by, so being out of sight of land was difficult for navigation. During the daytime they used the height of the sun and at night the position of the Pole Star to determine their latitude. These observations combined with a crude system of dead reckoning were the main navigational tools. It is probable, although no definite proof has been discovered for this, that they would have used some kind of log to measure the distance they had covered. The Vikings did not possess charts for navigation but they did have remarkably accurate tables of distances between places and so, if they knew how far they had come, they would have been in a position to know how far they were from land. The problem was that in times of cloud or fog, neither sun nor Pole Star was visible and, in conditions of storm, towing a log could become highly inaccurate. This would mean that Rognvald and his men would have been reduced to using the lead to determine the depth of water they were in, together with a variety of observations based on the natural features of the sea, to try and establish their whereabouts. To the experienced mariner the sea is not entirely a wilderness of waves. Different species of birds were used as an important source of information. Gannets, the common guillemot, great black-backed gulls and puffins would all have indicated the approach of land, and the direction of their flight would have provided a useful pointer to the direction of that land. Even the look of the sea could offer important clues. The set of the waves, the presence of overfalls or eddies, the direction of the current, the colour of the water, all these phe-

This silver disc brooch of Aedwen is inscribed with a curse, which sums up the dilemma for the archaeologist removing items from graves.

nomena could be used by the experienced seaman as an aid to determining his position. The presence of concentrations of plankton, ice floes or whales was also a useful tell-tale sign.

The day following the storm the sea was calmer but there was a large swell. By the time that Rognvald and his men became aware that they were approaching land it was already dark and so none of the usual indicators were observed. The saga particularly comments on the intensity of that darkness. 'It was very dark, and they saw signs of breakers surrounding them on all sides. Up to this time they had kept together. There was nothing to be done except to run the vessels on shore, and this they did. The beach before them was stony and narrow, enclosed behind crags. There was a rocky beach in front of them, and only a narrow foreshore and cliffs beyond. All the men were saved, but they lost a large quantity of their stores. Some of the things were thrown up by the sea during the night.' This description of the wrecking is tantalisingly brief but none the less provides some vital information for anyone trying to determine the exact location of the incident. The reference to breakers being all around suggests that they found themselves trapped in a bay or inlet facing a lee shore. The rocky beach, the narrow foreshore and the cliffs beyond also provide a precise description of the immediate terrain they encountered. Unfortunately, these characteristics are all very common attributes to innumerable bays and inlets of the Shetland Islands, which is where they had ended up, some hundred miles to the north of their intended destination.

Whether Rognvald was entirely unaware of where he was landing, or whether he knew all along he was approaching the Shetlands, but had decided to put in there in order to recover and regroup after the storm, is not made clear. A little further on in the *Orkneyinga Saga*, however, there is an extremely valuable piece of information that slips almost incidentally into the story. In the immediate aftermath of the shipwreck Rognvald's immediate concern was to find warmth and shelter for his men. Between the two boats he most probably had close to a hundred people with him. Clearly they would have to be distributed among a number of farmsteads and crofts. A farmer called Einar at Gulberuvik refused to accept the dozen men sent to him unless Rognvald made application to him in person. This refusal drew a scathing response from Rognvald. Most modern scholars are agreed that Gulberuvik refers to present day Gulberwick, a small bay to the south of Lerwick, that has numerous rocky beaches and cliffs within it that fit Rognvald's description of the immediate topography of the shipwreck. It seems reasonable to conclude that Gulberwick was the place where the *Hjalp* and the *Fifa* came to grief, although the information is far from conclusive. It is, for instance, self-evident that when Rognvald sent his men to Einar at Gulberuvik he had already quartered himself elsewhere. In which case, he may well have been in the vicinity of another bay nearby, such as the Voe of Sound to the east, or even the East Voe of Quarff to the south.

Another important factor to take into account when trying to determine exactly where the boats sank is that everyone survived. This was partly due to the physical structure of the boats. Being small and shallow-drafted they would have been able to get in close to the shore before grounding and

The Cuerdale Hoard attests to the Viking presence in Ireland but no Viking shipwreck anywhere in Europe has yet been found intact, with original cargo in situ, most probably because of the fragility of their structure.

becoming unmanageable. But it also suggests that they must have beached in a relatively benign sit-uation. Was this luck, or had Rognvald managed to pick out, in the dark, the piece of coastline most propitious for running on to? The *Orkneyinga Saga* does not make this clear but it seems quite prob-able that the spot was chosen with some forethought. There is another description in Egil's saga that has similarities with Rognvald's account. 'Then they sailed southwards past Scotland, and had great storms and crosswinds. Weathering the Scottish coast they held on southwards along England; but on the evening of a day, as darkness came on, it blew a gale. Before they were aware, breakers were both seaward and ahead. There was nothing for it but to make for land and this they did. Under sail they ran ashore, and came to land at Humbermouth. All the men were saved, and most of the cargo, but as for the ship, that was broken to pieces.' It seems this business of beaching was very proba-bly a common feature of Viking navigation in times of extreme stress.

The 1972 archaeological expedition conducted its investigations entirely within the confines of Gulberwick Bay. Even with a hundred volunteers, and divers spending up to five hours a day in the water, over an extended two-month period of searching they only managed to cover about a quarter of the Gulberwick coastline, examining a total area of probably little more than one six-teenth of a square mile. This was because the entire search was done by eye, each diver sifting sys-tematically through the sand and small pebbles as they went. Underwater metal detectors were tried but they turned up too many empty lager cans to be of much use. Sadly the expedition dis-covered no evidence of Rognvald's shipwreck. This does not mean that the wreck did not take place there. It does, however, underline the limitations of this kind of shallow-water searching. Not only was the area surveyed extremely small but also there were large parts of the bay that, although they fitted exactly with Rognvald's description of his landing place, could not be investigated at all because there were too many boulders or other logistical problems. It is difficult not to conclude that if the *Hjalp* and the *Fifa* are ever to be found it will most probably be as the result of some sharp-eyed beachcomber, trawling the shores and rock pools of Gulberwick Bay and just happen-ing upon a piece of Viking jewellery.

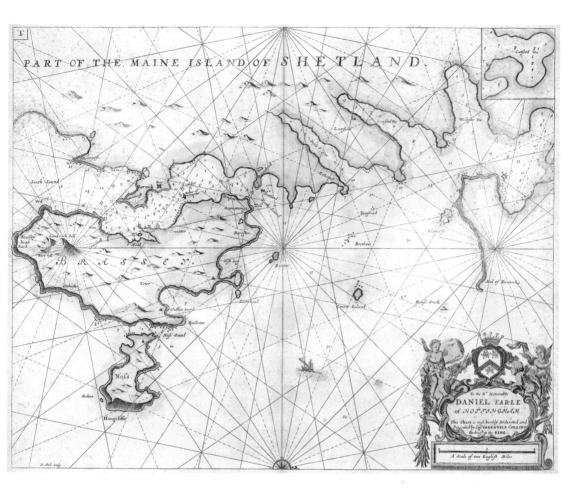

HJALP AND FIFA:
The treacherous fogs, currents and reefs of the Shetland Isles resulted in the loss of many Viking ships on its coastline. One of Greenville Collins's charts from a survey carried out in the late 1680s and published in 1693.

KRONAN:
Among thousands of everyday objects recovered from the wreck site, one of the most beautiful has to be this golden spoon.

Above
BONHOMME RICHARD:
The height of the battle off
Flamborough Head between *Serapis*
and *Bonhomme Richard*.

Left
GOLDEN LION:
Although from a later period, this
eyewitness depiction by Lieutenant
Meynell shows the appalling
conditions below decks in slave ships.

Right
CARLISLE:
The ships of this era were elaborately
decorated, as shown by this model of
a fourth-rate ship contemporary with
the *Carlisle*.

Overleaf
DUNWICH BANK WRECK:
A typical moderate-sized merchant
ship of the sixteenth century, in an oil
painting by Andries van Eeertvelt.

VLIEGEND HERT:
Some of the recent finds, now in the
Maritime Museum in Vlissingen.
These include an ivory ruler and
fragments of clothing, as well as the
eye-catching golden Ducats.

VROUW MARIA:
Colour impression of the
state of the wreck when
first found.

A TUBE TO THE BOTTOM OF THE SEA: THE NEW TREASURE-SEEKER.

The Latest Form of Treasure-Seeker.

AN ATTEMPT TO RECOVER £1,000,000 FROM THE SEA: THE NEW WRECKING-VESSEL, SHOWING THE REMARKABLE TREASURE-RAISING APPARATUS.

Our Illustration, which has been made from a drawing in the "Scientific American," by the courtesy of that paper, shows a new type of wrecking-vessel designed to enable a company that has a contract with Lloyd's to recover from the bottom of the sea some £1,000,000 in bullion and specie sunk in the British man-of-war "Lutine," which went down off the entrance to the Zuyder Zee, on October 9, 1799. "The most interesting part of the plant is the submarine tube and working chamber. The former is . . . five feet in diameter and ninety-five feet long. . . . There is a passage-way down which the operators may walk when the working compartment is on the bottom. . . . The working compartment . . . is about eight feet across, with large doors opening out from its bottom, and with provision for the admission of compressed air."

LUTINE:
Image of a machine devised for salvage of *Lutine*.

3

The Dunwich Bank Wreck

IN THE SUMMER OF 1595 two young Englishmen turned up at the court of the Holy Roman Emperor in Prague, which was then part of what was known as Germany. One of the men was Sir Anthony Sherley, the son of a councillor to Queen Elizabeth I. The other was Thomas Arundell, cousin to Sir Robert Cecil. They claimed they had come to Prague as 'soldiers of fortune' eager to serve the Emperor, Rudolf II, in his war against the Turks. Sherley had letters of recommendation from the Queen. Arundell was already known to the Emperor. They presented themselves as adventurers eager for glory. Tomaso Contarini, the Venetian ambassador in Prague, who made their acquaintance, wrote to the Doge that, as far as he could gather, 'they have come to

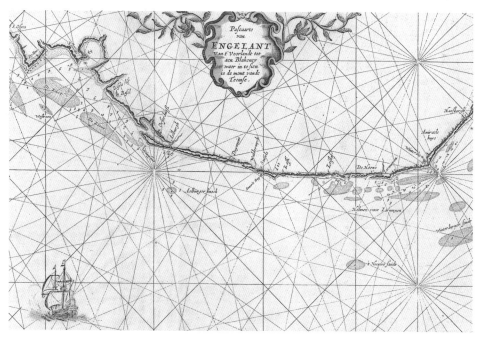

Part of a Dutch chart dating from the seventeenth century showing the coast of East Anglia. The top is approximately West.

these parts merely as young men anxious to follow the wars. One of them told me they had not gone to the wars in France, because those were civil wars. . . This war they thought greater and better worth seeing.' Actually, by the standards of the time, Arundell was not as young as Contarini implies. He was already thirty-six years old. There was also, among some of the Emperor's court, a suspicion that the two Englishmen were spies, or at best had come on a secret mission to try and arrange a peace. Queen Elizabeth was well known for her careful neutrality. A previous English visitor to Prague, supposedly on commercial business, had 'given poor satisfaction to his Majesty (Rudolf II) on account of his interference in politics'. Arundell and Sherley both admitted that there had been a lobby in England before they left that had objected to their being given permission to travel to Prague for fear this might upset the Turks and thereby jeopardise the interests of those English merchants who had business in Turkey. There was evidently more to this visit than simple adventuring. Arundell confessed in a letter written about six months later that, 'the Queen gave me leave to serve in Hungary for two years, and gave me instructions at my departure which I may not repeat, except to say that a wiser man than I would not have thought her the Emperor's enemy.' In such a complex and delicate political situation it is hard not to agree with Contarini's conclusion: 'It is difficult to understand the meaning of what is going on.'

In the event the two Englishman were permitted to go to the front line of the war, but suitable warnings were sent on ahead that a careful eye should be kept on them. They appear to have acquitted themselves with distinction. At the battle of Gran, 7 September 1595, Arundell personally replaced the Turkish crescent with the Imperial eagle and for his efforts he was dubbed 'The Valiant'. Arundell's own description of his efforts does not reveal him to be particularly strong on modesty, even if he was adept with the sword. 'I arrived at the camp at the very instant of the only battle between the Turks and us, and immediately put myself at the very front of the army, where, by reason of my plumes of feathers and my armour and furniture, all full of gold and silver, I was a mark for all men's eyes. I so conducted myself that day that Count Mansfeldt told the Emperor that an Englishman of good appearance was the first man of mark who charged the enemy.' It seems that battle at this time was conceived of as an opportunity for fashion as much as the furthering of political interest. The Emperor, however, was obviously sufficiently pleased by Arundell's performance that he made him an Earl with the rank of 'Comes Imperii', a position to which were attached numerous special privileges. He gave other volunteers gifts including sables, crystal glasses, plate and massy chains, (i.e., solid, presumably of gold). Arundell does not specify what gifts, if any, he himself received. He was, however, entrusted with an urgent message to the Queen that led him to interrupt his European tour of battlefields and return immediately into England, after what appears to have been little more than one day of actual fighting. 'The Emperor gave me messages to the Queen, which seemed of such importance that I could not allow myself to consider my own ease, but commenced my dangerous homeward voyage in an unseasonable period of the year.'

A typical merchant ship of
the late sixteenth century,
seen in this Dutch
engraving after Bruegel,
dated 1565.

Arundell's route home very probably took him through the town of Stoade (Stade) on the
Elbe situated just above Hamburg. It is also very probable that he would then have chosen to cross
the North Sea in a ship of Hamburg. Whatever his exact mode of conveyance was it proved disastrous. In Arundell's own words, 'when we were sailing near Aldborough in Suffolk a mighty wind
broke our ship on the shore, and, though my life was saved, I lost all I possessed through my
zealous desire to serve one, of whose bright beamed eyes one favourable look or smiling accept-
ance were a large requital to all passed perils.' It is characteristic of Arundell's egotism that he does
not say anything about what happened to the rest of the crew, passengers, or the vessel itself. In his
letter to Robert Cecil of 1 February 1596 Arundell again refers to the shipwreck, this time as an excuse for not coming to see his powerful cousin in person. But apart from mentioning that it had resulted in him catching a cold, and demonstrating his strong propensity for self-pity, it provides little
further information on the event itself, 'had I not suffered a shipwreck, and so lost all my apparel,

linen, horses, money, and whatever else I had, and withal gotten an extreme cold by tumbling into the sea for the safety of my life, I would myself have been the deliverer of these salutations.'

Arundell's extravagant line in flattery and self-pity cut no ice with Queen Elizabeth. Far from sympathising with his shipwreck, she promptly added to his problems and had him put in Fleet gaol. She was outraged that he had had the audacity to accept an earldom from a foreign power: 'she is much offended that he hath presumed to take any dignity from the Emperor without her privity.' So far as Elizabeth was concerned it smacked of treachery. In her own pithy phrase, 'I would not have my sheepe branded with another man's mark; I would not they should follow the whistle of a strange shepherd.' No doubt there were other less explicit but probably more powerful reasons for Arundell's sudden downfall. There were rumours that he was secretly a Catholic and had taken the opportunity while abroad to visit Rome. In the letter to Cecil noted above, Arundell hotly denied these accusations: 'I have neither been at Rome nor had to do with any of the Spanish or Popish faction.' But the problem was that Arundell had 'form'. He had already been in prison in 1580 for what was described as excessive zeal in the Catholic cause. Rather more damning was the letter of Samuel Symcroft to Arundell, undated but written after the Prague venture and carefully preserved among Cecil's papers, which suggests that the hot-headed Arundell may well have been mixed up in some kind of Catholic conspiracy.

After a few months cooling off in Fleet prison Elizabeth allowed Arundell to be released into the care of his father, Mathew Arundell, residing at Wardour Castle in Wiltshire. The father was most reluctant to undertake this unlooked-for responsibility. He was careful to distance himself from his son's wild behaviour. He particularly objected because it meant that he would have quartered beneath his own roof his son's wife, Mary Wriothesley, with whom he did not get on. He made a request that she should be kept at least 'two flight shots away'. Clearly Elizabethan family life was not all minuets and marzipan.

Arundell survived his cold dip in the North Sea and his disgrace, and appears to have continued to lead a tempestuous life, being one of those named by Guy Fawkes, under torture, as a co-conspirator. Despite his many escapades, he managed to die of old age in his own bed in 1639, something of a rare privilege in those days. There is one further small incident recorded in the annals of Dunwich Corporation that may well have been connected with the loss of his ship and may also help pinpoint the exact site of the wreck. In 1596 the Corporation acquired a large chest that had been washed up on the shore. The town of Dunwich's rights to wreck were limited to the short strip of coast from the port of Dunwich to Westleton abutting on the high sea of Cachecliff. The chest is still in existence today and can be seen in Dunwich Museum.

After 1596 the memory of the shipwreck of Thomas Arundell, like so many other similar shipwrecks, passed into oblivion. There is a distinct possibility, however, that recently it may have inadvertently been rediscovered. In 1974 two local divers, Stuart Bacon and Tom Church, were asked

by a Dunwich fisherman whether they could recover a net that he had lost on an underwater obstruction in the vicinity of Dunwich Bank. The divers discovered the net caught on a large concreted irregular hillock on the seabed. Conditions, as almost always in this part of the North Sea,
were extremely hostile. Strong currents combine with nil visibility to make diving an activity that
only the intrepid are prepared to undertake. In pitch black all work has to be carried out by touch
only. It is certainly not a job for the claustrophobic. The divers concerned, however, were used to
these conditions, having worked extensively on the underwater remains of medieval Dunwich that
toppled into the sea in the immediate vicinity. They recovered the net and presumed that the

When Stuart Bacon first
pulled up a section of
timber embedded with
fifty-six cannon balls in
1992, he realised that he
had discovered a
shipwreck rather than
part of the submerged
town of Dunwich.

object it had caught on was part of one of the many churches that are strewn across this part of the seabed.

Years went past and fishermen continued to trawl up worked stones that almost certainly formed part of the old ecclesiastical buildings, together with pieces of driftwood. The problem with the driftwood was that it was usually very difficult to determine its origin or exactly where on the seabed it may have come from. Then in 1992 a large section of frames and strakes was brought up from the vicinity of the same concretion that had been first discovered nearly twenty years earlier. It was only as a result of Stuart Bacon's careful record-keeping and long experience of the area that a connection could be made between the two events. The timbers were embedded with fifty-six cannon balls. They had definitely come from a shipwreck.

The area was now surveyed with a magnetometer and a positive reading was recorded. The divers involved decided to hire a dive support vessel and investigate the site in greater detail. As everyone concerned was an unpaid amateur, finance was something of an issue. Funding was raised from Nuclear Electric, at nearby Sizewell, and from Stuart Bacon's own small enterprise, Suffolk Underwater Studies. The latter had been set up by Stuart Bacon without the benefit of public funding, to promote the archaeological study of the Suffolk coast. A beautiful small museum has been created above Mr Bacon's craft shop in Orford and the centre has functioned for many years as a valuable information and collating point for local finds by enthusiastic members of the public.

By the summer of 1994 the group was in a position to hire the Dive Support Vessel *Sirius* for a total of three days. The first two days of diving achieved nothing. The concreted mound was relocated but no sense could be made of it. This was hardly surprising because conditions were as usual so opaquely black that underwater lights were unable to penetrate. Then, on the last day, there was a breakthrough. Seven metres from the datum point that had been put down Stuart Bacon's hand touched what felt like a smooth metal tube. He immediately began to think in terms of a cannon. Feeling his way along it he came to a fish-shaped handle. From that point on he had no doubts as to what he had found. He attached his safety line to it and headed for the surface. Later that same day the cannon was strapped and winched on to the ship. It was a superb bronze saker measuring 11 feet 6 inches (Spanish measurements).

The gun was conserved with the assistance of Nuclear Electric in a specially constructed tank and then put on display outside the Suffolk Underwater Studies Museum in Orford. The inscriptions on it had been severely abraded by the sand and so it was not possible to be certain of the gun's founder or the exact date it was cast. It has, however, been subsequently examined and written about in great detail by the ordnance expert Rudi Roth. Mr Roth is of the opinion that the gun was made by Remigy de Halut at Malines in the Spanish Netherlands some time between 1536 and 1556 for the Spanish Emperor Charles V. A remarkably similar-looking gun was salvaged from the wrecked Spanish Armada ship *La Trinidad Valencera* that came to grief in

In 1994 DSV *Sirius* was used to remove some of the sand that covered the wreck site.

Kinnagoe Bay, Northern Ireland, and was discovered and salvaged by Sidney Wignall in 1970.

The raising of the Dunwich Bank cannon immediately led to much fevered speculation as to what the wreck was that it had come from. The first thought was that it was another Spanish Armada wreck. The problem with this is that no Spanish armada ships are mentioned in the written records as having sunk anywhere near the Suffolk coast. It was then widely reported in the newspapers that it could be the wreck of the *Royal James*. This possibility cannot absolutely be ruled out. It is common knowledge that ships carried cannon that had been captured from other nations. However, all the sinking detail connected with the *Royal James* suggests that it sank further north and much further out to sea. Also no charred timbers have been discovered at the Dunwich Bank wreck site. Given the severity of the fire known to have occurred on board the *Royal James* one would have expected some evidence of burning. A more convincing theory suggests that it could be the remains of one of the Dutch ships that also sank during the battle of Solebay. A Spanish Armada ship is known to have been wrecked on the Dutch coast and so it is possible that the gun originally came from this source and had been used by the Dutch Admiralty ever since. Another possibility, and the one that I personally favour, is that it is a cannon from the wreck of the ship that Thomas Arundell was travelling on when he returned from the Continent. The position on the coast is consistent with the old records. Arundell mentions Aldeburgh rather than Dunwich but he may well have gone into Aldeburgh depending on the winds and tides when his ship sank. The date of the cannon also somewhat favours the Arundell shipwreck version of events. It is known from wrecks such as that of the *Kronan* that bronze cannon could stay in service for over one hundred years. However, an examination of the bore of the Dunwich cannon suggests limited use and so implies that it was still in the first quarter or so of its serviceable life. Of course, this does not definitively reveal how long it had been in existence when it was lost, because it is just possible that it had been on board ship more than a century, but very little used during that entire time, and so was still in the first quarter of its serviceable life even after a hundred years. Such a scenario is possible, but unlikely. Given the date of the cannon's founding, and an average rate of wear and tear, the cannon's sinking date would be closer to 1595 than to 1672, the date of the battle of Solebay. The main argument against the Arundell theory is that if Rudi Roth is correct about the founder then the cannon is Spanish in origin. Arundell was most probably returning to England from a German port in which case the ship he was on was most probably a ship of Hamburg or an English ship. But this negative argument against is far from conclusive. Mr Roth himself points out that both the *Trinidad Valencera* gun and the Dunwich gun are very similar in design to the guns manufactured by Gregor Loffler, master gunner to the German Imperial Emperor in the middle of the sixteenth century. A lot is known about Loffler's gun designs because of a remarkable book known as the *Geschutzbuch*, produced between 1550 and 1552, which contains 520 detailed drawings of guns, 145 of which were designed by Loffler. A copy survives in the Vienna National Library. The possibility then cannot be absolutely discounted that the gun is German not Spanish in origin, and even if it is Spanish, then again it is still possible that it had been captured by the English and was on board an English ship when it sank.

The Dunwich gun was recovered in 1994. One might have hoped that in the intervening time a little more might have been discovered about this fascinating and obviously important shipwreck. The sad truth is that little further of any substance has been achieved apart from the carefully drawn site plans and surveys produced by Stuart Bacon and his small group of volunteer divers. The explanation for this lack of progress is an extraordinary combination of bureaucratic timidity and academic opposition.

Working in extremely hostile conditions Stuart Bacon and his team of amateur divers have carefully mapped the wreck site. Considering that all the mapping and measuring has to be done by touch, something of the difficulties involved in this process can readily be imagined. Their fingertip underwater explorations have revealed the existence of a minimum of six cannon, at least three of which are made of bronze, excluding the one that has already been recovered. A number of other anomalous features has also been identified and plotted but because of concretion it has been impossible to determine what they are. Having got as far as they could with the predisturbance survey Stuart Bacon applied for a Surface Recovery Licence to bring up those objects that had already been mapped. The need for this was considered to be urgent. There was strong evidence that one bronze gun had already been stolen from the site and there was a fear that other thefts would shortly follow. It was also felt that artefacts on the site were being gradually but significantly degraded because of the continuous effects of sand erosion. The cannon that had already been brought to the surface showed severe effects of abrasion. Over and beyond these concerns relating to the vulnerability of the wreck site, there was also the understandable feeling that it would only be through further excavation that more could be learnt about the ship's origins and identity. The Department of Culture asked the advice of the Advisory Committee on Historic Wreck Sites. The Advisory Committee asked the advice of a specialist underwater archaeological unit based at one of Britain's leading universities. There was much exchange of paperwork. The Department finally agreed that 'an excavation of the site is required', but recommended that fur-

The bronze cannon that was recovered was an impressive eleven and one half foot long saker. This is its decorated muzzle.

ther preliminary work should be carried out first. Concrete blocks were to be put on the seabed as datum points rather than using the cannon themselves as the datum points, which is what Stuart Bacon had been doing. Conservation facilities were to be put in place. And, most importantly, a competent professional archaeologist was to head up the whole operation. The Department of Culture revealed themselves to be very adept at laying down proper procedures. What they were not so good at was coming up with any funding. Stuart Bacon and his colleagues were expected to carry out all the Department's requirements at their own expense.

With the benefit of grants from Shell UK and funding from a commercial company called Deep Sea Exploration, Stuart Bacon's team managed to fulfil all the criteria that had been set out. Most significantly they managed to persuade the world-renowned underwater archaeologist Margaret

Rule, famous for her work on the *Mary Rose*, to head the project. She was attracted to it because she recognised the enormous potential significance of the find. Having complied with the Department's wishes Stuart Bacon again applied for an excavation licence. Again it was turned down. This time a completely new set of objections were raised, fourteen of them in total. They varied from the academically obscure, 'reasons were not given for the methodologies proposed', to the bizarrely nitpicking, 'information about publication was vague'. Many of the objections centred on what were deemed to be the inadequacies of Stuart Bacon's predisturbance survey, completely ignoring the conditions of total darkness in which the survey had to be carried out. Margaret Rule has gone on record as stating that in her opinion the survey was more than adequate: 'I have seldom seen a better survey,' she wrote.

Stuart Bacon has devoted a large part of his life to the study of the underwater archaeology of the Suffolk coastline.

It now began to emerge that the Ministry had changed their minds about the need for excavation and had no intention of granting a licence under any circumstances. 'There is no clear archaeological justification for excavating the site' was the newly adopted position. Instead, they proclaimed the virtues of 'non-intrusive archaeological techniques'. Behind the Ministry's constant procrastinations and frequent moving of the goal posts one suspects the growing influence of the 'hard line' faction of the archaeological academic community that believes that no artefacts from shipwreck sites should be brought to the surface. Instead, the shipwreck is to be conserved *in situ* on the seabed. It is a shame that the Ministry did not expand a little bit more on just how these non-intrusive techniques work in conditions of near total darkness, and what successes have so far been achieved through their deployment in such conditions on other projects. It is equally unfortunate that they did not spell out the financial implications of conserving the hundreds of thousands of historic shipwreck sites that exist around Britain on the seabed. It is also perhaps legitimate to ask for whose benefit all this conserving on the seabed is to be done, if no member of the public ever gets to see the results.

Clearly feeling somewhat pressured both by the tersely critical remarks made by Margaret Rule and the serious concerns expressed by Stuart Bacon, not least as to the geological stability of the site itself, the Ministry did what Ministries do best and commissioned a desktop report on the stability of the site from a specialist organisation in monitoring seabed sediment movements. This report duly concluded that the site was 'relatively stable' thus appearing to support the logic of the government's favoured policy of doing nothing. Stuart Bacon, however, who is one of the few people to have over thirty years' first-hand experience of sediment movements around Dunwich Bank, strongly contested the validity of the report's findings. He sent the Department a scathing critique. The original writers of the report then responded stating that, 'Scientific knowledge of the processes controlling bank formation and development, and the transport pathways of material between the adjacent coastline, the banks, and further offshore, are not well understood, and remain largely speculatory.' If this is the case one does somewhat wonder what the point of the report was in the first place.

The Ministry now felt the need to commission the new advisers to the Advisory Committee to carry out a further predisturbance survey of the site. This new report confirmed everything Stuart Bacon had already said about the difficulties of diving on and adequately surveying the site, because of the strong tides, the lack of visibility and the obstruction of old fishing nets and other miscellaneous debris. The report states, 'It is likely that some degree of inaccuracy was caused by the interplay between the acoustic shadow created by the central mound and the effect of varying strengths of current upon the beacon array. . . The fact that the diver was not always able to see the object that was being recorded was also a problem.' Elsewhere it states, 'the uncertainty with regard to the number of guns arises from the fact that identification and reidentification of concrete features on subsequent dives was problematic in nil/low visibility conditions.' Reading this report one again begins to wonder just what the point of these repeated predisturbance surveys is when no one seems to come up with consistent data. Certainly Stuart Bacon is of the opinion that this latest report wrongly maps a number of the cannon.

Meanwhile, running alongside this sorry saga, a furore has been raging about the one cannon that has already been raised. Stuart Bacon informed the Receiver of Wreck about his find, as he was obliged to do according to the Merchant Shipping Acts. The wreck was then nominated by the Department of Culture Media and Sport (DCMS) as an historic wreck site in accordance with the provisions of the 1973 Protection of Wrecks Act. The bronze cannon, having been conserved, was exhibited outside Mr Bacon's Suffolk Underwater Studies Museum. The Receiver of Wreck was not happy with this as a permanent solution and so efforts were made to find a museum to

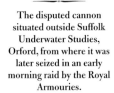

The disputed cannon situated outside Suffolk Underwater Studies, Orford, from where it was later seized in an early morning raid by the Royal Armouries.

house it. Stuart Bacon was agreeable to this proposal but was very insistent that it should be a local museum because the gun had more contextual meaning as a local exhibit. All parties seemed to be agreed on this one principle, namely that the gun should be kept as close as possible to the place it originally came from. Stuart Bacon was quite prepared to forego any salvage award, a reward that he was legally entitled to, and which could have amounted to a significant sum of money, so long as the gun stayed in the area.

The difficulty was that Norfolk Museum Services, Ipswich Museum, English Heritage at Orford Castle, Lowestoft Museum, Dunwich Museum and the National Trust all turned it down. They all had too many objects already to house and conserve for their slender budgets. No one was prepared to take on the giant Dunwich Bank cannon except for the Royal Armouries situated at Fort Nelson in Hampshire. The Receiver of Wreck duly vested title with the Royal Armouries. Stuart Bacon contested their right to do this. In the event the Royal Armouries turned up early one morning at Suffolk Underwater Studies, sawed through the chain by which the cannon was secured against theft, and carted it away. The people of Orford were understandably outraged at this high-handed seizure of what had become something of a local landmark.

The sad thing is that the Ministry has spent large sums of taxpayers' money commissioning seemingly endless reports and surveys of the site and yet nothing has been added by all this expenditure to our understanding of our maritime history or the public's enjoyment of its heritage. On the contrary, Stuart Bacon and his team of volunteer divers are now so disillusioned with the entire business that any future discoveries are more likely to be abandoned to the destructive effects of trawlers, dredgers, pipe layers, and pillagers than to responsible amateur enthusiasts trying to work within the law. Without any prospect of an excavation being carried out in the near future, it seems it will be some years yet before we know the true identity of the shipwreck on Dunwich Bank.

4

The *Blessing* of Burntisland

O NE OF THE LONGEST-RUNNING, most tantalising, and also most glamorous of treasure hunts, or archaeological quests as some of the more serious participants regard it, has involved the search for Charles I's lost coronation baggage. It lies by general agreement somewhere in the murky waters of the Firth of Forth not far from a line between Burntisland on the north side and Leith harbour on the south. This was the main ferry route before road bridges and rail-

ways made the crossing somewhat simpler to negotiate. But quite where the treasure lies along that line remains a conundrum. To date nothing of King Charles's travelling money, silver and gold dinner service, elaborately chased and inscribed goblets or general royal paraphernalia has been located. Charles was, of course, a notoriously unlucky king. Within a few years he was to lose his head, which no doubt made the loss of a few hundred items of his household goods pale into insignificance. Even so, at the time it

Charles I with some of his coronation regalia; oil painting in the style of Daniel Mytens. Charles did not make his coronation trip to Scotland until eight years after he had come to the English throne.

must have been a considerable inconvenience and it probably had something to do with his sub-sequent decision to accelerate his return to London. He himself explained this hasty departure south as prompted by a desire to see his queen and surprise her with his presence before he was expected. It may equally well have been something to do with the fact that his cook and many of his cook's servants had drowned, and he did not relish eating poorly prepared meals off inferior trenchers.

The underwater searches that have so far taken place to try and relocate poor Charles's travel-ling canteen have been well organised and technically sophisticated. The Royal Navy no less has lent the services of one of its mine-hunters, HMS *Cottesmore*, to scan the seabed, deploying the very latest in side-scan sonar technology. Appropriately enough Prince Andrew was at the time serving on board the *Cottesmore*. As a direct descendant of the Stuart king, and therefore a po-tential claimant of anything that might eventually be recovered, he had more than a passing inter-est in the success of the operation. Unfortunately, none of the twelve targets identified by *Cottesmore* on its 1994 survey turned out to be the desired quarry. Divers sent down to the seabed to investi-gate the targets turned up nothing more than the usual detritus found in a busy waterway: disused oil cans, rusting steel fishing boats, trawler nets, miscellaneous abandoned containers of all shapes and sizes, but no 280-piece silver and gold dinner service.

Continued burning optimism is, however, the driving force and main prerequisite for all suc-cessful shipwreck hunts. Despite the disappointment of the 1994 survey the search went on and by January 1999 the newspapers were again full of the story as to how King Charles's priceless kitchen equipment had at last been located. The team carrying out the investigation were so con-fident, it seemed, of having found their target this time round that they announced the details at a press conference on the 350th anniversary of King Charles's execution. The wreck lay one mile from Burntisland in 120 feet of water. The mound on the seabed was the exact shape and size that they had expected and the position was within their search parameters. The Royal Navy had again participated, this time making available the hydrographic survey ship HMS *Roebuck*. Donald Dewar, then secretary of State for Scotland, duly imposed a Protection of Historic Wrecks order on the identified site.

Once again disappointment followed the fanfares. By September 1999 no artefacts had been re-trieved that positively identified the site as being the baggage ship. Doubts began to be cast by third parties as to whether the mound really contained the right wreck. The *Independent* newspaper re-ported that a San Diego-based diver called Bill Warren claimed the wreck was of the wrong centu-ry. Somewhat undermining his own credibility Mr Warren also claimed that an American psychic had identified the true location of the *Blessing* and a Professor William Wallace of San Diego University had scientifically confirmed this position as being the correct one. Quite where the sci-ence came in to this process was unfortunately not explained in the article. The original Scotland-based group was not dismayed by these criticisms. They were still hopeful that they had got the right ship. According to the press reports, 'Alex Kilgour, spokesman for the Burntisland Heritage Trust, said that he was confident that a positive announcement on the identity of the 60-foot long, 15-foot wide, and five-foot deep ship could be made within two months.' His colleague, Ian Archibald, somewhat revealingly admitted at the same time, however, that their site had originally been identified by a dowser called Jim Longton, although the Royal Navy survey ship later located an anomaly in the same position.

Sadly it was not to be. The first flush of excitement slowly gave way to a renewed bout of disappointment. Month after month went past and still nothing was retrieved that positively proved that the site was actually that of King Charles's baggage ship. A prolonged silence once again descended upon the subject of the *Blessing* of Burntisland. Many of the original participants in the project still continue their interest and still believe that the elusive boat may one day be found. Understandably, however, they have become somewhat more circumspect in their announcements.

One of the difficulties when it comes to locating the remains of the *Blessing* is that although the

The return of Charles, when Prince of Wales, from Spain in October 1623. The small vessel ahead of the flagship *Prince Royal* is about the size of the *Blessing*. Detail from a painting by H C Vroom.

47

cargo is highly glamorous, the boat itself was extremely humble. It was a small wooden ferry boat probably single-masted, no more than 70 feet long and 100 tons in burthen. It would not have carried many, if any, cannon, perhaps just a couple of small swivel guns in the bow for signalling and defence in a minor skirmish. This lack of a significant quantity of iron cannon makes it a very poor magnetometer target. The boat's nails, the odd iron fitting, the anchors and the iron used in the construction of the numerous carts from the royal baggage train that was loaded on board would be about the sum of it, one or two tons at the most. It is probably because of this envisaged lack of iron that most of the surveys that have so far been conducted appear to have used sonar rather than magnetometer. The trouble with using sonar, however, on a project like this, is that the remains of a small 370-year-old wreck would almost certainly have been entirely silted over by a thick layer of mud. The Forth is, after all, a major river estuary. For detection purposes sonar relies on a deviating contour on the seabed. If no such contour is present then nothing will show up. Perhaps this is why the Burntisland Heritage Trust turned to dowsing. A sub-bottom profiler might have been more productive, but this technology is still pretty much in its infancy and beset with teething problems.

Another difficulty is the scantiness of the historical evidence. One would have thought that the near drowning of a king would have generated a large quantity of comment. But the event appears to have been passed over in the annals and records with surprisingly little mention. Even the boat's name, the *Blessing*, is open to question. There was certainly one *Blessing*, owned by a Captain Andrew Watson of Burntisland, who was actively involved in the ferrying of people across the Firth of Forth at this period. However, the available evidence would suggest that there were two small ferry boats in attendance on the king that day. Burntisland Burgh Records for Tuesday, 9 July, read 'Understanding that the King his Majesty is to visit. . . Ordaineth two boats to be provided for him and noblemen who should happen to go with him. And the said boats to be equipped by Capt. A. Watson. . . and a boat to be equipped by Capt. J. Orrock.' As Watson appears to have been the senior and more important of the two captains involved it seems reasonable to assume that the King travelled in his boat and that it was Captain Orrock's boat, following close behind that sank. The name of Captain Orrock's boat has not been discovered.

The story of the sinking and the events that led up to it, so far as it can be pieced together from the random historical scraps of information that have survived, is similarly confusing. Charles set out from London on 11 May 1633 for Scotland. It would be the first time he had been there since the age of three. This was an era when the Scottish elite liked to live in London, occupied most of the high offices of England and largely concentrated their formidable energies on ruling their wealthy southern neighbour, apparently considering this option as far preferable to inhabiting their own comparatively poorer and less powerful kingdom. Charles had come to the throne in 1625 on the death of his father, James I of England and James VI of Scotland. He had not as yet, however, even bothered to visit the kingdom of his birth for the purpose of being formally crowned King of Scotland. It is important to remember that Scotland and England were at that time still separate realms. A royal visit for the purpose of investiture was therefore already eight years overdue when Charles finally got around to it. His formal coronation was to be the stated purpose and ceremonial centrepiece of the royal tour. The underlying agenda was to bolster his power in the northern kingdom at a time when it was being increasingly threatened in the south.

The procession north was an impressive one. There were thirteen nobles who occupied some of the highest positions of state and two bishops, as well as a vast number of supernumeraries necessary to any royal progress of this kind, including six trumpeters, six chaplains, nine messengers, seven musicians, two surgeons, two physicians, an apothecary, eight cooks, grooms, pages, cup bearers, carvers, sewers and miscellaneous servants and ancillaries. There were 500 people in

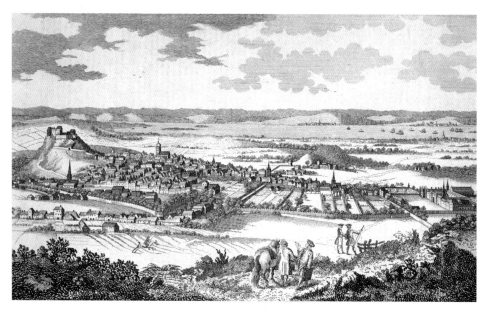

An eighteenth-century view of Edinburgh, with Burntisland visible on the other side of the Forth.

all, horses and carriages for the entire complement, and fifty cart loads of baggage requisitioned from the Office of the Ordnance. It is the cooks that especially concern us, as they appear to have suffered more than most when it came to the sinking. Further supplies, including large quantities of plates and cutlery, were transported by sea in a ship of Anstruther called the *Blue Doo*.

The entire entourage stayed at various stately homes en route. To be selected as a stopover was an expensive business. The Earl of Newcastle, for instance, at Welbeck House, spent £700 on a banquet in the king's honour. After-dinner entertainment consisted of the usual speeches and then, somewhat more unusually, 'a marriage between an exceedingly tall wench and a very low dwarf with quintance and dancing'. One cannot help but wonder whether the marriage was a love match or merely an arrangement for the amusement of the royal visitors.

By 8 June the King had arrived at Berwick, where he stayed until the 12th, before going on to Dunglas, Setton and Dalkeith, at each of which noble seats he spent one night. The roads were, in those days, in a very poor state, carriages frequently getting stuck in mud or turning over if a wheel slipped into a pothole. The roads in Scotland were, if anything, in an even worse condition than those in England. The Scottish Privy Council meeting in Holyrood House on 17 January 1633 were busy making last-minute and frantic orders for the repair of the highways: 'The Lords of Secret Council, finding it necessary and expedient for the honour and credit of the kingdom and for his Majesty's contented reception here, that the highways and passageways through which his Majesty's progress will lie be mended, helped and enlarged and made passable for coaches and horses.' As the cost of all this road-mending fell on the local inhabitants of the parish wherein the defects lay, it can be imagined that having the royal entourage pass through your locality was not regarded by everyone as an unqualified delight.

Despite all the logistical problems the descent upon Edinburgh appears to have been a triumph of stage management. A contemporary memorialist, James Balfour, described the occasion with breathless enthusiasm. 'The kingdom had not seen a more glorious sight, the streets being railed and sanded, the chief places where he passed were set out with triumphal arches, obelisks, pictures, artificial mountains adorned with choice music and other diverse costly shows.' Quite why Scotland should have any need for artificial mountains as a backdrop when it always appears to have plenty of the real thing is a little curious, but presumably the scene-makers had their reasons. A portable mountain or two was perhaps a useful way of obscuring those sights that it was considered unseemly for a king to look upon. Charles himself clearly made an impressive entry. James Balfour again sets the scene. 'Then came the King Majesty riding on a barbary, with one exceeding rich caparison and footcloth of crimson velvet, embroidered with gold and oriental pearls the bosses of bridle cusper and tye, being richly set with emeralds rubies and diamonds, and in his head a panache of red and white plumes.' It was all pretty fancy stuff.

Charles stayed a little over two weeks in Edinburgh. The coronation was successfully completed. Various royal appointments were made. Sumptuous presents were given to the King including 'a basin all of gold estimated at 5,000 marks, wherein was shaken out of an embroidered purse a thousand golden double angels, as a token of the town of Edinburgh their love and humble service,' wrote John Spalding. One can not help but wonder whether such lavish gifts were on board the baggage ship when it went down.

From Edinburgh Charles carried out a whirlwind tour of some of his domains visiting Linlithgow, Stirling, Dunfermline and Falkland. On 10 July he left Falkland in order to return to Edinburgh.

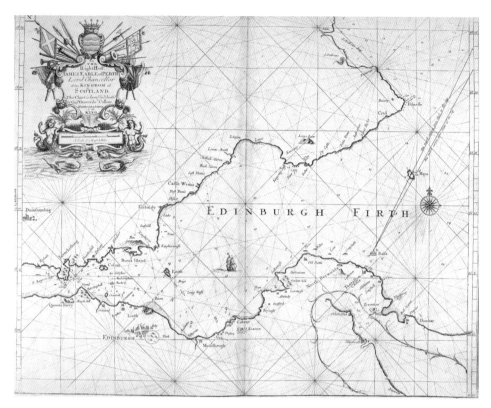

A Chart dating from the late seventeenth century of the Firth of Forth. 'Burnt Island' is
shown on the north side of the firth, and the usual ferry route went to Leith on the south.

To accomplish this he needed to cross the Firth of Forth and the best port for this purpose was
Burntisland, or Brunt Island as some of the original records refer to it. There was a regular ferrying service between Burntisland and Leith although the boatmen involved in running it were not
held in universally high esteem. A document of 1636 describes them as being unruly and com-
plains that 'they collected fares a mile or two out at sea and compelled passengers to pay double
under pain of detention.' When there was no wind they claimed extra money because they had to
row so hard and when it was stormy they claimed because of 'the risk run'. The same document
makes an interesting reference to the sinking of the King's ferry boat three years earlier, claiming it
went down not because of the bad weather but the negligence of the sailors. The number of Charles's
servants drowned is given as fifty and the loss of goods stated to be £100,000, a very considerable
sum in those days.

A rather more detailed and probably fairer explanation for the sinking is provided by James
Balfour, 'where his passage from Burntisland to Leith, he was in great jeopardy of his life by a sud-

den storm which did arise after a great rain that had been all the preceding night and morning, but spent itself in less than half an hour. His Majesty with no small danger recovered his own ship, which waited for him in Burntisland Road, later landing from it at Leith, only there was a little boat with some of the King's plate and monies, and 8 servants, lost.' The language is somewhat convoluted but the clear implication of what is being said here is that the King set out from the harbour in a small boat to travel the half mile or so to where his larger ship was anchored in Burntisland Roads, most probably in about ten fathoms of water. This larger ship may possibly have been the *Blue Doo* mentioned earlier. Another small baggage boat was following the King. A storm blew up. Charles managed to transfer to the larger ship but the small boat following sank. Another account related in the *Historie of the Kirk of Scotland* tells basically the same story: '. . . he came to Burntisland and passed over to Leith in a pinnace of his own; but the day being somewhat tempestuous, many going over the water at that time, a little boat, wherein there were sundry Englishmen, the King's servants, and rich coffers, were drowned in sight of the King's pinnace, which made the

A detail from Adam Willaerts' painting showing disembarkation from the *Prince Royal* in 1640. The *Blessing* may well have resembled the small craft in the right foreground.

King melancholy that night.' In John Spalding's account, on the other hand, the pinnace is not mentioned at all: '. . . came back to Burntisland, shipped, came over the water and safely lodged in the abbey that night. But, as he is on the water, in his own sight, there perished a boat following after him, having within her about 35 persons of English and Scots, his own domestic servants, and only two escaped with their lives. His Majesty's silver plate and household stuff perished with the rest.'

All these accounts tell basically the same story of a small boat sinking on the voyage between

Burntisland and Leith, with varying estimates of the number of King's servants and the value of goods lost. The problem is that when taken as a whole they allow for the construction of three possible sequences of events which have very different implications for sinking position. The first, which may conveniently be called the Balfour scenario, has the King transferring from a small boat to a pinnace, with another small boat, which was following on behind, sinking before or at around the same time as the King made his transfer. This places the sinking very close in to the shore and would almost certainly have allowed for subsequent salvage of non-perishable valuables. The *Historie of the Kirk* version on the other hand permits the possibility that the small baggage boat might have been lost after Charles had transferred to the pinnace, the small boat having been intended from the outset to make the entire voyage across the estuary. This makes it quite conceivable that the sinking occurred much further out into the Firth. The Spalding account leaves open the question as to whether King Charles transferred to a pinnace at any point in the crossing, which again has the result of making the sinking position much vaguer. The pinnace referred to here would have been a small, fast warship, not to be confused with the small rowing boat, also called a pinnace, carried on board ship, and much used by captains in the eighteenth century for making short trips.

Whether or not there was actually a royal pinnace in attendance that day at Burntisland is questionable, and not simply because Spalding makes no mention of it. The entire crossing from Burntisland to Leith is a distance of only seven miles. In some ways it would seem to have been undertaking an unnecessary risk for the King to transfer from small boat to pinnace, and then back from pinnace to small boat in order to land in Leith harbour, when the entire crossing could easily have been made in a small boat. Without transfers the time taken would probably have been no more than one-and-a-half to two hours. With transfers, which would involve the weighing of anchors and the setting of sails on a large ship, it would take much longer. We already know from the Burntisland Burgh records that the local council 'ordaineth two boats to be provided for him [the King] and noblemen who should happen to go with him' and that these boats belonged to Captain Watson and Captain Orrock. This suggests that the King may possibly have made the entire crossing in the small regular ferry boat belonging to Andrew Watson, with Orrock following on behind.

The privy Council of Scotland Records throw some further interesting light on the matter. Clearly preparations for the King's coronation visit were being discussed a full five years before he actually got round to making the trip. The baillies of Edinburgh had offered in 1628 to build a special 'bark' for the King's transportation between the two ferry points just as they had built such a ship for James I's visit in 1617. The offer had been sharply rejected by the Lord High Admiral, the Earl of Linlithgow, arguing that 'the charge of that business belonged unto him as his Majesty's Admiral.' The magistrates of Edinburgh seemed very happy to relinquish their responsibility, no doubt regarding it as being something of a financial burden. The following year the Lords of the Privy Council reveal themselves to be anxious that having claimed the honour, the Earl of Linlithgow does not attempt now to offload the financial burden on to the King himself. Reading between the lines of this dispute it appears that the Earl of Linlithgow may have regarded the right to build the pinnace or 'bark' as something of a perk, expecting to be handsomely reimbursed for his efforts from the King's exchequer, only to discover that the permanently impecunious King Charles was having none of it. In such a situation it seems conceivable that the royal pinnace was never actually built. On the other hand it has to be remembered that the purpose of the entire journey was essentially ceremonial. It would probably have been considered undignified for the King to make the crossing in a small ferry boat, even if it may have been quicker and more convenient. On balance it seems likely that there probably was a pinnace even if it had not been built by Linlithgow.

The situation is further complicated by the details of the sinking provided in Rushworth's *Historical Collections*. Rushworth, like Balfour, has the King transferring to a larger ship, this time called a warship rather than a pinnace, and he also refers to the fact that 'one of the King's boats with the King's plate was overset, and near 20 persons perished', a higher casualty rate than in Balfour but less than in Spalding. He mentions the crossing as taking place around midday and also states that the sudden storm was so localised that it was not even felt on land. What is most interesting about Rushworth's account, however, is that he remarks that three people were saved, 'sitting upon the keil which was upmost'. If accurate, and there is no obvious reason to disbelieve the truth of this assertion, then this is bad news for the would-be salvors. First, it introduces the possibility of the contents of the barge being tipped out and spread over a wide area of seabed outside any defined hull. Second, it suggests that the barge itself may not have sunk, or certainly not immediately. It may merely have turned over, causing a loss of contents and people. Certainly, the description of the weather in all the various accounts of a sudden but very shortlived tempest of wind is consistent with a boat capsizing.

Part of the difficulty with the Burntisland project lies in the fact that none of the accounts quoted were written by an actual witness of the sinking. The King's secretary, Sir John Coke, was travelling with Charles, and was very probably in the same boat with him but his mention of what occurred is so terse it adds nothing. He writes from Edinburgh to his co-secretary of state, Windebank, in London, 'Yesterday, in passing the sea from Falkland, a boat was cast away and some people and goods lost; but the King and all the Lords are in safety and good health.'

The records reveal one or two further glimpses into the grim tragedy of the loss but nothing that really helps pin down where the wreck lies. The body of John Ferries, the King's cook, was washed ashore. The place is given as 'The Wold' which does not significantly help to identify the position. There is included in his burial accounts a detailed summary of the possessions found on his person. '£45 in dollars and other white money, 5 × 12 pound pieces in gold, ane single angel, in all

In the seventeenth century witches were frequently held
responsible for shipwrecks and in 1634 some
Manchester women were arraigned for the storm which
had endangered Charles' life. This is the frontispiece of
The Discovery of Witches, published in 1647 by Mathew
Hopkins, the most infamous 'Witchfinder'.

£107–5s–4d; gold ring, rapier belt and hanger. Item a coat and breeches of camblet.' It seems like
a lot of cash for a cook to have been carrying but perhaps he was required to buy some supplies
from it.

One of the most sinister if incidental aspects of the sinking is the fact that the following year,
1634, a large number of Lancashire women were accused of witchcraft, one of their supposed sins
having been 'raising the great storm wherein his Majesty was in so great danger at sea in Scotland'.
It was not uncommon at this time for women to be accused of raising storms by means of witchcraft and put to death for their sins. Fortunately on this occasion they were found to be innocent
and released. Meanwhile the search for the *Blessing* of Burntisland continues.

5

The Burning of the *Royal James*

*T*HE 28 MAY 1672 WAS A BEAUTIFUL SUMMER'S DAY, the warmest of the year so far. The sea was 'as smooth as a fishpond' throughout, with only light easterly winds to ruffle the surface occasionally. Edward Montagu, the first Earl of Sandwich, on board the *Royal James* and in command of the Blue Squadron, rose early and put on his full regalia as if preparing for a great and ceremonious occasion. He was a Knight of the Garter, Vice Admiral of England and Admiral of the Narrow Seas. He was also a big cumbersome man and his steward Valentin assisted him with his wardrobe. Once dressed, the Star was pinned to his breast and the George hung around his neck, encrusted with thirteen diamonds. He wore the blue garter of the Order about his leg. His fingers were adorned with rich rings, including one with a large blue teardrop sapphire and one set with a small seaman's compass. He also carried a gold and jewelled pocket watch. He was not a man to frown upon ostentation; indeed he was noted for his lavish life style and personal generosity. His mood on that morning, however, was notably sombre. As he went to go on deck, legend has it that he turned to Valentin and said to him, 'Now, Val, I must be sacrificed.' If the anecdote is true then his prognostication was remarkably accurate. The *Royal James* was to sink later that day in a mass of flames and over 600 of its more than 900 men were lost, including the Earl of Sandwich himself.

The *Royal James* was a first-rate three-decker and one of the finest and newest ships of the fleet. It had been launched in the spring of 1671 and so was barely a year old when it sank beneath the waves somewhere off Southwold. It had been designed by the rising young naval architect Sir Anthony Deane in the shipyard at Portsmouth where Deane had the position of Master Shipwright. Deane was a close friend of Samuel Pepys who was himself a distant relation of Edward Montagu. Montagu was Pepys' first patron and instrumental in his rise to importance in the Navy Board. Deane and Pepys' careers were similarly to be closely intertwined. The social and professional world of the British Navy at this period was relatively small and closely knit.

At 1,416 tons the *Royal James* was the second largest ship in the fleet, only the *Royal Sovereign* being bigger at 1,492 tons. The *Royal James*, however, was longer than the *Royal Sovereign*. Its keel was 132 feet 6 inches, five-and-a-half feet longer than the *Sovereign*'s and it was by all accounts a fast and 'weatherly' sailer, though it did not survive long enough to be really put to the test. One feature of Deane's design that was particularly innovatory was the use of iron knees and pillars instead of the usual oak ones. This use of iron was not to become common in shipbuilding until over a hundred years later. The iron would provide a very helpful and distinctive feature for anyone trying to identify the remains of the hull today. The extra length enabled it to carry more cannon than any other ship at that time, 104 in total. The total cost of the hull came to £24,072. This was an enormous sum of money in those days, equivalent to many millions of pounds today, but interestingly the cost of the guns on board was greater than the cost of building the entire hull. In his *Doctrine of Naval Architecture* Sir Anthony Deane records the value of the guns, all of

them cast in bronze, as coming to £26,550. They would all have been engraved with the Stuart rose and crown. The coat of arms of King Charles would have been etched on the first re-inforce and that of his Master of the Royal Ordnance, Colonel George Legge, would have decorated the chase. Charles's monogram, CR, would have also been prominent and some-where along the barrel there would no doubt have been the broad arrow that designated the piece as being owned by the state. These guns form one of the main attractions for those searching for the wreck of the *James* but they are far from being the only lure. This was an age when war at sea was still conducted with a certain amount of lavish flamboyance. Sir Edward Montague was one of the most important courtiers of his day and would have had on board his own silver cutlery, plate and goblets

Edward Montagu, first Earl of Sandwich, after Peter Lely, Montagu was widely rumoured to have foretold his own death at the Battle of Solebay.

for the entertainment of himself and his officers. Treasury records reveal that Lord Sandwich alone lost personal property worth over £4,000 when the *Royal James* went down. Hardly surprising then that this wreck has been more extensively and continuously sought after than almost any other shipwreck in the North Sea area. Between the silverware and the guns there is plenty to stimulate the imagination of any aspiring treasure hunter.

In the summer of 1988 the newspapers were full of an amazing shipwreck find. The remains of the *Royal James*, it was claimed, had finally been located just a few miles off Southwold after many years of patient searching. The reports made good reading. Richard Branson, the billionaire and founder of the Virgin group of companies, had put up some of the considerable amounts of cash required to finance the expedition. A local company, Geosite Surveys, had provided cutting-edge technical support. Orlando Montagu, a direct descendant of Edward Montagu, the Earl of Sandwich, had provided a fascinating family link with the past. George Spence, a young diver who had sold his house to get the project under way in its early days, and had subsequently devoted years of his life to the *Royal James* quest, added the necessary element of tenacious human endeavour against insuperable odds. And finally, of course, there was that most vital of all ingre-dients to any good shipwreck story, the millions of pounds of valuables that were shortly expect-ed to come to the surface in the form of bronze cannon, gold coins, silver plate and jewels.

George Spence (centre) on the *Dawn Shore*. Spence has been searching for the *Royal James* wreck for over twenty years, so far without conspicuous success.

1988 was not the first time that there had been reports of the *Royal James* being found. Nor was it to be the last. Down the decades there have been any number of eye-catching news-paper headlines claiming that the wreck has finally been discovered and mentioning mouth-watering values of booty running to many millions of pounds. Yet to date all the money, all the time and all the rumours have come to nothing. The *Royal James* continues to be tan-talisingly reticent about declaring its present whereabouts. The Branson-funded expedition proved to be no different from the other false starts. Despite all the fanfares and trumpetings nothing more emerged of the missing vessel than a piece of anonymous charred timber. The trouble with charred timber is that it could have come from any one of several dozen vessels lost in this area of the North Sea during the fierce and bitter battles of the Anglo-Dutch wars.

Usually when a wreck cannot be located it is because the records are thin on the ground. This is not the case with the loss of the *Royal James*. I have collected upwards of 1,000 pages of primary source material relating to its sinking. There are eyewitness statements not only from those on board ship but also from those on shore. There are journals, log books, diaries, letters, newspaper accounts, official reports, eulogies and poems. There are also drawings, paintings and even tapestries that depict the progress of the battle at various points throughout the day. In fact there is such a wealth of documentation not just from the English side, but also from the Dutch and the French, that it is difficult to disentangle all the available material. In this case it is perhaps not so much a paucity of information but an excess which explains why the whereabouts of the *Royal James* has continuously slipped through the net. Amid such a mass of detail it is easy to miss the crucial clue.

The Third Dutch War started in earnest on 13 March 1672 when Sir Robert Holmes, lying in wait off the Isle of Wight, attacked the homecoming Dutch Smyrna fleet. The attack did not produce the opportunistic windfall that Charles had hoped for but from that point on open hostilities between the two nations was inevitable and war was declared four days later. On 28 March France also formally entered the conflict against the Dutch. Diplomatic relations had already seriously deteriorated before Holmes' attempted hijacking. The previous year there had been one of those odd incidents involving naval etiquette that today seem almost incomprehensible as a reason for war, but were taken very seriously by the Stuarts. One of Charles' royal yachts called the *Merlin* had been returning from Holland to England with Lady Temple on board and had passed through the Dutch fleet. Salutes were fired but the Dutch refused to strike their flags and lower their top sails in deference. Charles was apparently outraged and the luckless captain of the *Merlin* was committed to the Tower for not firing on the Dutch fleet in retaliation for the insult, even though the odds against him were so enormous that any such action on his part would have been almost certainly suicidal. In fact, the cynical Charles had been privately seeking an excuse for war for some time before this. Officially England belonged to a triple alliance which included Sweden and Holland. But secretly Charles was already in league with Louis XIV, agreeing to support France's ongoing struggle against the Netherlands in return for cash payments from Louis. Charles' prime motivation, as always, was to obtain a source of money that would enable him to become more independent of Parliament.

It was nearly another month before the main French, English and Dutch fleets were at sea. The intention of the English under James, Duke of York, with Lord Sandwich second in command, was to rendezvous with the French fleet under the command of Count d'Estrées at Portsmouth, the French coming from Brest. It was considered that the advantage in numbers they would then have over the Dutch would be overwhelming. Anticipating this, Admiral de Ruyter was keen to attack the English as they left the Thames Estuary and before they entered the Channel. Fortunately for the English de Ruyter was delayed, waiting for the Zeeland fleet under Banckert, and by the time the Dutch reached the Downs the English were already gone. De Ruyter declined to chase the English down the Channel not wishing to be cut off from his home ports.

The conjunction successfully accomplished between the English and the French the combined fleet came back up the Channel hoping to meet with the Dutch in open water with a favourable wind, under which circumstances they were confident of victory. The combatants first saw each other on 19 May in the vicinity of the Galloper Sand. The wind was from the south-west which gave the Anglo-French fleet the advantage of the weather gage. De Ruyter, however, was far too experienced an admiral to engage his ships under such adverse circumstances and so retreated towards the Dutch coast. Night fell and both sides burnt false lights to try and confuse the enemy. At dawn the following day there was a thick mist so that the two fleets remained obscured. Small-arms fire was exchanged and contact between friendly vessels could only be maintained by the ringing of bells and the beating of drums. At nine o'clock the mist suddenly cleared as the result of a sharp north-westerly wind springing up but the sea was now too rough to make an engagement possible. Once again de Ruyter retreated towards his coast and the allied fleet stood away. Lord Sandwich advised James against approaching too close among the notoriously treacherous shoals off

Air lift in operation off Easton Bavents. A seventeenth-century swivel gun was trawled up here in the 1970s and this area has subsequently been the focus of much of the searching for the *Royal James.*

544770
7787

For most of the year the waters off the East Coast provide the diver with little or no visibility.

Schooneveld. The English and French sailed back across the North Sea to anchor in Solebay more or less abreast of Southwold. The allied fleet was already running short of supplies of food and water. The plan was to revictual and then take up a position in the vicinity of Dogger Bank with the intention of controlling Dutch supply lines and possibly capturing the returning Dutch East India fleet which was expected to come via the north route, that is, up the west coast of England and round Scotland. This tactic would force de Ruyter to leave the protection of his sandbanks and give battle to the English and French in open sea. For some days de Ruyter did not know where the allied fleet had gone. Then one of his scouts captured an English collier that had passed the fleet in Solebay. The master of the collier gave the game away. Shortly after the receipt of this valuable information the wind began to blow from the east and de Ruyter immediately set sail.

Between three and four o'clock on the morning of 28 May 1672, soon after dawn, a scouting ship came at great haste into Solebay, top gallant sails flying and firing its guns in obvious alarm. The Dutch fleet had been sighted under full sail only a few leagues to the east. The allies, that is, the English and the French on this occasion, had been taken completely by surprise. Large numbers of men were ashore and the flagship of the English fleet, the *Prince*, was still in the process of being heeled over and cleaned. The blame for this fiasco was afterwards to be laid firmly at the feet of Sir John Cox, Captain of the *Prince*. According to the account given in James's memoirs, as soon as the wind started blowing from the east, James had realised the potential danger of being surprised upon the coast and had given an order for the fleet to stand out from the shore and be ready to give battle. Sir John Cox had argued against this, claiming that they were in no immediate danger. A packet boat had just come in with the information that the Dutch ships were still lying off their own coast, many of them with their yards and top masts down. Captain Cox considered that the combined French and English fleets would be better off making use of the time available to complete their supplies. James was persuaded. As a military leader James was undoubtedly brave but he frequently revealed himself as lacking confidence in his own opinions. The problem with Captain Cox's advice was that it was based upon faulty intelligence. Sir John Cox became, of course, a convenient scapegoat because he was shortly to be killed in the ensuing battle and so would not be in a position to defend his reputation. But James's narrative is consistent with the known facts as detailed in John Narborough's journal and certainly seems perfectly credible.

Another version of the events that led up to the battle of Solebay, one of the bloodiest naval engagements of all the Dutch Wars, is related by the seventeenth-century historian, Bishop Burnet. According to Burnet the day before the battle, that is, 27 May, a Council of War was held during which Lord Montagu, Earl of Sandwich, had urged that the fleet should put to sea and James had retorted by accusing him of cowardice. According to Burnet, Lord Sandwich was so stung by this accusation that he fought with particularly reckless valour during the ensuing engagement, making no effort to save himself when his ship, the *Royal James*, finally caught fire. By this means he proved his courage to all who had doubted it. There is no corroborative evidence that this Council of War ever took place let alone this actual conversation between James and Lord Sandwich, and as Burnet both contradicts himself within the space of a few lines and was always eager to rubbish James's reputation at every available opportunity the story was very probably little more than malicious. For James to have accused Sandwich of cowardice, because he recommended the ships stood out to sea so as to be better prepared for an attack, does not make any logical or navigational sense, and while James may not have been much of an intellectual, he was a good seaman. (If there had been a recent difference of opinion between the two men it is far more likely to have occurred when Sandwich recommended not following the Dutch fleet too closely in to the sands of Schooneveld when the wind was in their favour.)

There is, however, some interesting anecdotal evidence, that ties in with the Bishop's waspish remarks and helps to explain their possible origins. It seems that Lord Sandwich, normally a sanguine and jovial man, had a strong premonition of his own death. According to the Earl of Mulgrave, who was present at the battle, he was in a very melancholy mood the evening before hostilities started. 'He dined in Mr Digby's ship the day before the battle when nobody dreamt of fighting, and showed a gloomy discontent so contrary to his usual cheerful humour, that we even then all took

A contemporary Admiralty model of a three-decker, the *Britannia* of 1682.
This ship was marginally larger than the *Royal James* but very similar in design and layout.

notice of it, but much more afterwards.' John Evelyn's diary, a mine of information on so much to do with this period, helps to illuminate just what it was that was at the root of Lord Sandwich's depression. After lamenting Sandwich's death together with the deaths of Clement Coterell and Sir Charles Harbord, two young officers who had also been aboard the *Royal James* when it caught fire, Evelyn makes the following entry: 'And here I cannot but make some reflection upon things past: Since it was not above a day or two, that going at White-hall to take my leave of his Lordship (who had his lodgings in the Privy Gardens) shaking me by the hand bid me *god buy*, he should he thought see me no more, & I saw to my thinking something boading in his countenance; no says he, they will not have me live.' The 'they' referred to here are identified as the Duke of Albemarle and Lord Clifford. Both these men had the ear of James.

The cause of Lord Sandwich's gloom then went far deeper than any simple disagreement about pre-battle tactics. He had lost influence with James particularly since the scandal about misappropriated spoils from the Dutch East Indiaman that he had taken at Bergen. Perhaps most importantly of all Sandwich was, in principle, against the present war. Again it is Evelyn that supplies the details. 'He was utterly against the war from the beginning, & abhor'd the attacquing of the Smyrna fleete.' The legend that he died almost wilfully in order to prove his courage and loyalty was clearly born out of this mood of despondency and disaffection. Samuel Pepys, a kinsman and devoted supporter of Sandwich who in turn had given Pepys invaluable help in the early days of his career, makes his own contribution to the myths surrounding Sandwich's death in his *Naval Minutes*. Pepys notes that on 27 April 1694 he was dining with Lord Clarendon in his parlour where he had hanging a painting of the *Royal James* in its last hours as it burnt to the waterline. The conversation naturally enough turned to Lord Sandwich and the battle of Solebay that had taken place twenty-two years beforehand. Lord Clarendon referred to a dinner he had had a few weeks before the battle at Lord Burlington's house, together with Lord Sandwich and Sandwich's loyal officers Sir Charles Harbord and Clement Cotterel. After the meal they had walked in the garden, Lord Sandwich supported on either side by Harbord and Cotterel, 'for his greater ease, being then grown somewhat goutish or otherwise unwieldy'. They had talked about the forthcoming war. Lord Sandwich had complained about how he was now kept in ignorance as to the proposed tactics. He had then added somewhat ominously, 'This only I know, that I will die, and these two boys will die with me.' Was this Lord Clarendon embroidering the conversation two decades later for the benefit of another dinner party or had Lord Sandwich really foreseen his own death and that of his two supporting officers?

Whatever the truth one thing was very quickly clear. The French and the English were caught off their guard. The Dutch bore down from the north-east. The French Admiral D'Estrées, commanding the White Squadron, which was planned to have been in the vanguard of the action, set sail to the south-east. Sandwich, in charge of the Blue Squadron, headed towards the north-east. And James, Duke of York, commanding the Red Squadron, hurried in his wake as quickly as could be managed. The *Royal James* was the first ship under sail, probably somewhere between 4 and 5 a.m., and very rapidly found itself so far out in front that it was forced to bear up to leeward in order to bring itself back into line. Numerous different authorities are all more or less agreed that at around 7 a.m. the *Royal James* engaged the Dutch fleet, being the first ship to do so.

There is less accurate information on exactly where the ships were when the conflict started. Captain Kempthorne, in the *St Andrew* mentions how 'from 7 of the clock, we continued fighting on the same tack until about 10 or 11... standing still to the Northwards about two or three leagues from the shore'. However, Kempthorne was some distance astern of the *James* and unable to see quite what was happening because of the smoke from the guns. The *James* was presumably further to the north and further out to sea. According to Ralph Babett writing from Aldeburgh, the fight began four leagues north-east of Aldeburgh, which would place the action about on a level with Southwold. This seems a little unlikely because the *James* started from an anchorage off Southwold and had headed north-east for two or more hours before engaging, which would place the initial battle more probably six or seven leagues north-east of Aldeburgh. Babett's remarks demonstrate the difficulty of judging the distance of ships from a viewpoint on land.

During the first two hours of the battle the *Royal James* was subjected to an intense attack by three or four vessels in Captain van Ghent's squadron. The *Henry*, the nearest ship to the *James*, was similarly pounded and at one point was boarded and seized by the Dutch, although it was later retaken. After about an hour of this heated exchange of gunfire the Dutch attacked the *James* with two successive fireships, the most deadly and feared weapon in any sea battle at this period.

The first of these fireships the *James* sank with its lower deck guns and the second it also managed to disable sufficiently to avoid its deadly cargo. It was around this time that Sandwich sent off his barge to his vice admiral, Sir Joseph Jordan, in the *Royal Sovereign*, who was in the van of the squadron and not yet engaged with the enemy, instructing him to tack and weather the enemy and bear down on his assailants from the windward side. Captain Haddock of the *James*, the only officer of that ship to survive the terrible mauling of that day, was later to accuse Jordan of displaying a callous disregard for the plight of the *James*. He wrote that 'some time after [nine or ten o'clock] Sir Joseph Jordan. . . passed by us to windward very unkindly.' It was an accusation that was to prove extremely damaging to Jordan's reputation. Jordan admitted receiving the message and remarked in his own account that he had already been preparing to tack and weather the Dutch. His explanation as to why he did not go to succour the *James* was that he did not see the state of distress it was in and he was anyway busily engaged with other Dutch ships. Meanwhile Sandwich, in desperation, also sent off his pinnace to his rear admiral, Sir John Kempthorne, in the *St Andrew*, requesting assistance, but the pinnace never arrived with its desperate message and although Kempthorne seemed half aware that there was something wrong, his view was obscured by smoke, and moreover a number of ships in his division were having trouble getting into line.

Help failed to arrive and before very long the *James*'s situation had seriously deteriorated. At around 9 a.m. one of de Ruyter's more daring captains, van Brakel, who had led the devastating raid that had inflicted widespread damage on the English fleet when it had been moored at Chatham in 1667, left the Dutch line and crashed his ship, the *Groot Hollandia*, sixty guns, across the bows of the *Royal James*. 'About an hour and a half after we engaged we were boarded thwart our hawse by one of their men of war', is how Haddock puts it. The two ships were quickly entangled and the strong flood tide running from north to south would have the effect of continually forcing the Dutch ship closer under the *James*'s bowsprit. The *Groot Hollandia*, riding lower in the water, was able to pour shot into the hull of the *James*, while the *James*'s guns largely flew over the top of the *Hollandia*.

In desperation, Lord Sandwich suggested boarding the Dutch ship in order to free themselves of her. Captain Haddock dissuaded him. He pointed out that between 250 and 300 of their men were already dead and they would probably lose a hundred more if they tried to board. (The total complement of men on board the *James* was originally 800.) In addition, even if they did manage to successfully take the Dutch ship it was still unlikely they would be able to free themselves because of the effect of the flood tide. Third, attempting to board would involve removing men from manning the guns, which would not only be advantageous to the enemy, but also might give the impression of surrender and therefore precipitate a counter-attack from the Dutch. Lord Sandwich conceded the argument.

The situation, however, continued to deteriorate. Sometime between 9 and 10 a.m. van Ghent in the *Dolfijn* closed in, passing first along the windward side and then the leeward side of the *Royal James* and raking her with gunfire. By this stage the *James* had very few men left alive on the upper deck, so it was down to the gunners on the middle and lower decks to reply. It was around this time that Captain Jordan failed to come to the *James*'s assistance claiming, 'in the smoke and hurry we could not well discern what was done to leeward.' Sandwich appeared philosophical if not defeatist. On seeing Jordan turn away he remarked, 'we must do our best to defend ourselves alone.'

A little before midday Captain Haddock was shot in the foot and had to go below to receive treatment: 'my shoe full of blood, forced me to go down to be dressed' is how he graphically put it in the account he wrote up later. While he was receiving treatment he remembered that the tide must have changed and immediately sent up the order for the *James* to be anchored by the stern, which would have the effect of causing the now strongly flowing ebb tide to carry the *Groot Hollandia* away towards the north. The stratagem worked and Haddock then ordered the cable to be cut and the mainsail to be set and 'sail afore the wind', which would presumably have been in a south-south-westerly direction towards the shore. At this point Lord Sandwich, who was still directing the action from the quarterdeck, felt there was a good chance that after all the *James* might survive. Not only had they freed themselves from the clutches of the *Groot Hollandia* but van Ghent in the *Dolfijn* had been killed. Sandwich sent down a message to Haddock telling him 'to be of good cheer that he doubted not but that we should save our ship'. Just how cheery Haddock was feeling at that moment is not recorded but as 'At that time one of the chirugeons was cutting off the shattered flesh and tendons' of his toe, probably not very. What is clear is that despite all his dark prognostications about what the future held for him Sandwich was still far from throwing in the towel.

The breathing space for the *Royal James* proved to be short-lived. Vice Admiral Sweers in the *Olifant* took over the attack and was manoeuvring his vessel into a boarding position, when a third fireship, called *La Paix*, commanded by Jean Daniels van den Ryn, another of the heroes of the Chatham raid, successfully grappled the *James* on its port side. Sweers withdrew. Within a few minutes the *Royal James* was a mass of flames, 'a spectacle equally worthy of the compassion of both its friends and its enemies,' wrote de Ruyter with characteristic gallantry.

The consensus of opinion seems to be that the *Royal James* was grappled by the fatal fireship at around midday. Haddock refers to 'near 12 o'clock' but he has a great many different things all happening at around this same time, of which the fireship is the last event and so his testimony is not too precise. The Dartmouth drawings show the *Royal James* on fire at twelve o'clock. Jordan in the *Sovereign* saw ships on fire 'about noon'. 'Almost midday' is de Ruyter's opinion and old Mr Munns of Pakefield saw the *Royal James* 'blown up about noon off of Eastern Ness'. However, as always with so many witnesses, not everyone is agreed as to the time. An anonymous account by someone who had been on board the *St Michael* refers to seeing 'a great fireship of the enemy lay her on board. . . between 1 and 2'. Christopher Gunman in the *Royal Prince* records that at about

An oil painting by Ferdinand Bol of De Ruyter, widely regarded as the greatest of
all Dutch admirals. In command at Solebay, he was an astute and experienced naval tactician
who has left his own account of the battle.

two the *Royal James* was burnt by a fireship. Thomas Lucas who watched the battle from the cliffs
wrote that he saw that the *James* 'flew in the air at 2'.

Also around midday the bulk of the English and Dutch fleets, which up until then had been
firing at each other on a northerly tack, came into shallower water, an indication that they were

approaching what was described in various log books as the Red Sand. There is no bank called the Red Sand shown on modern-day charts or anything in its near vicinity under a different name. Greenville Collins's coasting pilot of 1686 does, however, show a shoal called the Red Sand about five or six miles south-east of Lowestoft. Dutch charts of the same period also show it, but a little further out and a little further south. Whether or not the bank ever actually existed pilots in both fleets clearly felt that they needed to tack if they were not very shortly to find themselves in difficulties. So both fleets turned and then proceeded to head south. As they came back in a southerly direction a number of ships observed the *Royal James* in distress. The amount of time that had elapsed between the ships tacking and then passing the *James* gives some rough indication of the distance the *James* was south of the Red Sand in the early afternoon. An anonymous writer on board the *St Michael*, for instance, records tacking 'somewhat past eleven' and then around two hours later he mentions, 'between 1 and 2 we were almost got up within cannon shot of the *Royal James*... and now, as we came near the *Royal James*, we though it safest to bear to leeward of her, which we did... and Captain Sadlington in the *Dartmouth*, coming under our lee, the Duke ordered him to tack and endeavour to save what men he could, belonging to the *Royal James*, many of which we saw swimming upon pieces of timber, and what they could lay hold on...' This would suggest that the *James* was at this point about two hours sailing south of the twelve-fathom line off the Red Sand, which is where the *St Michael* had tacked. Given the conditions and the somewhat vague time references this could equate to anything between six to twelve miles.

Spragge in the *London* was also in the vicinity of the *Royal James* about 2 p.m. 'About 2 o'clock could scarce weather the ruins of the *Royal James*, being all on fire. Was forced to bear away to leeward of her in company with the *Charles*.' Unfortunately Captain Harman in the *Charles*, in writing his account, does not mention passing by the *Royal James*. The best and most detailed account of the battle is without a doubt that contained in Narborough's journal. Narborough was first lieutenant and then made captain of the *Royal Prince* after the death of Captain Cox in the early stages of the battle. Between eleven and twelve o'clock Narborough records how the *Prince* was 'much disabled in the masts and rigging' and needed to withdraw from the battle in order to repair. It was at this point that the Duke of York, who had started the battle on board the *Royal Prince* transferred himself and his standard to the *St Michael*. Between twelve and one o'clock, the *Prince* having been hurriedly put back into some kind of service, Narborough tacked. 'When we tacked we had but 11 fathom water. I judged we were near Lowestoft sand called the Red Sand. I could not see the shore it was so dark with smoke.' The *Prince* now stood to the south with the benefit of a wind at ENE and 'at NE, a small gale.' (A gale was not a gale as we would understand the word today but

---

The *Royal James* was set alight by a Dutch fireship, the most feared naval weapon of the Anglo-Dutch Wars. Detail from an oil painting by Willem van de Velde the Younger.

nothing much more than a breeze.) Christopher Gunman, also in the *Prince* confirms the approximate time of tacking. 'At noon we were five leagues ESE of Lowestoft. We then steered SSE upon the ebb which likewise carried us off.' This emphasises how far out to sea the *Royal James* must have been when it burnt, because a few hours later, between 3 and 4 p.m., the *Prince* 'passed by the *Royal James* a little to the leeward of her, she being on a light fire and at anchor, for she rode with her head to the South by East and all the burnt yards and booms which dropped from her and the hull of the Dutch fireship which set her on fire drove astern of her to the Northward set. There was four of our boats and small vessels taking up the men which saved themselves by swimming and on rafts.' The *Prince* came up with the *James* between two and four hours after tacking away from Lowestoft Sand. Narborough's observation is extremely important because it establishes that the *James* had been anchored a second time, presumably from the bow or its head would not have been towards the south. Since being set on fire it had not therefore just been at the mercy of the wind and the tides but in a more or less stationary position.

On the evidence of Captain Haddock's account one would have imagined that the *James* was situated some distance to the north of Southwold when it was set on fire and presumably anchored up for the second and last time. It had originally left Southwold at around 5 a.m. heading in a northerly direction. It did not engage until 7 a.m. during which time even with light winds and a strong flood tide against it, it had probably made around two to three knots an hour. It was another two hours approximately before the *Groot Hollandia* ran across its bows. It seems reasonable to assume that it was probably some six or so miles north of Southwold by this point as well as at least nine miles out to sea. However, if this was the case and it anchored a second time as soon as it had been set on fire, which would be logical in order to facilitate the rescue of those seamen that remained alive, it is difficult to understand why it was two hours or more before ships such as the *Prince* and the *St Michael* came up with it again on their southward tack. The explanation may lie in the way Haddock compresses a number of events, the freeing of the ship from van Brakel, the setting sail and turning to the south, the engagement with Sweers in the *Olifant* and the fatal attack by the fireship, almost into one single moment, everything occurring just before noon. The confusion is understandable. Haddock was injured at this point and was not on deck but undergoing surgery without the benefit of any anaesthetic other than brandy. An intimation that there may have been some considerable gap between the getting free from van Brakel and the boarding by the third of the fireships is suggested by the evidence of seaman Robert Evans who made a deposition on oath at Landguard three days after the battle. He and fourteen others got off in the *Royal James*'s jolly boat and landed at Southwold. According to Evans 'they fought about two hours after they were clear [of van Brakel]'. The *Royal James* would have been on a southerly tack throughout this time and would have had the benefit of a light breeze, the wind having shifted from the east-south-east to the east-north-east. Progress would not have been very rapid. The *James* was

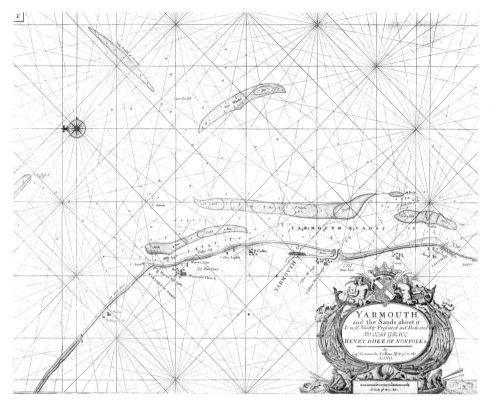

Both fleets turned to the south when they thought they were nearing the
notorious sandbanks off Yarmouth, as shown on this chart of the time.

heavily damaged and probably waterlogged by this stage. Even so this southerly tack may well have taken it back to around the latitude of Southwold. The fact that these seamen made for Sole Bay is an indication of where the *James* was when the ship was finally abandoned. At around 5 p.m. the Duke of York again changed ship, transferring from the *St Michael*, which by then was also in a bad way, into the *London*. Meanwhile, the *Royal James* continued to burn throughout the afternoon and into the evening.

Most of the searching for the *James* that has taken place to date has been in an area within one league from the shore. The key evidence for carrying on the search in this area has been the witness statements of two men that were both observers from the land, Thomas Lucas and Francis Chaplin. Lucas claimed that 'I saw the whole business, and was so near as I saw almost every broadside, and was in hearing and whistling of the shot.' This certainly implies that the battle took place close to land. However, Lucas's testimony is demonstrably unreliable. He claimed that Lord Sandwich had been saved which was proven to be untrue. He also claimed that the *Royal James*, having been set on fire 'flew in the air at 2'. De Ruyter, on the other hand, who was much closer to the action, specifically stated that 'it burnt without jumping in the air because van Brakel had pierced it with so many blows that all its powder was spoilt, and that even without the fireship it was already near sinking.' Lucas's whole account is full of bombast and exaggerated rhetoric per-haps compensating for the fact that he had missed being on board the *Dreadnought* as he had in-tended. Chaplin has a more low-key prose style. He writes from Aldeburgh at 3 p.m., 'The smoke drives right upon us now. . . We have seen seven ships fired but are not able to tell who has suffered. They began betwixt Southwold and this [Aldeburgh] and have so continued ever since. They are not a league distance from that place [Southwold] at this time. . .' This is nearer the truth but again misleading. No doubt the French squadron had been fighting Banckert's Dutch squadron in the vicinity of Aldeburgh. But the main fight had been taking place between Southwold northwards up to Pakefield. His letters, which he posted every two or three hours, again demonstrate the lim-

Montagu refusing to leave the ship. According to his page, Montagu feared he would not be able to survive in the water because he was overweight.

itations of a land viewpoint. From Aldeburgh it would have been very difficult to tell how far distant the fleet was from shore at Southwold. All the evidence of Narborough, Gunman and Kempthorne suggests that the battle took place between two and four leagues from land up and down the coast between Aldeburgh and the Red Sand off Lowestoft. Narborough puts the matter most succinctly: 'We fought all along from before Cathy and Southwold and Dunwich and Aldeburgh between 3 and 4 leagues distance from the shore.' It is my guess that the *James* probably sank in the rough latitude of Southwold but at a distance of nine miles or so from the coast.

There is one further intriguing but also very possibly misleading piece of evidence that has resulted in the search for the *James* being conducted close to the shore. In the 1970s two fishermen trawled up a Dutch bronze swivel gun three miles off Southwold. The gun had the arms of the de Bitter family engraved on it. The de Bitters were involved with the Dutch East India Company and it is thought that Sandwich may have obtained the cannon when he seized some VOC ships in 1665. The theory is plausible. Sea captains of that day were fond of trophies from their enemies, particularly cannon. However, it is hardly conclusive proof that the *James* sank only a league from land. Fishermen rarely know exactly where an item gets caught in their nets, only that it is in the net when they haul it up.

The exact nature of Lord Sandwich's death is shrouded in almost as much mystery as whether or not he foretold it. Several early reports stated that he was dead even before the *James* was set on fire, while other versions had it that he did not die at all but was safe on another ship. For some days there was a rumour that he had been captured by the Dutch and was a prisoner in Holland. The seaman Robert Edmunds stated that he had seen Lord Sandwich in the company of Captain Haddock in his own barge, but as this testimony was contradicted by Haddock himself it seems improbable. Lord Sandwich's page provided the most memorable and probably the most accurate account: 'He stayed aboard while the ship was burning, and there were but ten besides my Lord. He moved my Lord to leap into the sea, knowing he could swim; but my Lord, distrusting himself by reason of his fatness and unwieldiness said he would stay somewhat longer; but bade him to take care of himself. . . and soon kissed him and bade him farewell.' What is not disputed is that some two weeks after the *Royal James* sank, Lord Sandwich's body was discovered on the Sunk Sand by the master of a ketch dragging for lost anchors. It was estimated that his corpse had drifted over thirty miles from where the *James* had gone down. His rings were wrapped in his blue garter and placed in his pocket which suggests he had taken some care to try and preserve them. His Star, George and gold watch were also found about him. All these items were handed in to the appropriate authorities. He was fortunate not to suffer the same fate as his hapless colleague, Sir Cloudesley Shovell, whose body was to wash up on the Isles of Scilly thirty years later, and was subsequently pillaged of its jewels.

6

The *Kronan* Catastrophe

*D*URING THE FIRST HALF OF THE SEVENTEENTH CENTURY Gustavus Adolphus established Sweden as the major military power in Northern Europe and the dominant naval
force in the Baltic. At the basis of Swedish strategic maritime thinking at this time was the
theory of *mare clausum* or closed sea. What this meant in practical terms was controlling the Sound,
the narrow entry way through which all ships had to pass to gain access to the wealthy Baltic hinterlands. If a nation controlled the Sound it could also control the valuable corn and timber trade
of the entire Baltic region with countries such as Holland, England, Spain and France, all hungry
for these two basic commodities. This thinking naturally brought Sweden into conflict with its
close neighbour on the other side of the waterway, Denmark. In the early 1660s, in order to continue its naval dominance, Sweden embarked on a major new shipbuilding programme and the
centrepiece of this process of rearmament was to be the giant warship *Kronan*.

The *Kronan* was a three-decked vessel, nearly 200 feet in length, 42 feet in the beam and with
a gross burthen of 2,140 tons. This did not quite make it the biggest warship ever built to date but
it was a sizeable beast and its armament of 126 bronze cannon certainly made it the most powerful
floating weapon in the world when it finally came into action. It was this heavy weight of cannon,
230 tons of them, that was also possibly a contributory cause of its undoing. The keel of the *Kronan*
was laid down in the shipyards of Stockholm in the autumn of 1665 by a Dutchman, appropriately called Peter Kron. It was, however, a brilliant, even if somewhat temperamental Englishman,
Francis Sheldon, who was to be commissioned as the shipwright and architect of the project. This
was very much a period when engineers, builders, artists and miscellaneous specialists of all trades
and skills sold their expertise to the highest bidder, moving freely around the European courts.
Thus it was not uncommon to find Dutchmen working in England, Englishmen in Sweden and
Swedes in France, even at times when these countries were in conflict with each other.

It was not long before there were problems with the *Kronan* project. Payment of the labourers
in the royal dockyards had become notoriously erratic and as refusal to work was punishable by
death it was hardly surprising that there was a constant shortage of key skilled artisans. To make

matters worse, as well as financial problems, there developed a basic lack of trust between Sheldon and the Swedish Admiralty. The Swedish authorities thought Sheldon's building methods were too expensive. He used, for instance, too many iron bolts. Also the whole style and conception of the ship began to look wrong to them. The *Kronan* was designed to have a rounded stern and the fat belly of the ship was constructed so as to stand high out of the water. The Swedes were more used to the Dutch style of shipbuilding where sterns were flat and the beam of the ship was at its widest at the waterline.

The *Kronan* was not finally ready for the water until 31 July 1668. The launch was something of a fiasco. The sternpost and the keel were both damaged. The Swedish authorities blamed Sheldon. Sheldon gave as good as he got. He blamed the damage on the fact that the ship had been so long on the stocks it had become warped and misshapen. The reason for this delay was not Sheldon's fault but the constant interruptions to the building process as a result of lack of supplies. Sheldon was particularly tetchy at the launching stage because he was owed by this time considerable sums of money. The Swedes were as stingy in their payments as they were suspicious of his building methods. It had proved to be a highly combustible relationship. Both sides, however, had persevered with the arrangement. Sheldon stuck it out, because he saw it as his only way of getting what he was owed. The Swedes continued with Sheldon because realistically they had no alternative.

The launch might not have been the grand ceremonial occasion that the Swedish Admiralty had planned but it was still a sufficiently impressive event for the Danes to take a close interest. The Danish Ambassador in Stockholm wrote to Copenhagen in tones of suitable awe when describing the ship's size and the power and number of the guns that the rumours said it would have. It was, however, to be another four years before the *Kronan* was finally fitted out and ready for the sea. This included a year spent on the superb stern decorations, carved by the Dutchman Hans Jacobsson. England, Holland, Finland and Lübeck, in modern-day Germany, were all involved in the supply chain for the final stages of the equipment process. In its way it was a truly pan-European project.

By 1672 with hostilities again breaking out in Europe the need for the *Kronan* to be completed became urgent. The 126 bronze cannon were the last items to be loaded. They were winched into position by means of a giant wooden crane that amazingly still stands as a monument today on Stockholm's ancient dockside. Sheldon, no doubt feeling that his master work was finally completed, and despairing of ever obtaining his back pay, decided to return to England. When the Swedes heard of his proposed departure they tried to arrest him. But they were too late. Sheldon had already given them the slip. It was an acrimonious ending to what should rightly have been regarded as a great triumph. The *Kronan* was a magnificent construction. The Italian diplomat and travel writer, Lorenzo Magalotti, was full of praise for its qualities. He described it as combining the very best of English and Dutch shipbuilding traditions. His comments on Sheldon were

less flattering. 'The builder was an Englishman who has left here in a fit of temper. That is typically English and does not become a fine man.'

In 1675 the young Swedish king, Karl XI, in alliance with France, ordered his new fleet to seek out, attack and destroy the Danish fleet. He rightly considered that this was vital before the Danes had an opportunity of joining with their stronger Dutch allies. Under the command of Admiral Stenbock the Swedes anchored near Karl's Island, close by Gotland. The choice of

The catastrophic explosion which destroyed the *Kronan*,
as seen in a contemporary oil painting by
Claus Möinichen in Fredriksborg Castle, Denmark.

anchorage was hotly argued against by other officers in the fleet but Stenbock insisted. The result was unfortunate. The *Kronan* lost an anchor. Complaints were also made about the *Kronan*'s poor sailing qualities on this, its first real test on active service. The fleet wasted time trying unsuccessfully to salvage the lost anchor and, by the time they gave this up as a hopeless task, the Danish had disappeared. On returning to Stockholm Stenbock was fined and dismissed.

In the spring of 1676 King Karl XI appointed a bureaucrat, Lorentz Creutz, with no previous experience of active naval command, to head the Swedish fleet. Creutz had already made a reputation for himself as a ruthless and feared administrator. He had imposed a series of much needed economies on the bloated and inefficient state sector. Some of the measures he had taken, such as substituting dried peas and porridge for salmon in the sailors' shipboard diet, had not endeared him to the lower ranks, but he was not altogether bad. He had, for instance, made up some of their arrears of naval pay from his own pocket. His promotion, however, was bitterly resented by career admirals such as Uggla and Bar.

The Danish fleet had by this time been reinforced by a squadron of Dutch ships. On 25 May the two fleets first met off Rugen, Bornholm. The *Kronan* showed itself to be a formidable war-machine, its heavy artillery causing serious damage to two Dutch ships, the *Delft* and the *Oostergo*. The initiative was lost, however, when Creutz noticed that his son, in charge of the *Merkurius*, was in danger from a Dutch fireship. He had the *Kronan* brought to, in order to lend his son's ship assistance, and, in so doing, sent a wrong signal to the rest of his fleet which followed his own action. The consequence of this sudden interruption of the Swedish assault was that the joint Dutch–Danish fleet was able to escape.

The Swedish fleet now withdrew to Trelleborg. Creutz offered the King his resignation, at the same time blaming his junior officers for what had gone wrong. The king reaffirmed his faith in Creutz's judgement. It was decided that the Swedish fleet should withdraw northwards towards Öland and await the enemy there. There was no need for any waiting. The Dutch and Danish tracked the Swedes northwards, now strengthened by further Dutch ships and under the overall command of the formidable Dutch Admiral, Cornelius Tromp. When Tromp was satisfied that he had the advantage of the vital weather gage, he attacked. Early on in the course of the battle Admiral Bar in the *Nyckeln* went about and headed directly towards the enemy line. Admiral Uggla in the *Svardet* followed suit and then Creutz gave the order for the *Kronan* also to go about. According to Anders Gyllenspak, the only officer to survive the *Kronan*'s sinking, Creutz knew it would be disastrous, but felt that he had no alternative but to follow in order to keep the fleet together. Gyllenspak, the sailing master on board the *Kronan*, advised Creutz that before going about it would be necessary for the sail to be shortened and the lower-deck gunports closed. Without these precautions the *Kronan* risked heeling over in the strong winds, in which case water would flood into the open gunports. Warships in the age of sail were in a continual dilemma with regards the positioning of the lower gunports. The higher the ports were above water level the greater the risk that the ship would be crank, that is, liable to list over to one side or the other when it sailed. On the other hand if the lower gunports were positioned too near the waterline then there was the constant danger of the sea flooding in when the gunports were open. Three feet was the generally agreed minimum distance between waterline and lower gunports. The fact that the *Kronan* had already revealed itself to be crank on its previous voyage may have resulted in this distance being shortened and could explain why the sailing master on board recommended special caution before suddenly going about. Whether the gunports were in fact closed is unclear. The testimony of the survivors is contradictory but the nature of the sinking would suggest that it is very unlikely they had been shut. Clearly there was a confusion of orders given and Creutz's inexperience cannot have helped matters. The *Kronan* turned, heeled over in a strong gust of wind, the sea flooded in, and from that point on its fate was sealed. Once a large and weighty ship like the *Kronan* heels over

The title page of Cornelius Tromp's biography features his success at the Öland battle, the bottom panel showing the *Kronan* blowing up.

beyond a certain angle it becomes almost impossible to right it again. The order was given to try to redistribute the weight by hauling the guns from the port to the starboard side, but dragging two tons of metal up a steep incline was more than could be humanly managed. What probably happened was that the higher guns broke free and crashed downwards causing the weight imbalance to worsen still further.

Finally, there came a catastrophic explosion. Seventeenth-century warships in action were always like floating tinderboxes waiting to blew up. In the chaos on board the *Kronan*, when she first keeled over, a lighted fuse, or perhaps a candle, must have fallen into the magazine. The starboard side of the ship was blown out beneath the waterline and the ship sank like the proverbial stone, drowning all except approximately forty out of more than 800 people on board. The luckiest survivor perhaps of any recorded maritime disaster has to be Anders Sparrfelt, a thirty-one-year-old major in the Swedish army. The explosion was so great that he was catapulted into the air, soaring right over two nearby enemy ships, only to land safely in the sails of a third Swedish frigate called the *Draken*. Hardly surprisingly his near miraculous escape has passed into Swedish folklore.

During the next ten years sixty of the *Kronan*'s bronze guns were salvaged by a Major Paul Rumpf using a diving bell designed by von Treileben, who had recovered the majority of the *Vasa*'s guns about ten years beforehand. The *Vasa* lay in water about twenty feet deeper than the *Kronan* but its position, inside Stockholm harbour, was far less exposed than the *Kronan*'s. As the *Kronan* lay at between eighty and ninety feet, a good four miles from land, the recovery of even half the armaments was no mean achievement. Presumably the sixty or more cannon that were left behind were abandoned because of difficulties of access and diminishing returns on the effort expended. Salvage in the seventeenth century was a strictly commercial enterprise.

A curious postscript to the *Kronan* story is the strange development of relations between Francis Sheldon, its architect, and the Swedish authorities. One would have thought that having fled the country back in 1672, and then the *Kronan* sinking in such ignominious and questionable circumstances, the last person the Swedes would have again wanted to do business with was Sheldon. Equally one would have thought that after all Sheldon's outrage at the way in which he had been treated, particularly his outstanding arrears of pay, he would not be in a hurry to go back. And yet the year after the *Kronan* disaster Sheldon was back in Sweden, having been commissioned to build three more ships. The relationship proved to be just as stormy as it had been the previous time round. Only one ship got built and by 1682 matters had deteriorated to such an extent that Sheldon was actually put in prison for a while. Even this experience, however, failed to bring him to heel and in the end the Swedes seemed happy for him to pack his bags a second time and take his skills across the Sound to the enemy. In 1690, at the age of 78, Sheldon was still working in Denmark. He died at Chatham in 1692.

After 1686 the wreck of the *Kronan* appears to have been forgotten about until around 1950

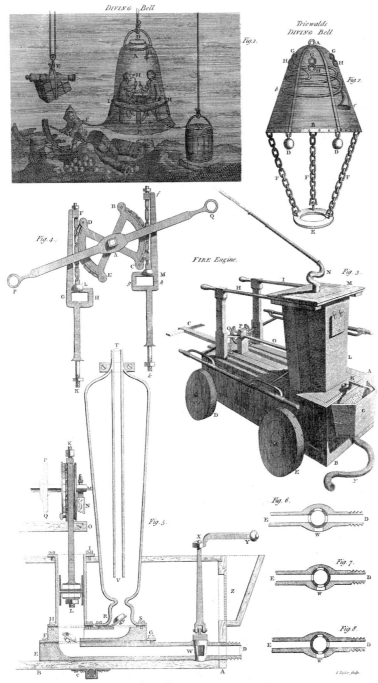

HYDRAULICS & HYDROSTATICS.

DIVING Bell

Fig.1.

Triewalds
DIVING Bell

Fig. 2.

FIRE Engine.

Fig. 3.

Fig. 4.

Fig. 5.

Fig. 6.

Fig. 7.

Fig. 8.

Print of a primitive
diving bell, similar to
the one used by
Major Rumpf to
recover some of the
Kronan's guns.

when the archaeologist Anders Franzen briefly looked for it. Franzen did not manage to locate the hull on that occasion and subsequently became distracted by other projects such as the excavation of the *Vasa*. However, in the mid-1970s his attention again returned to unfinished business with the *Kronan* and the unsolved question of where exactly it was lying. Documents in Swedish archives revealed that the battle had taken place east of the village of Hulterstad on the south-east corner of Öland and large numbers of drowned bodies had indeed washed up on the shores of this region. Even so it took two years of further seabed searching before the remains of the *Kronan* were finally located in the summer of 1980. One of the reasons that the search took as long as it did was the presence of thermoclines. These are layers of water of different temperature the presence of which play havoc with side-scan sonar readings.

The discovery of the *Kronan* has resulted in the excavation and recording of the most fascinating collection of historical artefacts. The cold waters and low salinity of the Baltic mean that destructive wood-devouring worms do not thrive and so the hull structure is remarkably well preserved. The clarity of the water with visibility to around twenty-five metres also makes it an ideal site for photography and underwater film. Two-thirds of the port side of the hull was still intact, standing in places approximately four metres proud of the surrounding seabed. The fact that so much of the hull was in such a good state was surprising seeing that there was plentiful evidence that it had been extensively trawled through by fisherman as well as subjected to the depredations of minesweepers.

The balance of the bronze guns has now been recovered. They form a remarkable collection both for their decoration and their diversity. The majority had been manufactured in Sweden as one might expect but a significant number came from Spain, Denmark and Germany, probably both through purchase and also captures of war. Even more remarkable was the diversity of date. The oldest had been cast in 1514 and so had been in service for over 150 years before it was finally lost. The newest had been produced in 1661. This diversity of date and country of manufacture underlines the difficulties involved when trying to identify a wreck from its ordnance alone.

When ships sink as quickly as the *Kronan* a large number of bodies are sometimes trapped within the hull. This probably explains why large numbers of skeletons have been unearthed. Bone analysis has predictably enough revealed that the skeletons are male and aged mainly between twenty and thirty-five. There are interesting exceptions, however. The youngest skeleton was of a boy aged ten, the oldest a man aged sixty.

To date 25,000 artefacts have been recovered and conserved in the museum of Kalmar. Some of the most interesting are also those that are most personally intimate. A gold ring, for instance, has been recovered with the initials LCD engraved on it. This ring must at one time have belonged to Lorentz Creutz's wife, whose family name was Duval and who died in 1675. There was evidence that the ring had been enlarged, presumably so that Creutz could wear it himself. It suggests an un-

One of the bronze guns recently recovered, in this case a 30-pounder of German manufacture.

expected trait of tenderness in a man otherwise noted for his stern and ruthless nature. Equally extraordinary is the back of a leather armchair with the Creutz initials and family crest. It is amazing that the leather has survived the intervening three hundred years. It is also revealing to discover that Creutz was the kind of man who liked to have his own creature comforts about his person even during a wartime voyage.

A number of wooden chests has been recovered containing the private personal possessions of various individuals who had been on board. One such chest had most probably belonged to the ship's surgeon, Peter Schallerus Grypenflycht. It contained a brass breastplate with the Swedish royal crest on it, together with numerous containers of glass, pewter and pottery, designed to hold a variety of potions and ointments. Another chest contained a leather belt and a pair of leather mittens, no doubt very useful in the cold climate of the Baltic. The unidentified owner, presumably an officer, was a man who liked to take good care of himself. He also had with him personal supplies of garlic, peppercorns and ginger, all well-established remedies for a variety of conditions that may afflict the mariner. It is these kinds of detailed items that help build up a human picture of the seventeenth-century seaman.

All these artefacts are, of course, of great scientific and historical value even if they do not have an obvious commercial value. The *Kronan*, however, turned out also to be a treasure ship of the more conventional kind. In 1982, in the remnants of a chest close to the stern was discovered a

Seventeenth-century warships were highly decorated, with the sculpture often carrying symbolic meaning. Classical allusions were common, with frequent references to the power and military virtues of ancient Rome, as shown in this wooden sculpture of a Roman soldier recovered from the ship.

hoard of 255 gold coins. The range of minting dates covers nearly two centuries from the late fifteenth century to the year of sinking, 1676. This provides further proof, if any were needed, that the wreck was definitely that of the *Kronan*, but again underlines how difficult it would be to identify a wreck from just one or two random coins. It is only because this is a large collection that it becomes possible to put a probable date on the loss. Most of the coins were Swedish ducats including a very rare ten-ducat piece, but a number were of Dutch origin and some came from as far afield as Turkey or Spain. There has been much speculation on just what these coins were doing on board. It would be normal for a ship of this size and importance to carry a certain quantity of coin for emergencies and every day purchases, but silver coin would be a more probable currency for such matters than gold. It has been suggested that the hoard was in fact a private collection of coins, perhaps Creutz's, and this explains the wide range of denominations. But it seems a little odd to take your coin collection into battle with you. If it was Creutz's gold it seems more likely that as a man of considerable substance he just liked to have a reasonable quantity of cash constantly about him. After all, if he was made a prisoner of war, which always had to be a distinct possibility when engaging the enemy, he might need some ready money to obtain his freedom. Gold was the easiest way of carrying a concentration of wealth. In 1989 900 silver coins were also recovered from a different area of the lower deck, again all compacted, suggesting that they must have originally been inside some form of container. It seems quite likely that this may have been ship-money but there can be no proof of this. In the year 2000 a smaller cache of forty-six gold coins was recovered. Again the ownership and the function of this separate find is a matter of pure conjecture.

Of all the many items that have been brought to the surface from the wreckage of the *Kronan* my personal favourite has to be the very Swedish-looking male figure of a portly, moustached and self-confident warrior dressed as a Roman. This marvellous sculpture was very probably one of the stern embellishments carved by Hans Jacobsson. There is something defiantly robust and blustering about the pose and gaze that wonderfully sums up the seventeenth-century seaman.

7

The *Golden Lion* of Amsterdam

O NE OF THE LESSER-KNOWN and more sinister of the numerous treasure ships that lie beneath the murky waters of the North Sea is the *Goude Leeuw* or *Golden Lion* of Amsterdam. The charred remains of this wreck, for it caught fire before sinking, lie in approximately one hundred feet of water in the vicinity of the Dogger Bank. Its somewhat tainted reputation derives from the fact that the chests of coin it was carrying were destined for the purchase of 500 slaves from the Dutch stronghold of Elmina on the West African coast of Ghana. The *Goude Leeuw* was the largest of a small fleet of five ships, chartered by the Dutch West India Company, to make the infamous triangular voyage. The first leg of the triangle was southwards to Africa to acquire slaves and gold. The second leg was across the Atlantic to the West Indies where the slaves were sold and a return cargo of sugar, cochineal, coffee, indigo and other Caribbean commodities were purchased. The third and final leg was the return voyage back to Europe.

A Dutch merchant ship of the same size and period as the *Goude Leeuw*.

The Dutch West India Company was the younger and poorer sister to the more famous Dutch East India Company, or VOC. It had been founded in 1621 and was governed by a board of nineteen, the Heeren XIX, as opposed to the VOC's Heeren XVII. It specialised in the triangular trade, but, except for the occasional boom year, such as 1628 when Piet Heyn captured the returning Spanish treasure fleet as a useful add-on to its regular business, the Company had never really prospered. The main reason for this failure was the high cost of the military infrastructure required in Suriname and Guyana in order to enable it to compete with the Portuguese, who had already been carrying on trade on those coasts for the previous hundred years and bitterly resented the intrusion of the upstart Dutch. By around 1670 the Dutch West India Company's financial affairs had reached such a parlous state that it went bankrupt and had to be reconstituted. The Company's greatest liability was, in a perverse way, also its greatest asset, for the Dutch State was well aware of its military importance in the struggle against the Iberian dominance of international trade, and so for strategic reasons was unwilling to let the Company simply disappear under the burden of its debts. It was therefore the Dutch government that invariably came to the Company's rescue during its long history of financial crises.

In the spring of 1689 preparations were being made at Groningen for the departure of the West India fleet of that season. The records in the Company archive provide a fascinating insight into the day-to-day problems faced by the Company officials when it came to dealing with their own employees. By June the *Goude Leeuw* was already loaded and almost ready to sail when senior Company personnel got wind that vital Company cargo was being left behind in the warehouse because there was apparently no room for it in the ship's holds. The suspicion was that officers of the ship, in collusion with independent merchants, had loaded private cargo at the expense of Company cargo. This was a persistent problem faced by the large trading companies of this period. Employees were generally rather poorly paid and so the attraction of sneaking on board some illicit cargo was considerable. These smuggled goods literally got a free ride and so the potential profit to be made on them was large. In order to combat the temptation there was usually a system in place by which certain favoured personnel, such as the ship's captain, were permitted to take an agreed amount of private cargo of a kind which would not compete directly with the Company's own goods and which took up little space. Specie, precious stones, jewellery and porcelain were all favourites for this purpose.

In the case of the *Goude Leeuw* the Company officials in Amsterdam clearly suspected underhand activity that went well beyond the usual quotas for permitted private trade. Inspectors were promptly despatched to Texel to unload the ship and examine it scrupulously for unauthorised cargo. The inspectors themselves were to be paid a premium for every smuggled item they located which, one might have reasonably objected, hardly made them the most objective of assessors. Presumably, however, this was considered to be the best way of preventing the inspectors themselves from being bribed to turn a blind eye to whatever it was that they found. The ship's officers wrote indignantly to the Company of their innocence claiming that the loading problems were entirely the result of all the provisions it was necessary to take on board to support such a large number of people. Colonists and troops as well as crew were all to be shipped out on board the *Goude Leeuw* and the other ships, and from Africa onwards there would be the addition of the slaves, although admittedly by then some of the trade goods would have been unloaded and anyway conditions for slaves on board ship were notoriously overcrowded and inhumane.

No smuggled cargo appears to have been discovered. Probably if such goods had been loaded they had been removed again long before the inspectors arrived. The space crisis was solved by the inspectors ordering the demolition of large quantities of water barrels. This enabled a further one hundred barrels of special Weesp brandy, a hundred chests of linen, and 10,000 lb of gunpowder to be taken on board, all vital commodities for the Dutch colonists in West Africa and the Caribbean. The staving in of the water barrels may well have had dire knock-on consequences for the second leg of the voyage, for an adequate supply of fresh water was the most important single resource in keeping the slaves alive during the horrors of their Atlantic crossing. In this particular case, however, the issue was never to be put to the test for the *Goude Leeuw* was never to reach Africa.

West India Company ships were significantly smaller than their counterparts that traded to India, China and the Spice Islands. Generally they were no more than 250 tons in burthen. Partly this was because the voyage was far shorter and therefore there was not the same need for a very large ship, but it also reflected the necessity for such ships to

Copper Manillas were the accepted currency of the African slave trade. Originally ornamental armbands, they came in different sizes, of varying value, and some were highly decorated.

negotiate the shallow river mouths of West Africa, where there were no deep-water harbours. The crews were also smaller. The crew of the *Goude Leeuwe* numbered only sixty. However, with troops, passengers and slaves also competing for the limited space, the overloading was probably generally far worse than it was on an East India ship.

The Dutch had taken possession of Elmina from the Portuguese in 1637. The local African kings were jubilant at the change, for they were by this time heartily sick of Portuguese dominance, but they were also equally anxious that the slave trade should continue to flourish just as it had done under the Portuguese. The ecumenical king of the Congo happily placed emblems of the Dutch reformed church together with Catholic images in his Catholic cathedral. In the last quarter of the seventeenth century many of the West African slaves were initially shipped to the tiny island of

The Dutch West African slaving centre of Elmina, seen in a print published in 1702.

Curaçao off Venezuela. This was where the *Goude Leeuw* was heading in 1689. The Dutch had a vast prison there capable of holding up to 3,000 slaves at any one time, before onward distribution not just to their own colonies in Suriname, but also to the Portuguese, Spanish, French and English colonies throughout the Caribbean and the American continental hinterland. As much as each nation vigorously tried to control its own colonial trade by buying products and slave labour only from its own national companies or through its own approved agents, in reality the continual shortage of slave labour meant that slaves were purchased from whatever source was available. The slave trade was, as a result, far more complex and interdependent than any simple model of it can explain. When the *Goude Leeuw* sailed, approximately 20,000 slaves a year were being exported from West Africa and the demand was steadily on the increase. Today, even though slavery continues to exist in many places in the world, it is difficult to think about the practice with anything but abhorrence. In the seventeenth century, however, it was generally regarded as a morally acceptable and legally sanctioned mercantile practice, and one that was essential to the continued wealth of the European and American elite. Emmanuel Downing, father to George, who was to give his name to the street that has become synonymous with the residence of successive British Prime Ministers, wrote to a friend, 'I do not see how we can thrive until we get a stock of slaves sufficient to do all our business.' In the words of one or two of the contemporary commentators one can sense a certain unease particularly if the slaves also happened to be Christian. On the whole, however, there was no sense of contradiction between being a slave owner and leading a philanthropic life.

When James II fled to France in the revolution of 1688 and William of Orange came to the English throne, war once again broke out in Europe, but this time, in contrast to the three previous occasions, England and Holland were allies against the common enemy of France, with Louis XIV supporting his ousted co-religionist. This meant that merchant ships had to exercise greater care than usual to be safe from enemy attack. For this reason the Dutch West India Company, knowing that they would be a prize target of any roaming French corsairs, directed its small fleet of five ships to take the northabout voyage around Britain rather than risk the hazardous Channel route with its long French coastline and series of enemy ports from Dunkirk to St Malo. In addition, the *Goude Leeuw* was supplied at the last minute with four extra small cannon, presumably for positioning on its quarterdeck. The small fleet, after endless delays, finally left Texel on 26 July, some five months after it had originally been scheduled to depart. The defensive precautions, however,

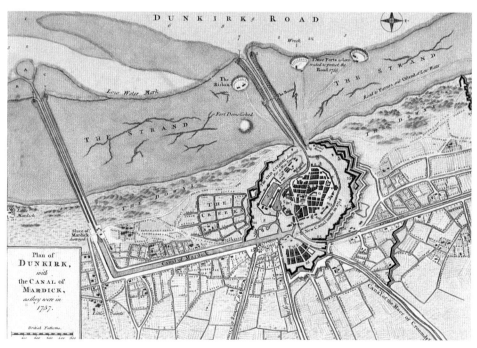

The privateering port of Dunkirk was a major centre for the French assault on Anglo-Dutch trade, the so-called *guerre de course*. As such it was the target of a number of Allied plans, but was protected by formidable fortifications.

were all in vain. A privateering fleet under the command of Monsieur D'Amblimont had left from Dunkirk, a week beforehand, with the intention of intercepting any rich allied shipping they might come across.

There were four ships in Monsieur D'Amblimont's squadron, the *Profond*, where D'Amblimont had his flag, and which was described as a flute mounting forty cannon, the *Sorcière*, Captain M. Herpin, with twenty-six cannon, the *Trompeuse*, Captain M. de la Motte, with twelve cannon, and the *Serpente*, Captain M. de Selingue, with twenty-six cannon. It is M. de Selingue's relation of the combat that provides the most detail. At three o'clock in the morning, which would have been first light, the French squadron sighted four vessels and a small galliot at about eighteen leagues to the north-west of Texel. The French were at that time situated at about fifteen leagues to the west-north-west of Texel, around twelve miles distant from their quarry. The wind was in their favour at south-west and they immediately set off in pursuit. M. de Selingue in the *Serpente* approached the West India Company ships first and identified the galliot as a species of pilot boat and one of the other vessels as a small Dutch flute. He continued to approach until he was just beyond cannon range. The West India ships lowered their main sails and hoisted their Dutch flags. Selingue came closer still at which the Dutch lowered their mizzen sails, a show of arrogance that surprised the Frenchman. They clearly meant to fight rather than flee. The two sides formed a line of battle with the French having the advantage of the wind. The *Sorcière* took the lead, followed by the *Profond*, then the *Trompeuse*, with the *Serpente* at the rear. In the ensuing melee, during which there was much jostling for the advantage of the wind, the poetically inclined M. de Selingue described his commander in the *Profond* as 'dancing a furious minuet'. The *Goude Leeuw* was soon in flames. Selingue was clearly gratified to learn from some of the survivors that he picked up that the fire had started at the same time that he had begun his attack, but as both the *Profonde* and the *Serpente* cannonaded the helpless Dutch ship it is slightly unclear as to which of them deserved the honours for sinking it. With the *Goude Leeuw* out of action, the *Serpente* now turned its attention to what Selingue grandiosely described as the Dutch rear admiral, but the *Profonde* intervened between the *Serpente* and the newly chosen victim, so the *Serpente* moved off and attacked the leading ship of the Dutch line, which was already being attacked by Herpin in the *Trompeuse*. Shortly afterwards the Dutch 'rear admiral' blew up very suddenly with considerable loss of life. This disaster prompted the only remaining large Dutch ship, which was probably called the *St Jan*, to surrender. Selingue was just in the process of sending a boarding party on to the *St Jan* when some survivors from the *Goude Leeuw* arrived beneath the *Serpente*'s bows and begged for mercy. In all Selingue took up seventy-six prisoners.

Selingue observed that the *St Jan* and the *Goude Leeuw*, both of Amsterdam, were designed to carry thirty-six to forty cannon but were only equipped with twenty-four each. The ship of Flushing, referred to as the rear admiral, had eighteen cannon and six perriers, the flute was armed with only six cannon, and the galliot just four. The Dutch were clearly inferior to the French in terms of number and weight of cannon and therefore probably never stood much of a chance in the battle. Selingue goes on to remark that the ship of Amsterdam that he took as a prize was loaded with '100,000 livres, argent de Hollande' (100,000 pounds, money of Holland). He adds that the *Goude Leeuw*, which had been destroyed, carried a similar valued cargo, but the Flushinger for Suriname, which also sank, was of less worth. The flute, which was also bound for Suriname, and which was also captured, he described as '*assez riche*' (rich enough). When it came to enumer-

French corsairs of the period often operated in squadrons - this is the famous Duguay Trouin in action - which made them formidable opponents for all but the most heavily guarded convoys.

ating his own losses he mentioned damage to sails and rigging and a large number of his men lightly wounded with only one man killed and one dangerously ill. He himself had received two bruises, one on his foot and one on his hand. He piously observes that his light losses were a miracle, but he was only half surprised, because he had put all his trust in Jesus Christ. The victorious French arrived back in the vicinity of Dunkirk on 3 August, capturing a dogger (fishing boat) on their way.

The captured ship, called *St Jan* of Amsterdam, was later sold for 9,000 ducats. This might seem cheap but it was in a severely damaged condition. The mate of the *Goude Leeuw* wrote from prison in Dunkirk to his former employers that for a few thousand ducats more the Company would probably be able to repurchase their old vessel from the party that had bought it. The prize

Dutch West Indiamen, depicted in fine grisaille detail by Van de Velde the Elder.

goods were relatively easy to dispose of. The prisoners of war posed more of a problem. There was talk of an exchange for French prisoners held in England, but the negotiations proved protracted and six months later nothing seemed to have been achieved. To the Dutch Company's credit they did send 3,000 Dutch guilders to Dunkirk for the support of the prisoners, a five-ducat allowance for each prisoner, which would suggest that there was a total of around 600 prisoners. One Daniel Verhagen, a Dunkirk merchant, was appointed by the Dutch West India Company to handle the funds. Meanwhile the Company had problems on other fronts. The owner of the *Goude Leeuw*, Cornelis Hobbe, was suing the Company for the loss of his ship. There was some suggestion that a number of the Dutch guns were out of action because of the ship being overloaded. No doubt Mr Hobbe considered the Company to have been negligent in this respect.

The papers of the court case have not been traced. They would probably make interesting reading. Meanwhile, the *Goude Leeuw* treasure continues to lie somewhere in the vicinity of the Dogger Bank.

8

The *Carlisle* Bullion

O N 4 FEBRUARY 1696 (1695 according to the old-style calendar) Dr Nathaniel Johnston wrote one of his regular news reports to his friend and patron the seventh Earl of Huntingdon, at the latter's grand house at Donnington Park. Most of the letter was taken up with an account of recent events in the House of Commons. At the end, however, he hastily added a postscript which contained some sensational news: 'I hear that we have lost the *Humber*, a ship of 80 guns, in the Straits shipwrecked. There was nothing saved in the *Carlisle* but the men, and it's said she had 150,000 of bullion and pieces of 8 and prize goods taken in the Straits.' Nathaniel had clearly been catching up on the latest admiralty gossip. The original manuscript is slightly torn but the words are still clearly decipherable. The lack of punctuation, however, in the final sentence makes it tantalisingly ambiguous. It is not clear whether the 150,000, presumably pounds, lost in the *Carlisle*, refers to the bullion alone, or the bullion and the pieces-of-eight, or the bullion and pieces-of-eight and prize goods collectively. By any interpretation, however, it

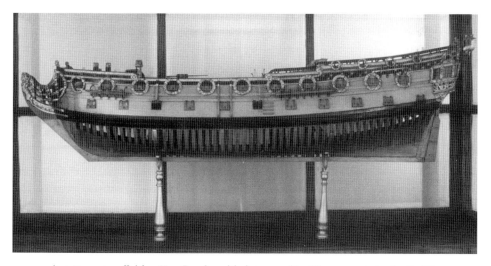

A contemporary official, or Navy Board, model of a 50-gun ship of the same period as the *Carlisle*.

still looks like a potentially very valuable wreck.

To understand the story of this bullion fully it is necessary to go back over a year. Europe was again at war, but England, having replaced James II with William of Orange on the throne, was now aligned with the Dutch and Spanish against the French. From a naval point of view most of the action revolved around attacks on trade to and from the Mediterranean and much of England's efforts were put into trying to safely convoy its merchant fleets, not always very successfully, while harassing the French.

In the autumn of 1694 Admiral Russell, who was in command of the allied fleet, received instructions that he was to overwinter with his ships in the Mediterranean. This was not very welcome news. He had already spent several frustrating months failing to bring the French fleet under Admiral Tourville to an engagement and had been looking forward to returning to England for some well-earned leave. The French fleet had withdrawn to Toulon. Russell was at anchor off Alicante. It was a cat-and-mouse game. But the French had the advantage that they were operating out of a home port. Then, in January, Russell received intelligence that four French warships had slipped away from Toulon to carry out escort duties in the vicinity of Malta. Russell immediately despatched six ships under the command of Captain Killigrew, in the *Plymouth*, to try to intercept. The *Plymouth* was a third rate, the other five were fourth rates, the *Falmouth*, the *Adventure*, the *Southampton*, the *Carlisle* and the *Newcastle*. On the morning of 18 January at 6 a.m., sailing off Pantalarea (Pantelleria), the *Plymouth* surprised two French warships, the *Trident* and the *Content*. As soon as the French realised that they had accidentally run into the enemy they fled. The *Plymouth* gave chase and being the fastest of the English contingent was the first to come up with the enemy. By then it was two in the afternoon and the rest of the English fleet had fallen some distance behind. The French, realising that they were not going to be able to outdistance the English, and seeing an opportunity for inflicting immediate damage on just one of their adversaries, lay to and opened their broadsides, causing much damage to the masts, sails and rigging of the *Plymouth*. The *Plymouth* fought back all sails standing, plying its forward guns against the *Content* and the after ones against the *Trident*. It was, however, a difficult situation. The *Content* was to windward making it almost impossible for the *Plymouth* to manoeuvre, while the Trident was close on the *Plymouth*'s stern inflicting considerable damage. One cannon ball took off the *Plymouth*'s tiller making necessary some urgent emergency repairs in order to maintain control of the ship. After about half an hour of this battering, the *Falmouth* arrived in support and quickly dealt with the *Trident*. A short while later, however, Captain Killigrew was shot dead. This was followed by the foremast coming down and the *Plymouth* was immediately compelled to drop out of the battle. The *Content* then bore away followed by the *Carlisle*, the *Newcastle* and the *Southampton*. The *Falmouth* and the *Adventure* continued their assault on the *Trident*. The captain of the *Trident* was the Count d'Aulnay, from Saintonge, brother to the Marquis de la Caze de Poure. Like Killigrew he was killed early on in the battle. The Count d'Aulnay's second in command was an Irishman. The Irish were frequently to be found fighting in the ranks of the French at this period. He continued the struggle against superior odds until 9 p.m. when the *Trident* finally surrendered. The small fleet withdrew into Messina with their prize. The *Content*, meanwhile, captained by the Marquis de Chalard from Brittany, sailed westwards towards the Isle of Marittimo on the westernmost point of Sicily, hoping to escape when night fell. Unluckily for him, however, it was a moonlit night and the English managed to continue their pursuit. The following morning at eight o'clock, the *Carlisle*, the foremost of the English ships, renewed hostilities. Against the *Carlisle*'s heavy cannon, the *Content* could only use six of its lighter guns. The rest were either disabled through falling masts and rigging or too low in the ship to be fired because of the increased rolling and pitching of the waves. Chalard himself described his ship as being at this point like a cart without wheels entirely governed by the sea. He called a meeting of his officers and it was decided at 4 p.m. to lower the French flag. Thirty-two out of his 380 men had been killed.

The first reports to reach France were that the *Content* had been sunk but these were later corrected. The French press was full of praise for the way in which both sides had conducted themselves during the battle. The English officers praised the gallantry of the French officers and the French for their part complimented the English on the courtesy with which they were treated as prisoners. They were even allowed to continue to wear their swords. This was an age when war was still conducted with a certain amount of gallantry and mutual respect. The English fleet left Messina on 10 March, leaving their prizes behind. The prisoners of war were all released and sent off back to Toulon. Only the Irishman was taken into permanent custody. He was regarded as a

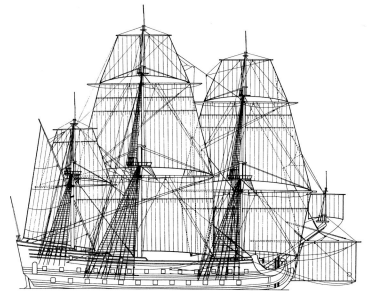

A French 56-gun ship of the same class as the *Trident*. A modern drawing by Veres László based on a contemporary plan.

traitor and so was destined to be hanged.

The English fleet arrived in Leghorn on 20 March, met there with a fleet of returning allied merchantmen and convoyed the latter back to Cadiz where they arrived on 18 April. In June the *Carlisle* and the *Plymouth* again sailed to Leghorn via Genoa arriving on 15 July. The *Plymouth* captured another French prize close by Corsica laden with sugar and ginger and the following month they captured near Toulon a Martinico ship, also laden with sugar. By 20 August they were in Barcelona. Then it was back to Cadiz and in early November another skirmishing cruise, this time the *Carlisle* in company with the *Dragon, Falmouth*, and *Adventure*. Meanwhile, in October 1695 Admiral Russell had returned with a number of ships to England and Sir George Rooke had come out with fresh reinforcements to take over command of the Mediterranean fleet, arriving at Cadiz on 28 November.

On 1 January 1696 (1695 old-style) the *Carlisle* finally departed from Cadiz for England in the company of the *Portsmouth* galley, a fireship called the *Crescent* and eleven merchant ships. Captain Norris of the *Carlisle* had instructions to call at Lisbon to see whether there were any other merchant ships ready to be escorted and then he was to continue his way northwards. Sir George Rooke took the opportunity of the *Carlisle*'s imminent departure to send a letter to his friend, Sir William Trumbull, in which he included the following brief note: 'I have sent you by the *Carlisle* a very small present of arracena wine and seville snuff, and if it does not prove as good as ever came to England, I shall be discouraged to employ my friends there in the like occasion. I have recommended it to the care of Colonel Crawford to convey it to you.' It seems most unlikely that Sir William Trumbull ever received his wine or his snuff although the letter itself clearly survived.

The *Carlisle* went into the river of Lisbon as instructed where about ten more merchant ships joined the convoy. They departed on 8 January and arrived safely in the Downs, close by Deal in Kent, on the 21st of the month. Captain Norris must by this stage have been eager to get home. His term of duty had lasted over a year. Besides he could look forward to a handsome share out of the prize money consequent upon his taking of the *Content* and other French ships. In the Downs a pilot called William Mumbray came on board to take over the navigation of the last few miles into the River Thames.

They weighed anchor at 8 a.m. on 27 January. The wind was blowing from the south-west by south. They stood through the Gull Stream and then steered north-east by north, followed by north-north-east and finally due north. At two o'clock in the afternoon, coming into about nineteen fathoms of water, they changed course again and hauled up to the north-west and then the west-north-west. Their pilot declared that they had already run the length of the Long Sand Head and, coming into shoaling water of about ten fathoms, they bore away north-west and north-west by north. At half-past three they saw Orford church and castle. At about four in the afternoon the pilot believed they were in the vicinity of the Sunk Sand. They came into fifteen fathoms of water but it quickly shelved again to twelve fathoms, then nine, then seven. A sinister rippling of the water was observed on their lee side. Captain Norris asked the pilot whether it might not be a sand bank but the pilot assured him that it was only an overfall. Captain Norris was not reassured. He requested that the ship was immediately put about and brought to an anchor. The pilot, however, refused to agree and said that the present course they were on would do very well to bring the ship up the river. At the next cast of the lead the water was only five fathoms and before they could haul up, or back a sail, the ship had struck. It proved to be the dreaded Shipwash sandbank, situated off Harwich, although the pilot remained adamant that it was the Sunk Sand.

They now backed all the sails, but the tide was falling very fast and they could not get the ship's keel off the sands. In panic they sent down the yards and the topmasts. The pilot claimed it was just high water when they struck but according to Edmund Foster, the first lieutenant, it was already a quarter ebb. They waited until the next high tide and at about 2 a.m. they got up their yards and topmasts again and backed their sails a second time and this time the ship came off the sand. It veered off into seven fathoms of water and they immediately let go their best bower anchor, their bower anchor and sheet anchor, and kept the pumps going and started bailing at all the hatchways. But by this time the sea was entering the ship so fast they were forced to heave the ship onto the sand again rather than risk her sinking in deep water. They spent the long dark night in this per-

The quarterdeck of an official model thought to represent the *Portland*, a similar ship to the *Carlisle*. Note the absence of a wheel, the ships of this era being steered by a 'whipstaff', a vertical lever used to put over the tiller. Because this device was below decks, it could make ships slower to respond to helm orders.

ilous situation fearing that any minute the ship would go to pieces. The following morning, at first light, they began to construct rafts on which to try to save themselves. They cut away their top-masts, mizzen-mast and foremast for this purpose. About three in the afternoon three fishing smacks came out from Harwich and took off all the men, about 400 in total, except three who were drowned.

The question inevitably arises as to whether or not the *Carlisle* really had such a large quantity of bullion on board when it sank on the Shipwash and if so from where did it originate. Dr Nathaniel in his note to the Earl of Huntingdon suggests that the bullion was seized from the French prize *Content* when it was captured. He does not refer to the *Content* by name mentioning only a French prize taken in the Straits. The term 'Straits' usually referred to the Straits of Gibraltar, and anywhere inside the Straits (i.e. the Mediterranean) and this is probably what Dr Nathaniel was thinking about. It is unlikely that he was referring to some other capture for it was the battle between Captain Killigrew and the two French warships that had received all the publicity in England the previous summer. Also, while the *Carlisle* did make one or two other minor seizures, there is no evidence that any other major French prizes were taken inside the Straits of Gibraltar. The problem with the theory that the *Carlisle* bullion originated from the capture of the *Content* is that nowhere among the first hand accounts of the battle contained in the Archives Nationales in Paris is there any mention that the *Content* was carrying a significant quantity of bullion. Indeed, there is no mention that these two French warships were carrying valuable cargo of any kind and if they had been it seems unlikely that they would have been abandoned in Messina. It is true that the presence of gold and silver is not always made explicit. But simple logic would suggest that if the *Carlisle* came back to Cadiz in April 1695 with a large amount of booty, it would not have been left on the ship for nearly another year before being transported back to England. Admiral Russell had returned in the autumn of 1695 with a large part of the Confederate fleet. If there was bullion to be transported back as a result of the capture of the *Content* and *Trident*, surely he would have taken it with him then. Dr Nathaniel's explanation as to the origin of the bullion does not really add up.

There is, however, another more probable explanation for the presence of the bullion reputedly on board the *Carlisle*. The English warship had been instructed to call in at Lisbon on its return voyage to pick up and escort any further merchant ships that may have been waiting there. It is highly probable that at that point it also picked up a large quantity of gold and silver. Merchants during this period were in the business of remitting large quantities of specie from Lisbon to London. The favoured mode of transport, because it was considered to be the safest, and this was especially the case during times of war, was an English warship. The captains of the warships liked doing it because they received a percentage of the value carried. It was a much coveted perk. It was also strictly against Admiralty rules unless there was a specially approved sanction to do it. In the *Carlisle*'s case this seems unlikely. However, like many aspects of navy business, a blind eye was usually turned to the practice. It was perks like these that helped keep wages down. If this was the origin of the *Carlisle*'s bullion it might also explain why it was that the whole business of its presence on board was somewhat swept under the carpet.

If one accepts that the *Carlisle* had indeed been carrying large quantities of bullion when it wrecked on the Shipwash Sand there remains a further difficulty for any would-be modern-day treasure-hunter hoping to recover it, even disregarding for the moment issues of legality and archaeology. This further problem relates to the possibility of salvage at the time of loss. It would be a great mistake to assume that just because the *Carlisle* went down over 300 years ago there would have been no attempt to salvage any valuables on board. The salvage industry may have been somewhat primitive but it was certainly very active at this period. This was, after all, the age of the great experimental scientist Edmond Halley and his diving bell. Basically this bell involved a

Even in the seventeenth century some underwater salvage was possible using various forms of diving bell, like the one shown here. The bell was replenished by sending down weighted barrels of air.

diver breathing air trapped inside an upturned wooden barrel. As the barrel was lowered the air was compressed by the increased pressure of the water, which enabled the diver breathing this compressed air to maintain an equilibrium between the air in his lungs and the pressure of the water on his rib cage. The barrel would be suspended a few feet above the wreck or the seabed and if the diver needed to leave his barrel in order to attach a rope, or use some other device, he could continue to breathe the compressed air by means of a tube between his mouth and the top of the barrel where the store of the air was contained. Fresh air was brought down in casks that were opened under water. This primitive technology had been used successfully in depths of up to around sixty feet. The *Carlisle* lay in water probably no deeper than ten to twenty feet at low tide. But the salvors on the *Carlisle* would have faced another far more intractable problem, which has frustrated many recovery projects on ships in similar depths and, even today, can still pose a serious obstacle. The rapid silting up of a vessel by sand has been the bane of many a salvage project. The ability of divers to recover the bullion on the *Carlisle* would have depended very largely on how quickly they gained access to that bullion after the ship had sunk.

Tracing old salvage records is extremely difficult. Exhaustive trawling through the archives has turned up two further clues relating to the *Carlisle* bullion. They both confirm that bullion and specie was definitely on board. They also confirm that some recoveries took place. An early newspaper called the *Post Boy* carried a report dated Harwich, 30 January: 'His Majesty's ship the *Carlisle* that ran aground on the Shipwash Sand is lost. Several smacks and the *Roebuck* went to her assistance from hence, but she was sunk before they got thither; the captains, pilot and all the men were taken on rafts on board the smacks, except 3, viz two sick men and a black, that were drowned, the rest landed here yesterday morning and went for London. All the plate and money in the Captain's cabin were saved.' This seems pretty categorical but in some ways it also raises as many questions as it answers. If the *Carlisle* was sunk by the time the smacks first arrived, and all the reports of the survivors at the court martial confirm that the decks were already under water at that stage, how was the money taken off? It is very unlikely that there would have been any divers in attendance at this initial rescue. Diving was a highly specialised activity and required some days if not weeks to organise. So either the newspaper is mistaken or the chests of specie, etc., had already been removed before the *Carlisle* slipped under the water. The latter is certainly possible. But the circumstances of the sinking make it surprising that amid all the confusion the officers had time to attend to the preserving of valuables, but not the lives of all of their men.

The second clue comes from a contemporary diarist. Under the date of 1 February 1696 is the following entry: 'The *Carlisle*, a man of war of 60 guns, the beginning of this week struck on a sand called the Shipwash, off Harwich, and sunk; but all her men except 3 were saved, as also a considerable quantity of bullion.' Again the reference to salvage of bullion is unequivocal. This diarist in his phrasing does leave open, however, the possibility that as well as a considerable quantity being saved a considerable quantity was also lost. At the end of the day you take your choice according to your inclination. Either you think like Dr Nathaniel that all was lost and, in that case, it must still remain somewhere beneath the Shipwash Sand, or you subscribe to the *Post Boy* version and think all was saved, or you can opt for the diarist who hedges his bets.

What is known is that one year after the sinking of the *Carlisle*, the events in the Mediterranean which Dr Nathaniel had presumed to be the explanation for the presence of bullion on the *Carlisle*, were again in the news and again money was at the centre of the row. The Lords of the Admiralty wrote to the Commissioners of the Navy informing them of the value of the *Content* and *Trident* prizes and the number of cannon that had been captured and instructed them to pay out the appropriate share of this booty to those who were entitled to it according to the terms of the recent Act of Parliament. The Commissioners promptly wrote back stating that the recent Act of Parliament only covered the capture of merchant ships not warships and that it was their understanding that where warships were concerned the standing allowance to the captors was limited to £10 for every gun taken, nothing being given for the value of the ship or cargo. Furthermore, they did not know who was entitled and who was not.

The distinction made here between a merchant ship and a warship seems odd in an age when merchant ships frequently carried more guns than a fourth or fifth rate. It also seems perverse to discourage attacks on enemy warships in favour of attacks on enemy merchant shipping when it is the warship that is more likely to involve stout resistance and possible injury to the attackers. As to the question of the Commissioners not knowing who was entitled to the awards, this was a potential hornet's nest, that the Admiralty had clearly wanted to offload onto the Commissioners, and the Commissioners had promptly handed back to the Admiralty. The problem was that the prize money was being claimed by Captain Norris of the *Carlisle* with respect to the capturing of the *Content* and Captains Grantham and Cornwall of the *Falmouth* and *Adventure* with respect to the taking of the *Trident*. Such an arrangement would exclude anything going to the officers and crew of the *Plymouth* or the family of the late Captain Killigrew who had lost his life in the attack. One of the naval commissioners, Josiah Burchett, who was later to write a detailed account of the war, sent a letter to Henry Killigrew, brother to Captain Killigrew, alerting him to the situation, and suggesting he take the matter up with the Admiralty on behalf of his brother's family. Henry Killigrew wrote to the Admiralty reasonably arguing that, as commander of the squadron and captain of the ship that first engaged the enemy, enabling the other ships to catch up and also engage, as well as very probably being the cause of the *Content* losing some of her masts, his brother's heirs deserved something.

The Admiralty, clearly nonplussed by the reply they got from the Commissioners, and feeling themselves possibly in something of a tight corner over the Captain Killigrew issue, did the usual thing and consulted their solicitors. Three months later the lawyers came up with an answer. 'It is the opinion of Mr Attorney and Mr Solicitor General that the captains, officers and company of his Majesty's ships which did actually take the *Trident* and *Content* are entitled to one third part of their value and ten pounds for each gun.' This seemed like a generous and fair settlement of the issue of warships vis-à-vis merchant ships. The second part of their decision, however, seems today to have been somewhat harsh. They concluded that the *Carlisle* had taken the *Content* and the *Falmouth* and *Adventure* had taken the *Trident* and that those who had been on board the

An oil portrait by George Knapton of Admiral Sir John Norris at the peak of a career undiminished by the loss of the *Carlisle*.

Plymouth, including the late Captain Killigrew, were entitled to nothing. Henry Killigrew, not satisfied with this answer, petitioned the Admiralty. The Admiralty, however, continued to stand by their previous decision. They declared that they had already referred the matter to Admiral Russell, the commander of the Mediterranean fleet at the time of the action, and it was Admiral Russell's opinion 'that captains Norris, Grantham and Cornwall were the only commanders entitled to the reward for taking the said men-of-war, in regard Captain Killigrew was slain immediately on engaging with the *Content*, and the said ship did not receive any considerable damage from the *Plymouth*.' Admiral Russell was,

of course, not himself an eyewitness, and as the main eyewitnesses that there were all had a vested interest in diminishing Captain Killigrew's contribution, it is difficult to have much confidence in the judicial process at work here. Indeed, the whole question of the sharing out of the prize money, seems like a rather shabby affair. This was, however, an age when privilege, patronage and bribery were frequently involved as much as principles of justice in any decision-making process.

9

The *Vliegend Hert*'s Gold

REASURE MAPS ARE USUALLY thought of as frayed pieces of parchment adorned with piratical hieroglyphics and covered in cryptic clues that involve digging holes at so many paces due east of a single palm tree or west of a fissure of rock. They are the very stuff of adventure and romantic fiction – and most usually the product of charlatans, freebooters or worse. As such they have proved to be of little use to any serious treasure-hunter. The value of old charts, however, to those wishing to track down the whereabouts of shipwrecks should not be lightly underestimated. They are often crucial for establishing the location of particular rocks, reefs, sandbanks or headlands that may be mentioned in a sinking report but the names of which have become corrupted, altered and lost over the centuries. It is only through the scrupulous examination of these ancient sea maps that the identity of some vital landmark can be rediscovered. On rare occasions an old chart will also provide more specific and graphic information. The place of a named wreck with sometimes the date of loss added will be actually marked, often by means of a quaint little drawing of a sinking ship. The purpose of these marks was partly historical record and partly to act as a very visual warning to navigators that a particular area was a place of danger.

Modern charts, of course, contain thousands of wreck marks, laid down with great accuracy, but they are of little use to anyone hoping to discover gold. The identity of the wrecks is generally unrecorded and the vast majority of them anyway relate to large steel ships lost during the two World Wars, very few of which carried any kind of treasure. They are recorded as a potential source of navigational hazard particularly to fishermen who risk snagging their trawler nets on such seabed obstructions. By contrast wreck markings on old charts are a rarity and when they do occur they are often of great interest. Edmund Gostelo's 'Map of the Islands of Scilly; showing all the rocks and ledges, with the soundings and bearings of the exact places where the *Association, Eagle, Romney* and *Firebrand* was lost' was certainly of assistance to Roland Morris in his search and rediscovery of Admiral Shovell's flagship. It should not be assumed, however, that old charts are an infallible method of relocating the wrecks named on them. None of the charts that show a position for the sinking of HMS *Victory* off the Caskets in 1744 have so far been proved correct.

A Dutch East Indiaman of the mid-eighteenth century.

The best kinds of charts as an aid to shipwreck location are without a doubt those manuscript drawings produced shortly after the sinking as a guide to a prospective salvor. It was just such a drawing, unearthed from the bowels of the Algemeen Rijksarchief (General State Archive) in The Hague, that came into the hands of John Rose and his team when they were searching for the *Vliegend Hert*, a Dutch East Indiaman that sank in 1735 among the sandbanks off Holland. As their excavation eventually led to the lifting of an entire chest full of rare gold coins this roughly drawn map could rightly be regarded as a fine example of a genuine treasure map. Even with the assistance of such a reliable and detailed guide, however, it took two years of searching before the wreck was discovered and another year before the chest was recovered.

On 3 February 1735, shortly after midday, the *Vliegend Hert*, Captain Cornelis van der Horst, weighed anchor and departed from the small port of Rammekens near Vlissingen in Zeeland, south Netherlands. The ship was owned by the Zeeland chamber, one of six such chambers that made up the VOC, the famous Dutch East India trading company that had been founded in 1600. The *Vliegend Hert*, named for Mr Johan van Buytenhem, Mayor of Vlissingen, whose coat of arms contained a flying deer, had been built in the Korendijk shipyard in Middelburg in 1730 and had already completed one round trip to the Far East and back which had taken almost exactly three years. It was of average size for a ship of its type, 145 feet long, 850 tons burthen, carrying thirty-six cannon, at least two of which were bronze. It was important that large quantities of iron should not be placed too near the compass in order to reduce the likelihood of magnetic error, and so some bronze cannon were still carried, to be positioned either side of the binnacle, even though they were far more expensive than their iron equivalent. Despite its racy name the *Vliegend Hert*, judging from the painting of its sister ship, the *Popkensberg*, was a typical broad-beamed, tub-shaped merchantman, designed for cargo capacity more than speed. The *Vliegend* was sailing in consort with a second, slightly smaller, ship called the *Anna Catharina*. Out in front of both ships was a pilot boat called the *Mercurius*, Captain Willem Gerbrantsz, whose duty was to guide the two valuable East Indiamen safely through the labyrinth of sandbanks for which the Dutch coast was notorious, and then down the English Channel as far as the Isle of Wight. It is a curiosity of the entire East India voyage that by far the most dangerous part for the Dutch was the first few leagues navigating through the difficult sandbanks of the southern North Sea. The English East India Company was hardly better placed as their ships had to negotiate the treacherous sandbanks of the Thames Estuary, including the notorious Goodwins.

3 February 1735 marked the height of the spring tides which would make the currents even fiercer than usual through the narrow channels that led from Rammekens to the open sea. Still more alarming was the fact that the weather was rapidly deteriorating. A gale had begun to blow from the east. Caution advised staying in port. But Cornelis van der Horst had already been waiting several days for a favourable easterly wind. Without it he was trapped in port. Now that the wind was at last blowing from the right direction he was understandably reluctant to miss the opportunity. It might be several weeks before it blew from the right quarter again. It was in this spirit that the small Dutch flotilla edged its way cautiously along the treacherous Deurloo Channel.

The two VOC ships were en route to Batavia, the hub of the Dutch East India Company's Far Eastern empire. They were due to call on the way at Capetown in South Africa where the Company had established an important trading post. The *Vliegend Hert* carried a crew of 167 men. In addition there were eighty-three soldiers and six passengers on board. Supplies for the long voyage, which

Spanish clipped coinage, known to the Dutch as 'spaanse matten'.

usually took up to around nine months, included dried fish, preserved meats, cheese, bread, rice, wine, beer and gin, not to mention thirty-three live pigs and twelve live sheep. The bulk of the cargo consisted of the basic raw materials for building and construction work such as bricks, wood and iron as well as military supplies, primarily saltpetre and weaponry, all vital for the establishment and defence of Holland's burgeoning colonial presence in the Far East. Taking up much less space but of far greater value were three chests containing silver and gold coin, the hard cash necessary for the purchasing of the much-coveted spices which would make up the return cargo. There were also some luxury items on board designed to make the life of the company's Far Eastern employees a little less austere. Fine French and German wines and Dutch gin were pre-eminent in this regard. Other items, that were later to be painstakingly recovered from the wreck site, included Chinese porcelain, Bavarian glassware, pewter plates and brass navigational instruments, but all these were most probably the personal possessions of the officers rather than trade items. By the mid-eighteenth century a ship's officers and company employees were possessed of greater wealth and desired a higher standard of personal comfort during the long voyage, than would have been the case a hundred years beforehand.

Towards late afternoon, as it grew dark, the weather dramatically worsened. The *Anna Catharina* was driven by a violent gust of wind on to the Dorpel sandbank where it was smashed to pieces within the space of just a few hours. Boats were launched but they were unable to survive the ferocious seas. All 175 people on board were drowned. The *Vliegend Hert* also hit the same sandbank, at about the same time, but remained intact a little longer, came off the bank and was able to anchor in deeper water. Cannon were fired to try and attract the attention of possible rescuers but it was a vain hope. The *Vliegend Hert* went down that same evening, shortly before midnight, and again there were no survivors. A merchant ship on its way to Toulon witnessed the dismal scene but in the circumstances of such tumultuous seas was unable to provide any help.

In 1979, John Rose, a successful restauranteur and experienced diver, together with Rex Cowan, a lawyer turned wreck-hunter, decided on the basis of the research information that they had gathered together that the *Vliegend Hert* was a target worth looking for. Many of those that they discussed the project with were sceptical. The waters of the Deurloo Channel were notoriously cold and murky. When diving it was rare that you could see further than a metre in front of your face. It was like groping through black pea soup. Such conditions make the location and identification of a shipwreck extremely difficult. Rose and Cowan, however, were not to be put off. Rose purchased a steel-hulled ocean-going catamaran, equipped it with the latest in side-scan sonars, magnetometers and navigational equipment, and began the long slow process of surveying the likely sinking locality. On 4 August 1981, after two years of patient searching, the magnetometer recorded yet another small anomaly, the latest in a series of several hundred such anomalies, all of which had been potential targets, and all of which had been dived on, checked out and finally rejected as being of no interest. On the face of it this latest anomaly was no more or less interesting than any of the others. It was then with no great sense of hope or anticipation that John Rose and his companion Steve Moore dived into the inhospitable grey waters of the North Sea. This time, however, they were in luck. John Rose almost immediately on reaching the seabed fell over a cannon protruding from the sand. A brief survey by hand of the immediate area revealed a total of four cannon, two bronze and two iron, heaped close together. The iron cannon had caused the anomalous reading. It was the bronze cannon, however, that provided the identity. They were both stamped with the VOC monogram.

During the next few months a variety of coins was recovered from the wreck site bearing dates from 1729 to 1734, providing further proof that they had indeed discovered the remains of the *Vliegend Hert*. The silver coins were black and corroded but the gold were in an excellent state, fine ducatoons minted in Utrecht. In one sense the most difficult part of the project was over. In another it was only just beginning.

Back in 1735 all the salvage groups employed by the Zeeland Chamber to try and recover the lost coin had been English. They included a James Bushell, a John Mitchell and a William Evans. The English clearly had possessed something of a technical advantage when it came to 'wreck fishing' during the first half of the eighteenth century. It is perhaps then only appropriate that it was an English group that finally recovered the *Vliegend Hert* treasure. The local Dutch press did

One of the near-pristine Ducatoons, dated 1734, recovered from the wreck.

not see it, however, quite in those terms. As soon as news got out that the *Vliegend Hert* had been located by English divers the Dutch newspapers were full of stories about how their heritage was being stolen by unlicensed 'English treasure-hunters'. The accusation was quite unfair. The entire project had in fact been undertaken with the knowledge and cooperation of the Rijksmuseum in Amsterdam and was conducted to appropriate archaeological standards. All recovered items were surveyed, logged and carefully recorded. The hostile reporting in the press, however, had the effect of encouraging local marauders to vandalise the site while looking for quick and easy loot.

The Dutch government eventually stepped in and provided the necessary site protection to allow the project to continue. The *Vliegend Hert* excavation was eventually to produce some unusual and fascinating finds including a primitive form of fish-can. Anchovies were discovered packed inside a stoneware jar, covered by a slate lid. This jar had in turn been placed inside a sealed lead casket, and the lead casket had then been squeezed into a wooden barrel. So much elaborate packaging certainly underlines the high regard the Dutch had for their anchovies. Rolls of tobacco on board the *Vliegend Hert* had similarly been encased in lead. Many of the rarest of the recovered

John Rose with some of the objects recovered from the *Vliegend Hert*. They include a chest full of coins, as well as personal artefacts like a shoe, a shaving bowl and a hip flask. Aspects of the ship's equipment were also represented by a barrel, the 'truck' (wheel) of a gun carriage and gauges to check the diameter of cannon balls.

artefacts can now be seen in Dutch museums such as the Stedelijk Museum in Vlissingen. The story of the *Vliegend Hert* salvage underlines the fact that the underwater heritage is at far greater threat from random trawling and unofficial looting than it is from a properly run and authorised commercial enterprise working alongside trained archaeologists. A policy of benign neglect which seems to be the policy at present advocated by the United Nations is actually no safeguard for the great variety of treasures lying on the seabed in busy waterways.

The *Vliegend Hert*, lying in sixty feet of water, has been located and excavated, but the *Anna Catharina*, in much shallower depths, remains elusive. The search continues.

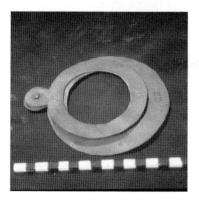

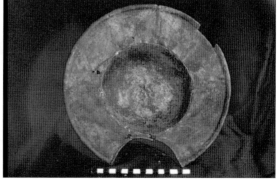

Lost Artworks of Catherine the Great

GERRET BRAAMCAMPS WAS NOT BORN to riches but he was an astute Dutch businessman who quickly made a fortune in the wine and timber import trades during the eighteenth century. Like many successful entrepreneurs, both before and since, he liked to surround himself with beautiful objects, and he invested a large part of his accumulated wealth in works of art. His large and elegant house on the Heerengracht in Amsterdam was a storehouse of superb paintings, porcelain, glass, gold and silver ornaments and miscellaneous 'objects of virtue'. His aesthetic sense was as well-honed as his commercial abilities and his collection was very soon the envy of Europe. On his death his entire collection was put up for sale. Detailed records of the auction and the prices fetched are still in existence. The paintings were sold on 31 July 1771 and the porcelain a week later. It was, in truth, one of the great sales of the century, and Catherine the Great, Empress of all the Russias, and an omnivorous collector of art objects, made sure that her agents were present to cream off the very best items. Her purchases were intended to enhance the fabulous collection she had already assembled in the Winter Palace in St Petersburg.

A View of the Winter Palace at St Petersburg, the intended home for the artworks purchased by Catherine the Great.

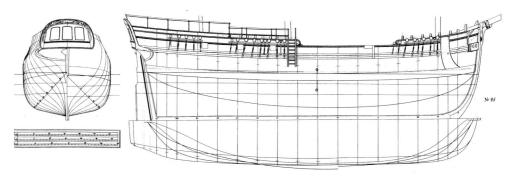

Plan from an eighteenth-century treatise of a northern European snow-rigged merchant ship of the same size as
Vrouw Maria. The snow was a two-masted rig with the after mast the larger, but conversion to a koff would have
involved cutting down the rig so that the forward mast became the main, in the manner of a ketch.

The auction records reveal that B. Tideman Johz and A. van den Bogarde were both extremely active making purchases on Catherine's behalf. Tideman Johz, for instance, acquired a Gerard Dou painting which shows a richly furnished interior in which a beautiful young woman is seated at a covered table. She is dressed in a yellow satin petticoat embroidered with ermine and is breast-feeding her baby. It cost 14,100 Dutch florins. There is a copy of the painting by Laquy in the Rijksmuseum, Amsterdam. Braamcamp and Catherine the Great both had a taste, or so it seems, for intimate domestic interior scenes. Another painting by Isaack Coedyk, purchased on Catherine's behalf by van den Bogarde, shows a room with a spiral staircase down which a man is creeping in order to take by surprise his servant and maid, who are flirting together. It was a bargain at 4,300 florins. Again there is a copy by Laquy, this time in the possession of the Fodor Museum in Amsterdam. Other paintings by Rembrandt, Gabriel Metsu, Adriaen van Ostade, Abraham Stork, Philips Wouverman, and Herman Zaftleven were also purchased on Catherine's behalf. Part of the Braamcamp purchases were sent to St Petersburg by land, but the bulk of them were loaded on to a relatively modest two-masted Dutch vessel called the *Vrouw Maria*. The *Vrouw Maria* sank en route. As all the art works mentioned disappeared without trace after the auction sale it seems reasonable to presume that they were all lost, together with the ship and numerous other treasured items. The latter may well have included rare pieces of porcelain, lacquerware, gold and silver artefacts, glassware, statues and rich furniture.

The master of the *Vrouw Maria* was a Dutchman called Reynoud Lorenz and the crew were also largely Dutch. The ship's home port was Amsterdam and it was there that loading commenced on Monday 12 August 1771. By 2 September the cargo loading had been completed, including the items purchased by Catherine. They were, however, unable to leave port because the wind was blowing strongly from the east. It was not until 5 September that the wind changed to the southwest and they were able to set sail. By 18 September they had passed Skagen, at the northern tip of Denmark, and on the 23rd they anchored at Elsinore beneath the Castle of Kronborg. Here the captain had to go on shore by dinghy in order to pay the 'Sound Toll'. These taxes were levied by Denmark on the cargoes of all ships passing in and out of the Baltic and the resulting customs records, which extend from the fifteenth to the nineteenth century, provide a most important source of information for today's economic and maritime historians. The tax receipts were a valuable source of revenue to Denmark until the United States put an end to the system in 1857 by refusing to pay. Other nations quickly followed suit. Denmark was no longer in a position to impose its will on the great trading nations of the world with their belief in the freedom of the seas. In 1771, however, there was no chance for a small ship like the *Vrouw Maria* to escape without paying. The entrance to the Baltic was guarded day and night by two Danish warships.

At Elsinore a pilot was embarked who stayed with the ship for the next few days in order to guide it safely through the treacherous waters of the Sound. This section of the voyage safely completed the pilot went ashore and the *Vrouw Maria* headed northwards up the Baltic. The Arctic winter was rapidly approaching and the days got increasingly shorter and darker. On 3 October at half-past eight in the evening, when the captain and most of the crew were at prayers, they ran on to a hidden shoal, among the bewildering archipelago of tiny islands off the south-west coast of Finland, which was then part of Sweden. The details of exactly what happened are all carefully recorded in the account supplied by the captain to the authorities in Stockholm, still preserved in the State Archives. The captain's account includes a transcription of his log book from the day he left Amsterdam until the ship was finally abandoned.

The *Vrouw Maria* was clearly far to the north of its correct course. On striking rocks panic broke out among the crew as for a moment they feared the ship would immediately go to pieces. They were lucky that a large wave very shortly brought them over the reef that they had struck and into deeper water. However, their troubles were far from over. The impact of the collision had caused the rudder to sheer off, which left their ship leaking badly and virtually ungovernable. They took in their sails and tried to anchor, but it was some moments before the anchors took hold on the sea bottom. They then set about manning the pumps. There were already three feet of water in the hold. The crew spent a backbreaking and perilous night pumping continuously. At first light the following day, which came at 7 a.m., they were confronted by the dismal fact that their ship was surrounded by reefs from which there was no apparent way out. To make matters worse, the wind was gusting from the south-west threatening to drive them on to more rocks at any moment, if the cable broke or the anchor gave way. The sky was dark and ominous. The decision was taken to abandon ship and try to save their lives. They lowered their two small boats, got together some warm clothing, blankets and food and set out for a nearby rock above the waterline. The captain does not mention firing guns, but it seems likely that he did, because that evening a local boat arrived crewed by five men. They promised to come back with help the following day. Meanwhile,

An artist's impression commissioned by the Maritime Museum of Finland showing the bow of the wreck as it appears now. The broken fluke of the surviving anchor is even mentioned in the historical record.

that evening, after the wind had dropped the crew managed to salvage ten barrels and one chest.

Over the next few days considerable numbers of local fishermen came out from the port of Åbo to assist with the salvage. It was a difficult business because the pumps were clogged with coffee beans and the water was swilling with sugar, all part of the general cargo that had been loaded in Amsterdam. The weather was erratic and the process of getting out the cargo was both difficult and risky. Salvage work must have been like groping in a huge basin of cappuccino. Then, on the morning of 9 October, they woke in their makeshift encampment on the barren rock to discover that the *Vrouw Maria* had been silently swallowed up by the sea during the course of the night. This put an abrupt end to any further thoughts of salvage. The goods that had been recovered were sold in Åbo later that same month. Some of them were items that had been destined for members of the Russian Court. No items from the Braamcamp collection, however, were listed. A complete catalogue of what was sold has survived in the minutes of the Åbo Municipal Court.

From Åbo Captain Lorentz travelled to Stockholm where, in the following December, he made a formal declaration as to exactly what had happened to his ship and its contents. From

Stockholm he and his crew eventually made their way back to Amsterdam. Meanwhile, diplomatic negotiations were taking place at the highest level to see what could be done about recovering Empress Catherine's lost treasures. The Swedish ambassador in St Petersburg, Baron Ribbing, wrote to the senior Swedish official in Åbo, Baron Rappe, to find out for himself what had happened and what the prospects were for recovering more of the lost goods. Count Nikita Panin, Minister for Foreign Affairs, also wrote in person to Baron Rappe, adding his personal weight to the seriousness with which this loss was being regarded in St Petersburg. Foreign Ministers did not usually get involved with the routine everyday business of shipwrecks, particularly where there was no loss of life, as in this case, but the *Vrouw Maria* was very much not an ordinary shipwreck. The count also had some of his own property on board as did several other members of the inner circle of the Russian aristocracy.

Sweden had, for the period, a relatively advanced system of local salvage societies, that were paid for from taxes collected from merchant ships. The district of Åbo's Salvage Society was headed by Charles Fithie whose father, Robert Fithie, had held the post before him. Interestingly the Fithies were not Swedish at all but English. Baron Ribbing instructed Fithie to go to the site of the *Vrouw Maria* wreck and see what could be done. However, by the time Fithie had reached the remote

The stern of the wreck. The rudder has disappeared, but there appears to be a loading-port to starboard of the rudder post, which suggests that the ship may have been fitted for the carriage of awkward cargoes like timber.

The hold area showing many of the surviving elements of the cargo.

island of Jummo, which was close to where the wreck had taken place, winter had descended. The entire area was frozen over. Fithie reported back that it would be impossible to do anything before the spring thaw came. As an experienced salvor he must have known all along that his journey would most probably be a waste of time, but presumably diplomatic pressure required that he should make a personal inspection. Baron Ribbing now had the unenviable task of informing the Empress, in a personal audience, that nothing could be achieved immediately.

In February there was a brief flicker of hope. Baron Rappe wrote from Åbo that the *Vrouw Maria* had been located at a depth of thirty fathoms and an attempt would be made to raise the entire ship as soon as the weather improved. This optimism was short lived. It transpired that a fisherman, who had been looking for the wreck by means of trawling his kedge anchor across the sea bottom, had hooked it up on an obstruction. But it turned out not to be the *Vrouw Maria*. It was instead probably one of the millions of rocks that covered the seabed in that area and which threatened to make any search for the *Vrouw Maria*'s remains extremely difficult. On 5 June 1772 Charles Fithie wrote to St Petersburg stating that in his opinion there was no longer any chance of finding the wreck. The Russian authorities were not satisfied. They requested that another neighbouring salvage organisation should be enlisted in the search. This further search was duly carried out but the results were just the same. Catherine had no choice but to reconcile herself to the loss of her treasures.

The *Vrouw Maria* was forgotten for over 200 years until the Finnish historian Christian Ahlström began his meticulous researches into the archives of Åbo and Stockholm in the 1970s, and unearthed the fascinating story concerning the shipwreck. He always believed that, using the information he had found and modern underwater searching techniques, it should prove possible to rediscover the location of the *Vrouw Maria*. It was not until the late 1990s, however, after linking up with the diver and side-scan operator Rauno Koivusaari, that a serious search for the wreck was started. In 1998 a large part of the delineated area was examined with sonar and there was only one wooden wreck found of the correct historical period. However, Ahlström considered that the find could not be the *Vrouw Maria*, because this ship had its rudder still intact, and Captain Lorentz's declaration quite clearly stated that the *Vrouw Maria*'s rudder had come off as it went over the reef. Ahlström was right. The wooden wreck that had been located was not the right one. One of the advantages of carrying out careful historical research prior to a seabed investigation is that it can save a lot of time investigating the wrong vessel.

Ahlström, however, despite his careful researches over a period of twenty years was still not completely satisfied with the amount of data he had so far collected. He was worried that he would not have sufficient evidence to enable him to discriminate the *Vrouw Maria* from other eighteenth-century wooden wrecks. After all, a rudder breaking off was a very common occurrence when a ship hit a reef, and the next wreck found might not be so easily dismissed. He now enlisted the help of the Gemeente Archive (Municipal Archive) in Amsterdam to try and discover whether further details of the *Vrouw Maria*'s structure could be located. The *Vrouw Maria* was a very common name for eighteenth-century Dutch ships. Amazingly, however, a sale document was found that linked one particular *Vrouw Maria* with a Captain Lorentz. This document also provided considerable structural details concerning the vessel. It had been approximately eighty-one feet long and twenty feet broad and although it had started out life as a snow it had been largely rebuilt in 1748 as a koff ship.

In June 1999 Rauno Koivusaari again set out for the sinking area in his ship, somewhat combatively called the *Teredo* (after the shipworm that destroys wrecks under water), and renewed his side-scanning operations. This time he struck lucky early on. Within only three hours of starting a new search a contact was made and divers sent down. An eighteenth-century wooden vessel of the correct measurements was discovered on the seabed lying at a depth of forty-one metres and this time without a rudder. Further confirmation that it was definitely the *Vrouw Maria* that they had found this time, if any further proof was needed, was provided by the way in which the main mast showed evidence of having been previously rigged as a snow, and, even more remarkably, a small kedge anchor was noticed hanging from the ship's side which had one fluke missing. A document referring to this defective anchor written on 18 August 1766 was one of the documents relating to the *Vrouw Maria* that had been unearthed in the Gemeente Archive in Amsterdam. It was part of a detailed inventory of the ship's equipment that had been taken at that date. Rarely can the historical record have matched so exactly the rediscovered object.

It was an extremely exciting find, not least because of the remarkably good condition of the wreck. The *Vrouw Maria*'s lower masts are still standing, its hatches are clearly visible and numerous intact boxes and barrels can still be observed inside the hull. The forehatch is still open just as Lorentz had described it being left open in his 1771 report when his crew first tried to salvage what they could of the cargo. It is as if time has stood still. The hull itself is in almost perfect shape apart

The after deck showing the shaft of two suction pumps and a decorated beam over
what would have been the entrance to the master's cabin.

from some damage to the stern end caused by the original impact when it hit the reef. The reason for this remarkable state of preservation is the low salinity and low temperature of the Baltic water that means the wood-devouring teredo worm cannot flourish. Also the wreck is sunk at such a depth that the ice does not reach it and so does not break up the timbers.

Three items were lifted from the wreck site: a clay pipe made in Gouda, a lacquer seal with the initials of a textile manufacturer in Leiden and a metal ingot. The first two items being of Dutch origin again fitted with the identification of the wreck as the *Vrouw Maria*. The metal ingot turned out to be zinc. The Sound records held in Denmark had mentioned zinc as being part of the *Vrouw Maria*'s cargo as it passed through on its final voyage. The Sound records did not mention any items of the Braamcamp collection because such items, being destined for the Russian court, would have been allowed to pass through free of tax.

Christian Ahlström makes the important point in his latest writings on the find of the *Vrouw Maria* that underwater archaeologists, using scientific archaeological approaches alone, would never have been able to come up with the kind of detailed information about the wreck which he has managed to unearth using historical sources, although they may well make equally important discoveries of a different nature. He goes on to state that he does not understand 'the age old, inexplicable animosity between history and archaeology' and makes a plea for greater cooperation between the two disciplines when dealing with post medieval finds. It appears that so far his plea may have fallen upon deaf ears.

Rauno Koivusaari immediately reported his find to the Finnish Maritime Museum in Helsinki as required by Finnish law. From that point the Maritime Museum has taken over control of the project. Some superb underwater photographs of the wreck have been taken, but to date no attempt has been made to excavate the wreck or bring the cargo to the surface, nor does it appear that there is much likelihood of this happening in the immediate future. The whole project seems to have become bogged down in a legal quagmire.

Koivusaari and his divers have put forward a claim for a salvage award to the Finnish courts which they believe they are entitled to according to the Finnish Maritime Code of 1994. The Finnish State has argued on the other side that the Protection of Antiquities Act 1963 excludes salvage law and the law of finds, and so no award should be paid. This line of thinking is very much in accordance with the UNESCO Convention on the Protection of the Underwater Cultural Heritage of 2001 which is totally opposed to anything that suggests shipwreck finds might be exploited commercially, or that the finder benefit in any material way. The trouble with the UNESCO approach is that, while its aims may be highly laudable in theory, in practice it will accomplish very little except to encourage pillaging and black-market exploitation of underwater cultural finds, instead of responsible reporting.

The mystery that surrounds Catherine the Great's lost treasures looks likely to continue for some time yet.

11

The Myth of the
Bonhomme Richard

OHN PAUL JONES is widely regarded as the first great hero of the American Navy, and the *Bonhomme Richard*, his most famous command, has consequently acquired something of the legendary status of Nelson's HMS *Victory*. Hardly surprising then that its remains have been much searched-for over the last thirty years, although reports of the wreck having been found have so far proved premature. The area of search is a difficult one and the depths of water involved are beyond conventional diving capability. This probably explains why it has so far stubbornly eluded all man's attempts to relocate it.

The moonlight battle off Flamborough Head. The *Bonhomme Richard* is obscured by the British frigate *Serapis*, while Landais' ship *Alliance* seems to fire indiscriminately into both.

The *Bonhomme Richard* is not a treasure ship in the usual meaning of that phrase. When it sank it was not generally thought to be carrying large quantities of gold or silver or intrinsically valuable artefacts, although there have been suggestions that there was a significant sum of French currency on board. The real allure for those wanting to hunt it down is its immense historical interest. Recovered artefacts would no doubt be much coveted by American collectors and museums. An examination of the remains of the hull may also finally put to an end one of the great naval controversies of all time. Did the *Bonhomme* sink because of the treachery of the Frenchman Captain Landais, who at the time was supposed to be fighting on the same side as the Americans? Commodore John Paul Jones certainly thought so and brought charges against Landais, in his famous 'Charges and Proofs Respecting the Conduct of Peter Landais'.

John Paul was born in the parish of Kirkbean near Kirkcudbright in Scotland on 6 July 1747, the son of a gardener. He went to sea at the age of twelve and was soon working on American ships in the West Indian slave trade. He seems to have been an able and competent seaman but his early life contains numerous mysterious lacunae, including suggestions that he may have been mixed up in more than one murder. He was never actually arrested for any wrongdoing, but it is from around this period of his life that he adopted the alias Jones.

On the outbreak of the War of Independence John Paul Jones was a fierce advocate of the American cause. In 1775 he became an officer in what was called the 'Continental Navy'. The next year he obtained his first command, a small twelve-gun sloop called the *Providence* rapidly followed by promotion to the captaincy of the *Ranger*, an eighteen-gun sloop-of-war. He then embarked on a series of skirmishes and raids around his old Scottish stamping ground, including a botched attack on the Earl of Selkirk's house, all of which gained him considerable notoriety, either as a hero or as a pirate, depending on your political standpoint, but achieved very little in the way of serious damage to Britain's commercial interests. Jones's crew were less impressed by his successes than he was himself and, when money became short, they quickly became mutinous. The captaincy of the *Ranger* was transferred to its first lieutenant, called Simpson, and Jones went to L'Orient. France had formally entered the war against Britain in July 1778. It was at this point that John Paul Jones obtained a promise from the French authorities that he would shortly be provided with the command of an entire squadron. John Paul Jones was nothing if not ambitious.

The immediate problem he faced was a dire shortage of suitable ships. He wanted something fast with a powerful battery of guns and large enough to carry a substantial crew and boarding troops. He rejected a series of worn-out hulks and finally compromised on the *Duc de Duras*, an old French East Indiaman of about 900 gross tons and approximately 145 feet long, built in 1766. The *Duras* had already completed four round voyages to the east which was usually considered to be the maximum a ship could manage before being broken up. It was a far cry from the glamorous warship that Paul Jones had imagined for himself but he was given little choice in the matter.

Paul Jones changed the ship's name from the *Duras* to the *Bonhomme Richard*. This was an astute piece of flattery aimed at Benjamin Franklin who was formally heading up American naval interests in Paris. Franklin's book *Poor Richard's Almanac* had been translated into French as *La Science du Bonhomme Richard*. Changing names was easily accomplished. Conversion and fitting out was a little more protracted. It took the next six months and included cutting ports on the gun-deck for the housing of six newly acquired but somewhat old eighteen-pounder cannon. These cannon turned out to be a bad idea. The ports were positioned dangerously close to the waterline and may well have been a contributory factor in the *Bonhomme Richard*'s eventual sinking. As for the cannon themselves the first time the *Bonhomme* was seriously engaged, they exploded. It looks a little as if the fledgling commodore had been suckered into a bad buy.

A Victorian portrayal of John Paul Jones as the head of a piratical gang robbing Lady Selkirk.

By August 1779 Paul Jones's small fleet was ready to sail with instructions to attack enemy shipping as well as create an invasion diversion. The idea was to distract attention from the much larger Franco-Spanish invasion fleet that was planned to strike the south coast of England. The diversionary fleet of five vessels consisted of the *Bonhomme Richard*, forty guns, the *Alliance*, an American frigate with thirty-six guns under Captain Landais, the *Pallas*, a frigate of twenty-six guns under Captain Cottineau de Kerloguen, the *Vengeance*, a brig of twelve guns under Captain Ricot, and *Le Cerf*, a cutter with eighteen guns under Ensign Varage (the *Le Cerf* never made it to the battle of Flamborough Head, having parted from the rest in a storm and returned to L'Orient). The legal status of this tiny fleet was hybrid and confused. It was financed by the French government and Jones's instructions were given to him by the French Navy Minister, Sartine, but the *Bonhomme* flew the American rebels' flag, the Stars and Stripes, Captain Paul Jones later claiming to be the first American ever to hoist this iconic emblem. The confused status of the fleet was to cause much friction between Captain Landais, a Frenchman, who regarded his commission as coming directly from the American Congress, and which therefore made him, in his own mind, an independent, not required to take orders from anyone, and Paul Jones, a Scotsman, who had adopted America as his native country, and who had been appointed to overall command by the French. The proud and prickly Landais clashed badly with the egotistical swashbuckling Jones right from the time they first met. This personal conflict was to become almost as notorious as the battle itself.

Early in the year 1779 Landais had made the voyage from America to France with a troublesome crew, a number of whom he had been forced to commit to irons. Two American officers were among those that Landais had disciplined. Paul Jones had been unsupportive of Landais's action. Landais had insisted on a court of enquiry and the court found in his favour. The rebellious officers were dismissed. It was an inauspicious beginning to the relationship between Landais and Jones, but matters were rapidly to get worse. The small squadron departed from the island of Groix on 19 June 1779. At midnight on the following day in a sudden squall of wind the *Richard* and the *Alliance* collided. The accident was far from mortal but both captains blamed each other. Jones claimed that the *Alliance* should have given way to the flagship. Landais claimed that Jones's signals were unintelligible. The fleet returned to La Groix to make emergency repairs. Jones assembled a court martial but the court found Landais innocent, blaming instead Jones's first lieutenant who had been on the deck of the *Richard* at the time of the accident. Jones then performed a complete volte-face and criticised the court for being too lenient in their punishment of Lieutenant Robert Robinson. He now insisted that Robinson was dismissed from the service.

The squadron set out a second time on 14 August. Orders were to sail to the west of Ireland, around the top of Scotland and then back down into the North Sea. The arguments continued. Paul Jones was keen to make daring raids on land, burning and pillaging as he went. Landais, and the other French captains, preferred to concentrate on the capture of merchant shipping. The latter was less risky, potentially more lucrative and was anyway more in line with their training and past custom. The early stages of the cruise proved uneventful. A few small prizes were taken but nothing of any significance. Signals continued to be widely misunderstood.

The British press, meanwhile, was full of scaremongering stories about pirate Jones and his wicked intentions. There was panic along the north-eastern coastline as hasty measures were taken to improve the country's defences. But in reality the threat was much exaggerated. At one point Jones did sail close into Leith harbour, planning to attack and ransom the port. But on this occasion he was thwarted not by his officers but a last-minute change of wind. Frustrated yet again, Jones sailed on southwards as far as Spurn Point. The entire cruise was in danger of becoming something of a non-event. Then Jones's luck changed and his reputation was made forever.

At around 3.30 p.m. on Friday, 24 September, the weather was clear and pleasant with light breezes of wind, and the *Bonhomme Richard*'s small schooner was sent to intercept a brig that had been observed towards the south-west. The schooner had no sooner been despatched than the British Baltic convoy hoved into view, escorted by two warships, the *Serapis* with fifty guns under Captain Pearson, and the *Countess of Scarborough*, a twenty-gun sloop-of-war under Captain Piercy.

The fleet was carrying vital supplies for the navy. This was the moment that Paul Jones had been waiting for. It was the opportunity that was to transform not just the importance of his cruise but was to earn him a lasting place in American naval history.

The merchant fleet headed towards the coast under the protection of the guns of Scarborough Castle. The two British warships positioned themselves between the fleet they were protecting and Jones's squadron of four ships. At around six in the evening Jones came up with the enemy. He hoisted a blue flag, a blue pendant and a blue-and-yellow flag, which was apparently the signal to form a line of battle, though whether Captain Landais understood it as such is open to question, for a conventional battle line was never formed. Around 7.00 p.m. firing started. The *Bonhomme Richard* engaged the *Serapis* and the *Pallas* took on the *Countess of Scarborough*. The legend of Jones's bravery has been built upon the fact that the *Richard* was a far inferior ship to the *Serapis*, yet took on the more powerful enemy and vanquished it. Certainly in terms of nominal firepower there was some truth to this. The *Richard* carried forty guns. The *Serapis* was designed for forty-four but probably carried closer to fifty. Also the *Serapis*'s guns were heavier and more powerful. It had twenty eighteen-pounders whereas the Richard only had six. This disparity was further increased when early on in the battle one of Jones's eighteen-pounders blew up, killing several of his men. After this setback he felt obliged to discontinue use of the remainder of his specially purchased eighteen-pounders. This certainly gave the advantage to the *Serapis* in the early stages of the battle and if the *Serapis* had managed to keep a steady distance from the *Richard* throughout their engagement it would very probably have emerged as the eventual winner. However, the *Richard* had the advantage of being on the windward side and at one point it completely took the wind from the *Serapis*'s sails, cut across its bows and collided. The *Serapis*'s bowsprit became enmeshed in the *Richard*'s mizzen-mast rigging and could not disentangle itself. From that point on the two ships were locked together stern to bow and while the *Serapis*'s guns continued to pound the *Richard* below the water line, the *Richard*'s superiority in manpower and small-arms marksmanship now became crucial. When the two ships closed they were about three miles east-by-south from Flamborough Head. Captain Pearson lowered his anchor in the hope that the wind and tide would carry the *Richard* away from him, but the wind and tide just drove the two hulls tighter together.

It was an extremely bloody battle that now ensued with considerable loss of life on both sides. Jones's marksmen dominated the deck-fighting making it virtually impossible for anyone on the *Serapis* to poke their head above the hatchways without having it shot at. But the *Serapis*'s cannon continued to blast holes in the hull of the old East Indiaman so that the holds were gradually filling with water. A number of fires broke out on both ships. At one point panic seems to have overtaken some of the *Richard*'s crew, fearing that their ship was about to sink. A gunner by the name of Henry Gardner attempted to lower the ensign in surrender; seeing which, Paul Jones supposedly tried to shoot him, and, when his pistol failed to fire, he knocked him unconscious by hurling

it at the back of his head. This incident no doubt led to the later picture in the chap-books that showed Paul Jones shooting dead a Lieutenant Grub for mutinying. It was also possibly this incident that led to Captain Pearson calling out to ask whether the *Richard* had struck. This gave Paul Jones the opportunity for making his famous response, which has subsequently guaranteed him his immortality, 'Struck Sir? I have not yet begun to fight.'

It got dark about eight o'clock. It was a brilliant moonlit night and large crowds of onlookers, attracted by the noise of gunfire, watched the battle from the cliff tops. Eventually it was Captain Pearson who surrendered, just before his main mast collapsed and after one of Jones's men, an intrepid fellow called Hamilton, and like his captain another Scotsman, had crawled along the yard arm of the main mast and lobbed a grenade through an open hatch, killing a large number of the *Serapis*'s crew. The *Countess of Scarborough* had already surrendered about half-an-hour beforehand to the *Pallas*, a significantly better-armed vessel. It seems probable that Pearson could see no sense in further prolonging the slaughter of his men. He could not have known how close the *Richard* was to sinking and, indeed, that tough old Indiaman did not finally go down for another thirty-six hours. The court martial that was later held into the loss of the two British warships exonerated Captain Pearson's behaviour in all respects. His only error, if error there was, was to allow the *Serapis* to be grappled by the *Richard*.

The real controversy concerning the battle of Flamborough Head has centred on the character and behaviour of Captain Landais on the *Alliance*. Jones, in his 'Charges', claimed that Landais had on two occasions during the course of the battle drawn close to the action, and on both occasions had raked the *Richard* with gunfire rather than the enemy. It was Jones's contention that Landais had been hoping to sink the *Richard*, so that he could then take the *Serapis* himself, and claim both the prize money and the glory. This version of events seems somewhat extreme even by the standards of Landais's admittedly eccentric character. Under the circumstances of the *Serapis* and the *Richard* being locked together it would have been difficult for the *Alliance* to engage the *Serapis* without running the risk of also damaging the *Richard*. Landais was aware of this and it was one of the reasons why he did not immediately enter the fray. When he did open fire he maintained that he used grapeshot against those on the *Serapis* deck to minimise collateral damage. Paul Jones argued that Landais fired his heavy cannon into the *Richard*'s exposed port side. It would be interesting to examine the *Richard*'s hull, always presuming that it has survived reasonably intact on the seabed, to see whether the damage to its port side was consistent with fire from the *Serapis* or the *Alliance* and how many French cannon balls are lodged in the *Richard*'s timberwork. Captain Pearson, for his part, certainly regarded himself as having been attacked by two ships, not just one, and stated that it was the *Alliance*'s return to the battle that was critical in his decision to surrender. It seems not at all out of the question that Jones may have elaborated Landais's supposed treachery in order to maximise his own triumph.

Jones's version of events does not really make any sense. It is almost inconceivable that Landais could have thought he would get away with deliberately sinking the *Richard*. Landais was clearly a difficult and haughty man, and the two captains clearly loathed each other on a personal level, but there is nothing about Landais's behaviour, or his later writings, to suggest that he was completely insane, which he would have to have been to open fire on his own side in such a situation.

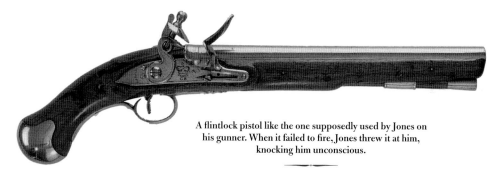

A flintlock pistol like the one supposedly used by Jones on his gunner. When it failed to fire, Jones threw it at him, knocking him unconscious.

It is quite possible that some of the grapeshot from the *Alliance* went astray and injured some of those on board the *Richard*. Landais admitted as much in his memoirs. Some damage from friendly fire was almost inevitable in such a tight and confused situation. But this is a far cry from the accusations of treachery and cowardice that Jones formally levelled against his fellow captain. Nor does it explain why, if Jones really thought that Landais had treacherous intentions during the battle, he sent to Landais for the loan of a carpenter after it was over, to which request Landais promptly responded, sending across James Bragg. Similarly, he asked Landais to take on board the

Alliance a large number of the *Serapis*'s prisoners and supply the prize crew and officers for the *Serapis*, to which requests again Landais acceded. One would have thought that if Jones really believed Landais to be a traitor he would have had him promptly arrested and put in irons. Instead he entrusts him with a series of vital responsibilities and Landais obliges by undertaking them.

Jones's behaviour during the battle was undoubtedly brave but his later tirade against Landais suggests a rather unattractive obsession with presenting his own role in the most heroic and glorious light possible, even if it meant unnecessarily denigrating his colleagues. It clearly suited him to have combated two enemies, both Landais and Captain Pearson, rather than just one. Jones certainly was not lacking in self-publicising skills and his later manipulation of the press, writing endless self-promoting letters and accounts of what had happened, suggests that he was one of the first to understand the full importance and power of the media as a means of self-aggrandisement. He quickly became a subject of popular ballad and a folk hero, even among large sections of the British nation. But the verdict of history is a pretty fickle business. Perhaps if more attention had been paid by posterity to Jones's neglect of his own injured men aboard the *Serapis*, while he went off to enjoy the entertainments of Amsterdam and pursue his own fame, his reputation may have not been so glorious. This neglect is testified both by Captain Cottineau of the *Pallas* and Charles Dumas, the representative of the Continental Congress in The Hague. Their letters on the subject do not reveal Jones in the best of lights.

This portrait by Charles Grignon of Captain Richard Pearson reveals him to be a man of less than commanding demeanour, yet his country regarded his convoy defence as heroic and he was awarded a knighthood and given command of the Royal Navy's finest frigate.

Captain Pearson surrendered about 10 p.m. on 24 September. The carpenters were immediately set to work trying to stop the leaks on the *Richard* and the pumps were kept going throughout the night. The situation, however, became steadily worse. By 2 p.m. the following day Paul Jones abandoned his command in favour of the *Serapis*, but left orders for those at the pumps and the carpenters to carry on with their work. At 7 p.m. he returned to the *Richard* and found the situation there continuing to deteriorate. He gave orders for the sick and wounded to be taken off together with all those valuable items that were easily transportable. It was at this point that one would imagine that any money that had been on board was removed. At 10 p.m. the officers and men that belonged to vessels other than the *Richard* were ordered to abandon the ship. By 4 a.m. the following morning the water had risen to the level of the lower deck and there was clearly to be no chance of saving her. The remainder of the *Richard's* own crew now also took to the boats and by 10 a.m. every man had left. One hour later the *Richard* went down. There remains just one small mystery in connection with the sinking. Shortly before the *Richard* disappeared, and after all the men had left it, Paul Jones sent another boat from the *Serapis* to the *Richard* for the purpose of re-boarding. Whether he had just remembered some valuable that had not been retrieved, or whether it was sent to make doubly sure all the men were safe is not evident. Whatever the explanation, the boarding party did not have time to re-enter the *Richard* for she went down too quickly.

In the summer of 1976, the well-known wreck-hunter Sidney Wignall organised a major search for the wreck of the *Bonhomme Richard*. The designated search area was about three miles off the coast of Flamborough Head covering about twenty-five square miles of seabed in total. The survey company, Decca, lent its latest equipment and most skilled personnel for the project. An impressive array of Trisponders, Aquafixes, Hi-fixes, Satnavs, Data loggers, Track plotters, Echo sounders, Digitizers, and other high-tech gadgets of the period – that already seem somewhat antique – were deployed. A ten-day search turned up one main target, a sunken hull measuring approximately 120 x 30 feet lying in 180 feet of water. Excitement was increased by the fact that the wreck mound was discovered in an area from which a local fisherman had retrieved

A rather generalised portrait of John Paul Jones printed in the Netherlands, where he was regarded as a hero.

a muzzle-loading gun with the date 1775 inscribed on its brass trigger. The dimensions of the mound on the other hand were a little on the small size for it to be the *Richard*, although the size of mounds are often deceptive. Usually the build-up of sand results in them being larger than the original dimensions of the hull, but if the hull has broken into two or more pieces then, of course, the size may be significantly smaller. First-hand witness accounts of the sinking, however, do not suggest that the *Richard* broke up before it went down. The aim of the project was to salvage the *Richard* for the bicentenary celebrations of the famous battle. The fact that 1979 passed by without any further news emerging concerning the discovery of the *Bonhomme Richard* suggests that the mound was very probably the wrong one. Perhaps 2029 should be set as a new target date.

12

The *Guernsey Lily*

I N THE AUTUMN OF 1799 the Anglo-Russian army under the command of the Duke of York was defeated at the battle of Bergen-op-Zoom by the French Revolutionary army led by General Brune. The defeat led to the hasty evacuation of British troops, cavalry and equipment from the port of Helder in the north of Holland. It was the end of an ill-conceived and poorly executed campaign to free Holland from the dominance of France. Napoleon was by this stage of the French Revolutionary wars in control of a large part of Continental Europe and it was only at sea that Britain still held any real sway.

The evacuation got under way in the first week of November. The weather was stormy and in the circumstances the British were lucky to lose only one ship. This was the *Guernsey Lily*, a hired transport, and therefore not Admiralty-owned. The *Lily* struck on the Cross Sand off the Norfolk coast, came off, but was leaking badly and quickly sank in Yarmouth Roads, 'as nearly as possible three miles due east of the jetty'. Fortunately all the crew and troops were saved. The latter included soldiers of the Royal Artillery under General Farrington, a professional army officer who was to serve in the army for the impressive total of sixty-eight years.

The *Lily* was a small three-masted ship, 218 tons burthen, armed with eight cannon but also carrying a number of brass field pieces back from Holland. The master was called William Wilson, the owner was a Geoffrey Blackman of London and its home port was Woolwich. On learning of the loss of his ship Mr Blackman wrote to the Admiralty suggesting they might like to raise it, by which means the Admiralty would be able to recover the valuable ordnance on board as well as remove a dangerous obstacle from a major shipping lane much frequented by men-of-war. He was no doubt also hoping to recover his own vessel or at the very least some of its equipment and fittings, although he understandably refrained from spelling out this motive. Lord Duncan at the Admiralty neatly parried this overture offering 'every assistance' should Mr Blackman see fit to weigh the *Guernsey Lily* at his own expense. Meanwhile, he made enquiries as to what the official view of the matter would be regarding any proposed salvage. The Board of Ordnance replied making it very clear to Lord Duncan 'that the vessel not being the property of the crown the expense

A Dutch print showing the humiliating withdrawal from Holland by the 'Grand Old Duke of York's' Anglo-Russian invasion force. One of the ships in the offing would be the *Guernsey Lily*.

of raising her can not be defrayed by the public'. On the subject of how to recover their own property that was on board when the *Guernsey Lily* sank they remained strangely silent. There appears to have been at this point something of a bureaucratic stand-off between all the various departments involved and the interests of private persons. Lord Duncan contented himself with attaching a buoy to the wreck 'to prevent serious consequences', namely the possibility of a large man-of-war running on to a protruding mast or some other part of the abandoned wreck. Accidents of this nature were a common problem in busy shipping lanes. The wreck having been marked to all intents and purposes the *Guernsey Lily* and its contents seemed to have been quietly forgotten.

The wreck is not heard of again for the next thirty-three years. Then, seemingly out of the blue, the edition of the *Norwich Mercury* for 11 August 1832 carries a detailed and informative article concerning a small cutter captained by a man called Bell, which was anchored in Yarmouth Roads. The six-man crew of this small vessel included several persons 'singularly expert in the art of diving'. It appeared that the business of this cutter was to 'sail about from place to place, to offer her assistance to the recovery of lost treasure, etc.' It had arrived in Yarmouth with the specific purpose of 'endeavouring to obtain a portion of the treasure lost in the *Guernsey Lily* transport, which (some of our readers may recollect) got on the Cross Sand, floated off, and afterwards foundered in the centre of Yarmouth Roads, in 43 feet of water.' The article is careful to point out that the operation is being carried out with the permission of the Admiralty. These are not any old looters and wreckers but officially approved salvors. The newspaper article also goes on to provide considerable detail of what the *Guernsey Lily* had been carrying when it sank: 'the transport was laden with horses, ammunition, (in which were included 25 brass field pieces) a stock of wine, &c.' The precision of the information, much of which was later to be confirmed by actual recoveries, suggests that the correspondent's sources were reliable and well placed.

It was not just the thought of the treasure, however, that was considered exciting. Of equal importance to the readership of the *Norwich Mercury* was the technical innovation involved. The unnamed correspondent provides a detailed description of the salvage process employed.

The method which these divers use in descending is curious: – The cutter is first placed
immediately over the wreck; the diver then, habited in an India-rubber air tight dress, having
a tube attached at the back of the neck to receive the air, (which is constantly kept pumping
in) descends from a rope ladder, and gives signals for certain things to be sent down by a
small line, which is attended to by those on the deck of the cutter; by this line baskets and
other utensils are sent down for the use of the diver, and sent up again with wine, & taken
from the wreck. The diver's head-dress is curious; it is composed of copper, and is a complete

A British hired transport of the Napoleonic period taking on ordnance stores. Transports were given official numbers
which were painted on the quarters for identification.

covering, made much after the manner of the ancient helmet, only that it is made larger than the head, and has in its upper part three glass windows; it weighs 50 lbs. He has two other dresses on besides that above mentioned. He carries down with him about 120 lbs of lead in two bags. With all this weight, he declares, that when in the water he appears perfectly free from weight or encumbrance of any sort.

The diving suit that is being described here is the one which was invented by the brothers Charles and John Deane. Although not named in this article John Deane was the senior diver working on the *Guernsey Lily* project. His elder brother Charles meanwhile was in the same year working on the wrecks of the *Boyne* and the *Royal George*, both Royal Navy warships. The India-rubber suit mentioned was produced from the new material that had been created by Charles Macintosh (of raincoat fame) and was being used not so much for its air-tight qualities as to keep the diver comfortable and dry. There was no attempt with this diving system to make a watertight seal between the diver and the helmet as had been tried with previous pieces of diving apparatus such as the Lethbridge barrel, often with disastrous results. The key to the Deane's success was that the air was not being breathed at atmospheric pressure but was kept in equilibrium with the outside pressure of the water by means of a system of valves and tubes to and from the helmet, and an air-pump on the surface. It was the pressure of the air in the helmet that kept the water out of it, not the strength of the seals around the neck. Any failure to keep this equilibrium would cause bleeding from the eyes and nose and in extreme cases the body would be crushed up into the helmet. The fate of an unfortunate English diver called Tope in 1859, who had only been submerged in the water for one minute, graphically depicts the dangers of getting it wrong. 'The corpse presented such a dreadful spectacle; blood was oozing from the eye, nose and mouth. . . we found the head very badly swollen, the face and neck so filled with blood as to resemble liver, while the remainder of the body was as white as unclouded marble.'

The helmets were engineered by Augustus Siebe. The Siebe family were to be central to the production of diving helmets and suits for the next hundred years. The best description of how the Deane's diving apparatus worked is probably that given in the *Proceedings of the Institution of Civil Engineers* for 2 March 1833, where the relative merits of the diving bell and Deane's diving helmet were compared:

Mr Walker observed that the objections to the use of the diving bell, were its great weight; and also when down, the circumstance of not being able to observe anything laterally, from being confined in the bell; which objections are obviated by Deane's apparatus. Mr Walker had descended with it several times in 12 feet water, to examine the piers of Blackfriars Bridge, and found it very useful.

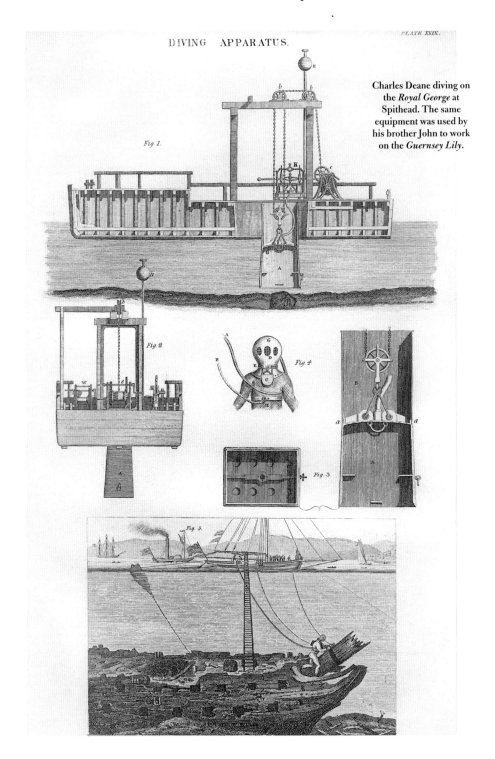

DIVING APPARATUS.

PLATE XXIX.

Fig. 1.

Fig. 2.

Fig. 4.

Fig. 3.

Fig. 5.

Charles Deane diving on the *Royal George* at Spithead. The same equipment was used by his brother John to work on the *Guernsey Lily*.

The apparatus consists of an india rubber dress (of the kind manufactured by Mr Mackintosh of Glasgow) worn over a dress of flannel for the purpose of keeping the diver dry and warm; and of a helmet strapped on over the head supplied with air through a flexible tube, in the manner of the common diving bell. The air enters the helmet at the back of the neck, and is conveyed by a small tube to the eye glasses, over which a constant current passes, to prevent the diver's breath from condensing upon them; the superfluous air escapes by a waste (air) pipe, and also under the lower edge of the helmet, at which level, it keeps the surface of water, and thus prevents any from entering the india rubber dress, the collar of which reaches above it. To the helmet are attached lead weights to the amount of 80lbs; the diver descends by means of a rope ladder, and has a rope fastened to his waist for the purpose of making signals. Mr Deane said the greatest depth to which he has descended was 11.5 fathoms, from which depth he brought up one of the hoops of the bowsprit of the *Royal George*; which was produced. The apparatus cannot be used when the tide is running strong; if it goes at the rate of only 1 mile an hour, it makes the diver very unsteady, though loaded with a weight of 80 lbs: a man ought to bear at least 20 lbs on the bottom to enable him to walk with freedom.

The Deane referred to here was Charles rather than his younger brother John.

The divers on the *Guernsey Lily* went down alternately twice a day taking advantage of the slack tides. Very shortly their efforts were met with some success. The *Norwich Mercury* declared that 'there has already been brought up a large quantity of wine (the bottles curiously tattooed with large and small oysters, which have been tasted and are excellent), some copper, iron handles of chests, pieces of gun carriages, etc.' The punctuation here is a little ambiguous but it is more probable that it was the wine that had been tasted and found to be excellent rather than the oysters. Oysters were cheap everyday fare whereas the wine would have been regarded as something of a luxury. Presumably the cool even temperatures at the bottom of the North Sea provided ideal conditions for the preservation of a good vintage. The gun carriages would have been part of the army's ordnance being shipped back and their presence would have been anticipated. The presence of copper is somewhat more surprising. It is most unlikely that the *Lily* was simultaneously shipping a copper cargo while involved in the evacuation of retreating troops and their baggage train. It more probably indicates that the *Lily* was copper-sheathed. The recovery of the iron handles of chests must have raised hopes that the dollars were not too far away. Certainly their discovery was still very much at the forefront of everyone's expectations. 'They hope soon to be in possession of the brass guns, valuable plate, and the dollars which it was known the transport had on board for the purpose of paying the troops.'

The activities of the salvors caused a considerable stir among the local populace of Yarmouth town and the surrounding areas. 'Great numbers of persons from different parts of the country have been off to view this novel and singular undertaking. Boatmen are in constant attendance to take off, at mod-

The Yarmouth sea front, as seen in a nineteenth-century etching.
The diving operations generated much interest among the local citizens.

erate charge, those persons who wish to witness this effort of human ingenuity and enterprise... The first descent was on Saturday, and has been repeated every day since, which has proved a great treat to numbers of all ranks who have attended to observe this surprising, perhaps unequalled exhibition.'

It was not long before the salvors were rewarded with more tangible evidence of success. The *Norfolk Chronicle* of 18 August recorded admiringly, 'On Tuesday one of the brass guns was brought up in a perfect state of preservation, and was fired off as a triumphant token of success.' Brass guns were worth serious money. In their exploitation of their own rapidly increasing notoriety Deane and Bell revealed themselves to be astute businessmen. Aware that their activities had entertainment value, over and above the strictly commercial return on the objects recovered, they began to charge the many tourists who had flocked to Yarmouth and chartered boats to see for themselves what was going on. 'The operations of the divers have created so much interest that the persons engaged in the undertaking have thought it necessary to lay a heavy charge upon those who choose to witness the descent which takes place, weather permitting, at high and low water.' Clearly they did not see why it should be only the local boatmen who profited from the spectacle that they were putting on. They were also sharp enough to exploit the ready market that existed among collectors for all the miscellaneous shipwreck artefacts and cargo oddities that they brought up. 'A very good market is also made of the different materials, which are brought ashore and sold to the curious as reliques.' According to the *Norwich Mercury* Deane and Bell were free to dispose of these 'reliques' as they wished. 'The Admiralty, we understand, has handsomely given permission to Capt. Bell to make what use he pleases of the articles found, only conditioning that the brass guns (if recovered) shall be given up, for which they will return their value.' Such an arrangement, if true, was clearly advantageous to the salvors, but seems of dubious legality. The Admiralty, of course, would have been entitled to give away items originally in their ownership such as cannon balls and shot for which they would no longer have had any possible use, but ship fittings such as copper sheathing would have been another matter. This would have presumably belonged to Mr Blackman or his heirs. There does not, however, appear to have been any consequential legal dispute.

The dispersal of such 'reliques' would of course be anathema to the modern-day archaeologist. It has to be said in defence of Messrs Deane and Bell, however, if their activities need defending at all, that John Deane produced a series of the most detailed and beautiful watercolour drawings of many of the more interesting items recovered. What he did not do, of course, was plot the exact position on the seabed from where each artefact was recovered. But it is questionable to what extent our scientific knowledge would have been increased even if he had. It is also interesting to observe the veneration accorded to shipwreck artefacts by ordinary members of the public, even in the early nineteenth century. It has to be remembered that this was in an era when shipwrecks around the coast of Britain were a daily occurrence and the *Guernsey Lily* was not of significant antiquity or associated with any large or dramatic loss of life. And yet the reverence accorded to these miscellaneous and intrinsically worthless items that were being salvaged was clearly very considerable. There is obviously a deep-rooted human fascination with the recovery of the past from the bottom of the sea that seems to go beyond rational explanation.

Some of the claims reported by the press are of questionable authenticity. 'We should have said that the diver, when under water, finds his strength so increased that he can bend two ends together of the large iron crow (of 3.5 feet long and 1.5 inch in size) which he takes down with him to part the wreck.' This reads very much like the diver having a private joke at the expense of the gullible journalist. Conditions at the bottom of the sea were understandably a mystery to the general public and so the diver could claim almost anything and it would be hard to disprove what he said. The same problem still exists today. The breathing of air under pressure seems to produce a tendency towards exaggeration. The quantity and nature of the recoveries made, however, were clearly verifiable. Within another week several more cannon had been lifted. The *Norwich Mercury* of 25 August admiringly records, 'Mr John Deane, the intrepid diver. . . has in spite of the blowing weather during the greater part of the week, succeeded in obtaining, besides a considerable quantity of shells, round grape, and canister shots, five brass guns, the latter as perfect and as fit for immediate use as on the day they were lost.'

John Deane clearly had a natural flair for good public relations. Early in September 1832 he is again attracting favourable press. 'We understand that Mr J. Deane has intimated his intention to commemorate their Majesty's Coronation on the 8th inst, by firing a royal salute at one o'clock, on board the cutter employed on his diving service, from the guns he has recently brought up.' What better way to draw attention to the brilliance of the salvage operation than by a very public display of loyalty using the reclaimed cannon? One gets the very strong impression that Deane and Bell were thoroughly enjoying all the hype that surrounded their glamorous operations. At the same time they were keen to point out that their salvage work also had another more utilitarian and practical aspect, but one that was none the less vital to the economic welfare of the nation. 'The importance of this service, besides the object of the present undertaking, is of the first consequence to the general shipping interest, from the wreck laying in the best anchorage of that admirable roadstead, and since the buoy being removed, which originally marked the situation of the wreck, numerous anchors and cables have been lost by getting foul of it; it has been ascertained by the diver that every part injurious to the navigation may be entirely removed.' John Deane was clearly touting for further wreck clearance business when he had finished salvaging the valuables that had been lost with the *Guernsey Lily*. Meanwhile, hope of recovering the dollars and silver plate had not been lost. The *Kentish Chronicle* of 2 October mentioned that 'letters have been received from those enterprising young men, Messrs W and G Bell of Whitstable dated Yarmouth in which they speak in confident terms of the success of the enterprise in which they are embarked in conjunction with Mr Deane. . . and expect in a short time to possess themselves of treasure to a considerable amount.'

Unfortunately, as with so many treasure stories, the trail at this point goes cold. There is no evidence that any dollars were ever recovered. By October the season for carrying on salvage operations would have been near to an end. The following year John Deane and the Bells are involved in other projects such as the *Hope* lost in the Scillies returning from Africa with elephants tusks and also the highly valuable *Enterprise,* a slaver lost on the coast of Ireland with a large number of dollars on board. There is no suggestion that they ever went back to the *Guernsey Lily*.

There remain the usual three alternative explanations for the absence of any further reference to the treasure. There is the possibility that the dollars and plate were never on board in the first place. It is perfectly logical that a retreating army would have had considerable sums of cash with it for the purchasing of supplies and the payment of troops while abroad. However, it is noticeable that none of the letters that survive among Admiralty records appear to make any mention of dollars. It seems almost inconceivable that if there had been significant quantities of money on board there would not have been some attempt at salvage at the time of loss. The wreck was even in 1799 well within recoverable depths. The logic of this is not conclusive, however, because it is always

Troops embarking for an overseas expedition around 1800. The personal gear of the officers in the foreground gives some idea of the kinds of finds that the *Guernsey Lily* site might have turned up.

possible that other correspondence concerning attempted salvage in 1799 may have become lost during the last 200 years. Another possibility is that the dollars were present but were salvaged between the sinking and the arrival of John Deane. The third and, of course, the most intriguing possibility is that the treasure remains somewhere beneath the sand. It is evident from John Deane's own correspondence that a total of seven guns only was recovered from the wreck. This leaves eighteen guns unaccounted for. The obvious explanation for these guns not being recovered is that they were buried too deep in the sand. The Deanes' diving apparatus was relatively sophisticated for its time but they would not have had any equipment for shifting large quantities of sand. If the majority of the cannon were out of reach there has to be a very good chance that the dollars also lay buried and inaccessible.

One of the keenest observers of the operations that took place off Yarmouth during the summer of 1832 was the barrack master, Captain George Manby. He had already invented the famous piece of shipwreck life-saving apparatus that bears his name. It involved firing a rope from land to a stricken ship which after being secured could then be used as a safety line for the disembarkation of those on board. His inventive mind and close observation of John Deane's diving system led him to devise a sectional rigid ladder for descending to the seabed instead of the rope ladder used by Deane. The Deane brothers used it for a while but it was more cumbersome than its rope predecessor and never really caught on.

By the end of the 1832 diving season a total of seven cannon had been recovered and handed over to the Board of Ordnance for a payment of £40 14s 6d, which was essentially the scrap value of the bronze. It then occurred to John Deane, who had a good eye it seemed for any quick profit opportunity, that the project had stimulated so much public interest that the salvors would have done better selling the cannon on the open market to a collector of antique weaponry. He negotiated to buy the guns back off the Board of Ordnance for the same price that he had just sold them and then approached the wealthy John Powell Powell of Quex Park, Birchington, in Kent, to find out whether or not he might be interested in purchasing them. His subsequent letter was both deferential and subtle, 'the guns are six pounders and are perfectly sound and serviceable, tho in the same dirty state as when we recovered, and from the whole of the circumstances connected with them, they are esteemed highly curious, as they cannot be matched in any part of the world, and as we intend now to dispose of them, and as they are exactly adapted for the use of a yacht. . . we beg leave to introduce them to you, and the other Noblemen and Gentlemen connected with the Yacht Club, and understanding that you have a fine powerful yacht, to ask if you would like to have them for her.' In a postscript he added that he had visited Quex Park the day before and considered that the cannon would look equally fine if placed in front of the hall, and suggested that Mr Powell might also like to purchase some of the shot they had recovered. It was a clever pitch, emphasising as it did both the appropriateness and the uniqueness of the offer. Mr Powell clearly fell for it. One of the cannon is still on display in the Powell-Cotton Museum at Quex Park today. It appears to have survived perfectly adequately without the benefits of modern conservation techniques. The inscription states: 'This GUN & Six others were recovered A.D. 1832 by Messrs Deane and Bell in 10 Fathoms Water from the *Guernsey Lily* Transport wreck in Yarmouth ROADS on her return from the HELDER A.D. 1799 after the expedition commanded by H.R.H. The Duke of York and were given by the Board of Ordnance to the Salvors as a reward for their skill.'

The Deane brothers were to go on to more famous and yet more lucrative diving projects, including the *Mary Rose* and the *Royal George*. It was their invention of the copper diving helmet, however, crucial in the development of diving technology, that was to be their most important legacy.

13

The Lure of the *Lutine*

T
HE *Lutine* IS PERHAPS the most famous of all lost treasure ships. In part this is because of the very large quantity of gold that was undoubtedly on board when it sank. In part it is an acknowledgement of the subsequent 200 years of almost ceaseless effort to recover that gold. All this expenditure of energy, money and imagination has been largely fruitless except for two or three years at the beginning of the nineteenth century and two further lucrative seasons during the 1850s. The French word *lutine* means an elf or sprite, and certainly so far as its many salvors are concerned it has lived up to expectation as something mischievous. However, so long as the evidence for the bulk of the treasure still remaining beneath the sand continues to be convincing to at least some of those that study it, no doubt the legend will continue to tease.

The name *Lutine* has also acquired fame through its close association with the venerable marine underwriting institution, Lloyds of London. Lloyds are reputed to have paid out without quibble on the loss. 'The immense sum. . . was discharged by the underwriters with honour and promptitude', according to Mr Angerstein, Chairman of Lloyds, giving evidence to the House of Commons Select Committee enquiry into Marine Insurance in 1810. It was Lloyds' immediate payment that helped establish it as a byword for financial soundness and probity. The underwriters astutely capitalised on this publicity coup by hanging the *Lutine* bell in pride of place in

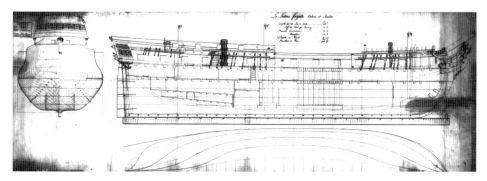

The official plans of the frigate *Lutine* as drawn up by the British after the capture of the ship.

their offices, when it was presented to them by salvors in 1858. Since then the *Lutine* bell has become almost synonymous with marine disaster. It is tolled once to indicate a loss, twice on occasions for celebration, such as the ending of World War II. Even the insurance payout, however, is not perhaps as clear-cut as Lloyds themselves would have everyone believe.

The *Lutine* was built in French naval dockyards in 1779 and had been in service for fourteen years before being captured by the British fleet under Admiral Hood at Toulon. Toulon at the time had gone over to the Royalist cause and the French authorities there handed the *Lutine* over without a shot fired, together with a large number of other warships. It was a major coup for the British navy. In 1795 the Admiralty had the *Lutine* refitted as a fifth-rate frigate. It was 143 feet 3 inches in length on the gun deck, 38 feet 10 inches broad, with a draft of 12 feet 1½ inches, and a gross burthen of 900 tons. Plans of the *Lutine*, made when it entered service for the Royal Navy, survive in the National Maritime Museum, and reveal it to have been an elegant ship with raised foredeck and quarterdeck. It was equipped with thirty-two guns instead of the previous twenty-six, although, according to Steel's Navy List for 1799, the actual number carried when it sank was thirty-eight, made up of twenty-six twelve-pounders on the main deck, four twenty-four-pounder carronades together with four six-pounders on the quarter deck, and two twenty-four-pounder carronades and two six-pounders on the foredeck. Shortly after it was captured it was refitted and copper-sheathed. The sheathing was carried out in rectangles approximately 4 feet by 14 inches and the weight of each square foot was recorded in ounces on each separate piece of metal, together with the initials of the contractor involved, the date of the work and the arrow mark of the British government. Two pieces of the sheathing that were recovered weighed respectively 28 ounces and 32 ounces, which were two of the standard weights in use at the time. The cost of sheathing a ship the size of the *Lutine* would have been in excess of £1,000.

To understand the nature and full significance of the *Lutine*'s last voyage it is necessary to know something of the political and commercial background that led up to it. Since the occupation of Holland by French revolutionary forces Amsterdam had abruptly ceased to be the main financial centre of the Continent. Its place had been largely taken by the rapidly expanding financial market at Hamburg. In the autumn of 1799, however, a number of the big trading houses in Hamburg were facing a severe liquidity squeeze. Between 25 September and 4 October many of the most famous names in banking and trade had gone to the wall including John Kirchenpaner, Aaron Simon, Saffe & Grape, Kleinwort, Guyener & Co., Goverts & Co., Abraham Lazarus, Joachim Schroder, Fredrick Ochme, Ofenbrug & Negenborn, Gadechens, Schoyer, Riez and Johann Rodde. The last-named merchant alone had failed owing 2.2 million marks banco (the Hamburg unit of currency at the time). *Lloyds Evening Post* of 16 October 1799 soberly recorded that 'the failure of the house of Johann Rodde, will be more severely felt in London than any that has preceded it.'

British merchants suddenly found themselves faced with an urgent need to ship gold and silver to Germany to shore up the failing credit of a number of major concerns there. On 1 October the Bank of England had already 'come to the resolution of lending assistance to the merchants to the amount of one million and a half (sterling)'. The papers of 18 October recorded a deteriorating situation. 'The intelligence from Hamburgh is still of a very unpleasant nature to the commercial world.' In the same edition it was mentioned that 'some London merchants have, it is said, resolved immediately to send over, for the relief of Hamburgh, one million and a half sterling in coin and bullion.' One million and a half sterling was the equivalent of twenty million marks banco. It also has to be borne in mind that by the time a news item reached an eighteenth-century newspaper, even if it was of a domestic nature as in this case, it was still very often more than a week old. It is highly probable that at least a portion of that one-and-a-half million sterling referred to here, was on board the *Lutine* when it left Yarmouth on the morning of 9 October bound for Cuxhaven, the main port for Hamburg.

The *Lutine* had been busily employed on the Cuxhaven run even before it left on its final voyage. On 2 October it escorted the *Prince of Orange* packet boat, Captain Thomas Bridge, to Cuxhaven. It is recorded that the packet boat sailed 'without mails in order to keep up a free communication with the continent'. The phrase is a strange one and open to numerous interpretations. There were passengers on board including a Mr Hartlett, the King's messenger. It is not evident whether either the *Lutine* or the packet boat were on that occasion carrying bullion. It is approximately 300 miles from Cuxhaven to Yarmouth making a 600-mile round trip. The *Lutine*'s turnaround

Hamburg, the destination for *Lutine*'s bullion.

time for this voyage is impressive for within six days it is again in Yarmouth ready to return a second time to Cuxhaven. In the early hours of 9 October the *Lutine* again left Yarmouth for Cuxhaven. On the evening of the 8th it was said that there was a brilliant ball in the great cabin of the *Lutine*, attended by some of the more stylish French émigrés such as the Duc de Montmorency and the Comte de Luxembourg, also known as the Duc de Chatillon, as well as wealthy merchants such as members of the Goldsmid family, though given the limited accommodation aboard a fifth-rate frigate it is difficult to believe that it can have been such a grand occasion. The frigate was commanded by Captain Launcelot Skynner. He had been made a post captain in 1795 and had served two terms in the West Indies in command of *La Pique* and the *Beaulieu*. He clearly had an affinity with French-named ships. His first officer was Lieutenant Charles Aufrere, son of Anthony Aufrere who lived at Hoveden Hall in Norfolk. The second officer was Lieutenant Kinmeer, and the surgeon was a Walter Montgomery of Edinburgh. The crew numbered around 240 men. Their names are all recorded in the *Lutine* pay books still preserved in the National Archives at Kew, London. Against each member of the crew serving on 9 October 1799 are the details of those who received the outstanding pay due to them: widows, brothers, mothers and even, in some cases, grandfathers, are all represented.

Some of the wealthy passengers and merchants who attended this farewell also stayed on board for the voyage, including the Duc de Chatillon and Daniel Weinholt, son of the indigo merchant John Weinholt. Weinholt was later reported to have been sending out £40,000, all of it uninsured. Another young relative of a wealthy merchant accompanying a shipment of funds was the nephew of Mr Goldsmid.

Lord Duncan, in charge of the fleet at Yarmouth, gave the *Lutine* the order to make the voyage. He wrote to the Admiralty on 9 October explaining that he had been asked by the merchant community to make a vessel available to transport funds to the Continent to bolster their failing credit, 'there being no packet for that purpose. . . ordered the *Lutine* to Cuxhaven with the same, together with the mails lying here for want of a conveyance.' In a previous letter dated 4 October he had also expressed his intention of using the *Lutine* to oblige the Hudson Bay Company who had requested 'a convoy for their homeward bound trade from the Orkneys to the River [Thames]'. It is unclear whether the Cuxhaven voyage was to supersede the trip to the Orkneys or whether the one was to follow on from the other. The escorting of merchant ships by Navy ships in times of war was of course standard practice but to have ordered an Admiralty ship to make a voyage by itself purely for the convenience of the merchant community, as with the Cuxhaven voyage, appears somewhat irregular and begs the question as to whether the *Lutine* had any other orders to fulfil on that voyage at the same time.

Whatever the exact orders may have been none of them was accomplished because towards midnight, with a gale blowing from the north-west, the *Lutine* struck on a sandbank to the north of Vlie

Bosun's Mate of period. Only two of the *Lutine*'s crew were picked up, and only one survived long enough to be interviewed.

Island or Fly Island as the British called it. It went to pieces almost instantly, only one man surviving. News of the disaster was sent by Captain Portlock of His Majesty's Ship *Arrow*, which was stationed off Vlie Island at the time of the disaster, via Admiral Mitchell, on board the *Isis*, to the Admiralty. The *Lloyds Evening Post* of 21 October carried the following report: 'The ship sailed from Yarmouth Road on the morning of the 9th inst. for Hamburgh, having on board 140,000 £ in specie. The wind being at NNW and a heavy gale *La Lutine* was driven towards the Vlieland on the coast of Holland, and a strong lee tide setting in during the night she went ashore not withstanding the exertions of her officers and crew and was in pieces before morning.

'All who were on board perished except two men who were picked up. A nephew of Mr Goldsmid, who was going over with the specie from the respectable house of his uncle's, for the relief of the Hamburg merchants in consequence of the late failures is, we are sorry to find, among the number of those who are lost.'

Another account remarks, 'we learn from good authority that there was six hundred thousand pounds sterling in specie on board the *Lutine*, which had been shipped by individual merchants in this country ... there were also several merchants on board.' So began the enduring legend and also the great confusion over the treasure of the *Lutine*.

At the centre of much of the subsequent debate about the *Lutine* has been the question of what quantity of gold and silver was originally on board. *The Times* of 11 October printed a report from Yarmouth dated the 9th stating that 'The Hamburg and Bremen mails of the 7th have been sent from Yarmouth to Cuxhaven in HMS *Lutine* which sailed from here this morning with bullion and passengers for Hamburg.' This was followed by a further report in the edition of 16 October, dated Yarmouth, 13 October: 'The *Lutine* sailed a day or two ago with upwards of 10 tons of money both gold and silver.' Both these reports are of particular interest because they were made before any news had been received of the *Lutine*'s loss. A ton of gold at the time was roughly equated with £100,000. Ten tons, assuming that the bulk of the cargo was in gold, which subsequent salvage operations have proved to be the case, would therefore have been equivalent to £1 million. This is a significantly higher figure than the £140,000 mentioned by the *Lloyds Evening Post* or even the £600,000 which the *Lloyds Evening Post* also posited as a possibility. The edition of the *Lloyds Evening Post* of 23 October revised the figure downwards to the lower of the two estimates. 'We are happy to learn that the loss of specie on board the *Lutine* frigate was not near so great as was reported in some of the public papers. The whole amount was 600,000 dollars, about £140,000 sterling. This is the return made from the bullion office.' This statement sounds definitive enough. The reports printed in the *Naval Chronicle* follow basically the same pattern as those in the *Lloyds Evening Post*. Initially the response is one of deep despair. 'In the annals of our naval history, there has scarcely ever happened a loss attended with so much calamity, both of a public as well as a private nature. We learn, from good authority, that there was six hundred thousand pounds sterling in specie on board the *Lutine*, which had been shipped by individual merchants in this country for the relief of different commercial houses in Hamburgh. There were also several merchants on board.' However, a later report moderates this view. Entitled '*Lutine* Loss Overestimated,' it continues, 'The loss of specie on board the *Lutine* frigate was not so great as was first imagined. The return from the Bullion Office makes the whole amount to 600,000 dollars; about £140,000 sterling.' Most of the other reports from around the time of the loss follow a similar fluctuation. The matter would appear to be fairly conclusive if it were not for a residual sneaking suspicion that it may have been politically convenient to minimise the loss. Clearly the commercial situation in Hamburg was already dire even before the *Lutine*'s fateful voyage and in order to boost shaky credit-worthiness it may well have been decided to play down this further disaster. It also has to be remembered that Britain was at war and the wreck of the *Lutine* lay in waters that were about to be abandoned for a second time to the enemy. It would hardly be patriotic to reveal the full nature of the disaster. In its edition of 25 October the *Lloyds Evening Post* almost admits this line of thinking. 'The rapidity with which the loss of specie on board the frigate for Hamburgh was announced and magnified, ought to serve as a warning to us, not to believe the idle rumours that interest and malevolence combine to invent and disseminate, in order to despair and vex those who love their country.' The forced optimism of this particular publication even led it to speculate that the *Lutine* had not sunk at all. Its correspondent writes, 'It was on Wednesday reported though we scarce know how to indulge a hope of its confirmation, that the *Lutine* frigate may have escaped. The circumstance which give birth to the idea, arises in the account given by the only individual who was supposed to have escaped from the wreck. This person was washed overboard by a tremendous wave, which carried away the spars and whatever was loose upon the deck. When he recovered himself there was no frigate anywhere to be descried, neither was visible, nor has there since been found, any part of the vessel, any bodies, or other circumstances which could lead to suppose there had been a wreck.' This desperate hope was not to last for very long.

A further complication as to values on board arises when one takes into consideration the statement made by Mr Angerstein, Chairman of Lloyds and respected Member of Parliament, to the select committee of the House of Commons on Marine Insurance held in 1810. Mr Angerstein gave in evidence, presumably as an example of the deep pockets of Lloyds underwriters, that the sum of £300,000 had been underwritten on the *Lutine* frigate by a combination of Lloyds and the two chartered companies, London Assurance and the Royal Exchange Assurance. One would have thought that Mr Angerstein would have been in a very good position to know the truth of the matter. The £300,000 mentioned only refers, of course, to insured cargo and would not include sums that went uncovered.

The situation becomes even more confused when one comes to examine a Royal Dutch decree of 14 September 1821 which vested rights to the remaining treasure of the *Lutine* in a group of salvors known as the 'decretal salvors', on condition that fifty per cent of what was brought up was handed over to the Dutch crown. In this document the value of the *Lutine* cargo is mentioned as being twenty million guilders or £1.6 million sterling. Nor is any light thrown on the matter by a booklet written by Colonel H. M. Hozier, secretary to Lloyds, and published in January 1895. This refers to notes made by John Mavor Still, Lloyds agent at Amsterdam around the middle of the nineteenth century, provided to Brandt Eschauzier, son of Pierre Eschauzier, Burgomaster of Terschelling and the original 'decretal salvor'. According to Mr Still's notes there was £900,000 on board insured at Lloyds, £160,000 insured at Hamburg and £128,333 for British troops at Texel, making a total of £1,188,333, still not including, presumably, private uninsured cargo.

It is not just the sum of money originally on board that is unclear. There is equal muddle about exactly where the *Lutine* was heading. Most of the newspaper reports suggest that the *Lutine* was heading directly for Cuxhaven and Admiral Duncan's despatch would confirm this. The *Naval Chronicle* on the other hand states that the *Lutine* had on board 'an immense quantity of treasure for the Texel'. The position of loss is consistent with both possibilities. Captain Skynner may have been heading for Texel but failed to find the entrance to the Den Helder Channel or considered it too dangerous to try and negotiate such a narrow passage in such a fierce gale and so stood off to the north a little. Equally well he may have been directing the *Lutine*'s course directly for Cuxhaven but been driven by the north-north-westerly winds on to a lee shore.

The idea that the *Lutine* was carrying the payroll for the British army on the Continent has been the cause of much subsequent controversy. The origins of this rumour, that first appears in the *Naval Chronicle*, seems to derive from the published report of the single survivor, a Mr Schabrack. Captain Portlock of HM sloop *Arrow* wrote a letter, which was sent to the Admiralty by Admiral Mitchell on board the *Isis*. Mitchell was commander of the fleet that was stationed off Holland at the time the *Lutine* sank. Captain Portlock provides the following information: 'This man [the survivor] when taken up, was almost exhausted. He is at present tolerably recovered and relates that

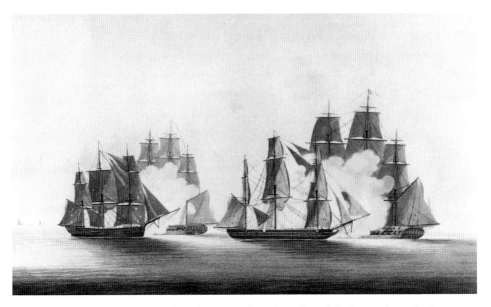

Captain Portlock's sloop *Arrow* (centre), an unusual experimental vessel that became famous in 1805 for a self-sacrificing convoy defence against heavy odds that ended with the sinking of the sloop.

the *Lutine* left Yarmouth Roads on the morning of the 9th inst. bound for the Texel, and that she had on board a considerable quantity of money.' The *Naval Chronicle* provides further information on the survivor in a report from Hamburg dated 28 October. 'Captain Clarke, of the bye boat, arrived at Hamburgh, reports that the cutter *L'Espiegle*, picked up at sea, near Borkum, two men on their oars, the only survivors of the crew of the *Lutine* frigate, one of whom expired soon after his arrival at Yarmouth. The other deposed, that being under a press of sail, at about 8 knots an hour, the vessel struck upon a rock and instantly upset.' The log book of the *Arrow* suggests that the second man was already dead before he reached Yarmouth. 'At 10 am came alongside a schoot with 2 men one dead the other to all appearance dead but by the exertions of the surgeon he recovered.' This entry is particularly important in that it makes it clear, in a way that Captain Portlock fails to do in his letter, that he must have had his information concerning the *Lutine* heading for Texel directly from the survivor himself. Clearly this gives it greater credibility than if he had received it through a series of third parties. Elsewhere in the *Naval Chronicle* the further information is provided that the 'survivor is Mr Schabrack, a notary public'. As a notary public one would have thought he would have had a proper understanding of the importance of precise statements of truth. On the other hand it has also to be remembered that he was no doubt somewhat traumatised by his recent experience.

There is a further small twist to this business of just where the *Lutine* was heading that has never previously been remarked by any of the many authors who have written on this loss. In the edition of 28 October *Lloyds Evening Post* reported that the 'mails on the *Lutine* had been found floating near the wreck'. A few days later it carried the further report that 'the underwriters of a considerable portion of the money lost in the *Lutine* have refused to pay their quota of insurance', alleging that the vessel 'departed from her declared course in sailing with government despatches for the Texel, previously to her making for the port of Hamburgh'. It is unclear whether the underwriters were basing their concerns on the reported words of Mr Schabrack or the evidence provided by the mail that had been fished out of the water from the vicinity of the wreck. At the very least this rather qualifies one's view of Mr Angerstein's proud boast that Lloyds' liabilities had been 'discharged by the underwriters with honour and promptitude'. It looks rather more like the more familiar story of an insurance company quibbling over the small print.

That the British government was actively in the business of shipping money to Holland for paying the army around the time of the *Lutine*'s departure is evident from surviving Admiralty documents. The treasure appears, however, to have gone on HMS *Amethyst* not the *Lutine*, and to have been composed exclusively of silver rather than silver and gold. Captain Cook of the *Amethyst* acknowledged receipt of silver coin on 3 October, departed from the Thames on the 6th and arrived at Texel on the 9th, the same day that the *Lutine* sank. Meanwhile, Admiral Duncan, on board the *Kent* in Yarmouth Roads, was busily organising further shipments of bullion to Hamburg on behalf of the English merchants. On 10 October Lieutenant Terrel, commander of the armed cutter *Courier*, also stationed at Yarmouth, transported one hundred barrels of specie, each barrel containing £5,000. On Sunday, 14 October, Lieutenant Wood, in command of the *Nile*, transported bullion on behalf of the house of Goldsmid & Co. from Gravesend to Cuxhaven. And on 22 October, after news of the loss of the *Lutine* had been received in England, there was a further shipment, 'equal to that unfortunately lost in the *Lutine*'. Frustratingly neither the amount nor the ship involved is given.

There are other question marks about the sinking of the *Lutine* over and above the ongoing arguments concerning the exact value of the treasure cargo on board and whether or not it was ordered to Texel before going on to Cuxhaven. They are, however, more easily answered. There has, for instance, been the persistent rumour that there was much drinking and partying going on during the *Lutine*'s final voyage and that this was a contributory cause of the sinking. The origin of these rumours appears to be a letter written by a Mr E. B. Merriman to the Committee of Lloyds and quoted by Colonel Hozier in his 1895 pamphlet. Mr Merriman writes, 'The merchants interested in the fate of the crew and passengers learned, as a result of enquiry, that the last that was seen of the *Lutine* was about midnight or later, of a clear night by the crew of a fishing boat that passed her quite close, and were attracted by the fact that on board the King's ship, instead of silence with all lights out, there was brilliant light, and evidently much joviality in the state cabin.' The clear implication of this is that there was disorder and dereliction of duty by the officers on board. A more detailed examination of the evidence, however, gives little weight to this theory. First Colonel Hozier describes Mr Merriman as being 'intimately acquainted with many of those interested in the cargo of the *Lutine*'. However, in the same breath, he also remarks that Mr Merriman's letter had only been recently received. As the *Lutine* sank almost one hundred years before Colonel Hozier's pamphlet the chronology does not exactly fit. Perhaps more importantly it has to be remembered that the *Lutine* did not leave Yarmouth until the early hours of the morning of 9 October. The fishing boat, even accepting its existence, was very probably close inshore and would have seen the *Lutine* at the very beginning of its voyage. In such circumstances it is only logical that there would still have been lights on in the great cabin. The fact that some of the young male passengers on board may have been indulging in a little revelry hardly undermines the competence of Captain Skynner and his officers. Also the last independent sighting of the *Lutine* before it sank was probably not the one made by the mythical fishing boat off Yarmouth, but by Lieutenant James Anthony Gardner in the warship *Blonde*, lying off Texel. Gardner recalled in his *Recollections* written in 1836, 'A short time before we sailed we saw the *Lutine*, 36, Captain Launcelot Skynner, at the back of the Haaks, and if I am correct, the evening she was lost.' Gardner makes no mention of revelry and partying.

Then there is the story of the Dutch crown jewels. In March 1869 London newspapers carried reports that the Prince of Orange had sent jewels to London to be reset and polished by Messrs Rundell & Bridges of Ludgate Hill. These jewels were said to be on board the *Lutine*, carefully sealed inside an iron chest, on their way back to Holland, when the ship sank. There is, however, no corroborating evidence for this story and it seems to be just part of that dark web of mystery, intrigue and exaggeration that builds up and forms a concretion around all notorious treasure ships.

Captain Nathaniel Portlock wrote to his commanding officer giving the circumstances of the wrecking. 'It is with extreme pain I have to state to you the melancholy fate of his Majesty's ship *Lutine*, which ship ran on the outer bank of the Fly Island Passage on the night of the 9th instant in a heavy gale of wind to the NNW... the wind blowing strong to the NNW and the tide coming on, rendered it impossible with schoots or other boats to get out to her aid until daylight in the morning and at that time nothing was to be seen but parts of the wreck.' The log book of the *Arrow* provides a few valuable further details. The winds are recorded as being from the west-north-west to north-west, strong gales and squally. At half-past nine in the evening the report of guns to the north-north-west was heard and at the same time 'rockets and port fires from a ship making signals of distress' were seen. After Portlock had finished his letter he realised he had omitted to mention the possibilities for salvage and so hastily added a postscript. 'I shall use every endeavour to save what I can from the wreck but from the situation she is lying in I am much afraid little will be recovered.' He was clearly feeling somewhat poorly himself and not exactly in the mood for

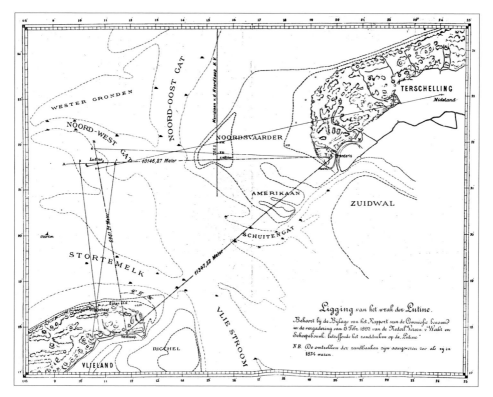

The precise position of the wreck as finally charted in the 1890s.

arduous undertakings. He closed his letter, perhaps somewhat tactlessly in the circumstances, 'I am sorry to have to state that I suffer a good deal from a rupture that I have lately received, and wish if the service will admit it to take a few weeks [leave] in the hopes of getting better.' Two days later Captain Portlock was successful in salvaging from the wreckage a barrel of flour, two casks of wine and one of rum. These would all have been floating on the surface of the water. On the following Tuesday they picked up some letters that had been on board the *Lutine*. It must have been these letters that prompted the underwriters to have second thoughts about their liability.

Portlock's comments about the difficulties of any salvage operation were almost certainly correct. The season for carrying out such work was already over. It was not until the following summer that any recoveries were made and then it was the Dutch who undertook them, claiming the wreck as their own property. Operations were put in hand under the supervision of the West Terschelling Receiver of Wreck, F. P. Robbe. After the removal of large quantities of wood, rigging, rope and other obstructions, gold bars and dollars began to surface. The wreck lay in about twenty-six feet of water. The work was carried out from small boats using tongs, nets, poles and levers rather than a diving bell. It was primitive equipment of the kind that had been used on such jobs for several centuries. The fishermen who carried out the work experienced all the usual frustrations of salvors. When the tides were right the weather was hostile and when the weather was calm the tides were wrong. To add to their problems the bullion proved to have been poorly packed and the iron hoops to the barrels constantly gave way, causing the precious contents to spill back into the sea. Despite all the problems during the years 1800 and 1801 bullion worth £55,770 was recorded as having been recovered. But the following year produced no tangible results, the wreck was rapidly silting up and very soon the project was abandoned.

Although earlier diving bells had some limited success, arguably it was the introduction of the Siebe helmeted diver in the mid-nineteenth century that made underwater salvage practical.

The *Lutine* appears to have been forgotten until, in 1814, Robbe's successor, Pierre Eschauzier, thought it might be worthwhile to have another go. The wreck was relocated with some difficulty and only seventeen gold coins were recovered and no gold bars. It was not exactly an encouraging result. Seven more years went by and nothing further happened. Eschauzier, however, had not in the meantime forgotten about the *Lutine*. On the contrary he appears to have become completely obsessed with the idea of its treasure and in 1821 he persuaded the Dutch government to issue the infamous royal decree which vested all salvage rights in himself, with the government receiving fifty per cent of all proceeds, and Eschauzier finding all costs of any salvage project. It was this royal decree that first suggested that the contents of the *Lutine* might be worth as much as £1.6 million. Eschauzier had been very impressed by recent work carried out by English divers using diving bells and was hopeful that he would be able to salvage the vast fortune that remained within the *Lutine* using this new equipment. He formed a consortium and issued shares in the time-honoured manner of treasure-hunting schemes. It was to be the first of countless such arrangements set up to recover the *Lutine* treasure. Over the next few years diving bells were deployed on numerous occasions but every time the wreck was rediscovered, it proved to be covered up with an impenetrable layer of sand three or four feet deep. Meanwhile, the Lloyds underwriters had heard about all this renewed activity and began to lobby the Dutch government as to their own claims on the treasure. In 1823 the Dutch crown, not wanting to fall out with their powerful neighbour just across the water, agreed to make over its own fifty per cent interest in the remaining treasure to the British crown, and the British crown in turn made over their rights to the aggrieved Lloyds underwriters. The Dutch were very careful to have it recorded, however, that they only did this out of kindness and generosity and not because the British had any legal right to the treasure that was, after all, in their territorial waters, and had been claimed as rightful booty during a time when Holland and Britain were at war.

Eschauzier continued to be obsessed by the *Lutine* treasure and constantly monitored the depth of the sand over the wreck. There were years, such as 1834, when it shifted entirely and bits of the wreck appeared again above the seabed. It was 1834 when the Bell brothers, with their diver John Deane, were invited over by the Eschauzier consortium to try their luck. However, by the time they had reached the site, the wreck was once again silted over. It is interesting to note that the well-informed Bells showed more interest in a Portuguese wreck that was lying close by than they did in the *Lutine*, much to the outrage of Eschauzier.

In 1837 Eschauzier died, enthusiastic and confident to the end that he would shortly recover the vast treasure that remained beneath the sand. For the next twenty years a succession of dreamers and chancers showed a similar interest in recovering the residual gold, but nothing came from their under-funded and ill-conceived efforts. Then in the spring of 1857 some fishermen pulled up by accident a part of the *Lutine* wreck which revealed that it had once again come completely free of the sand. An engineer called Taurel, together with Brandt Eschauzier, son of the late Pierre, promptly embarked on a new salvage operation. The wreck was said to be lying on a north-north-west–south-south-east axis. Using mainly helmeted divers forty-two bars of gold, sixty-two silver bars and 15,350 gold and silver coins were recovered during the next three years of operations. Engineer Taurel designed and constructed an expensive bell specifically for the *Lutine* salvage, but it proved to be useless. It was impossible to position it on top of the wreck. Even so, the total value of treasure recovered during this phase was calculated at £44,124. By 1860, however, the wreck had again silted up and the returns slowly dwindled away to nothing. Operations dragged on in a desultory manner for several more years, but nothing significant was brought to the surface.

In the late 1860s a new visionary engineer entered on the scene called Willem Hendrik Ter Meulen. He had invented what he called his sand-diving machine which was actually more like a sand-drill than a sand-diver. It consisted basically of a long copper pipe, or probe, perforated with small holes. The idea was that water was forced into the pipe by means of a steam pump and, jetting through the small holes under pressure, it cleared a tunnel down through the sand. The drilling concept was wonderfully effective. The difficulty came with the next stage, which involved a hapless diver descending down a narrow shaft between walls of sand to the wreck below. Not much thought seems to have been given to the risks of the tunnel collapsing in on the diver. Perhaps it

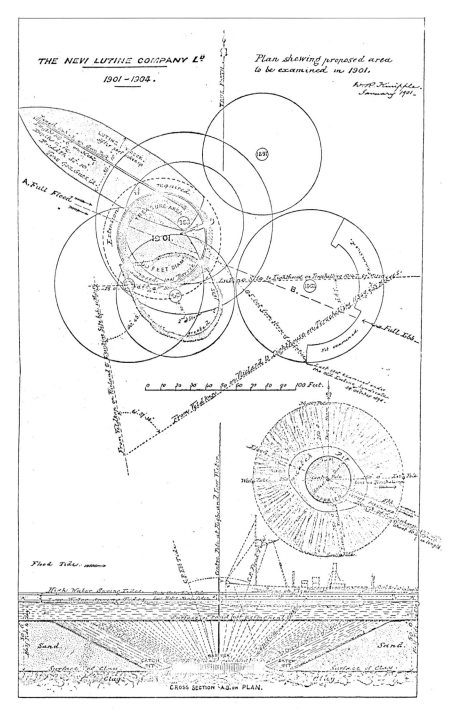

Plan of salvage operations for 1901-4.

is fortunate that, by the time Ter Meulen's consortium had purchased a small paddle steamer called the *Antagonist* on which to load his sand-drilling equipment, the sand over the *Lutine* wreck had silted up to such a height that there was not enough depth of water for the *Antagonist* to anchor in. The water depth was now just over three-and-a-half metres suggesting that another four metres of sand had built up over the wreck. There was, however, one small and lasting achievement made during this period. The position of the *Lutine* was recalculated as lying in 53° 21′ 33″ 974 North, 0° 10′ 41″ 804 East of the steeple of Westerkerk in the centre of Amsterdam, and stone markers were positioned on Vlieland and the Noordsvaarder, named Lutine Veldkamp and Lutine Brandaris respectively.

In 1886 two steam-suction shell dredgers called the *Tyd* and the *Friesland* were deployed over the wreck and during the next few years they brought up some 11,000 gold and silver coins, but, interestingly, no bars. They also brought up a large number of miscellaneous artefacts including weaponry, carpenters tools and personal items such as a gold signet ring, a silver watch, an earthenware pipe, and a seal with the name T. Ellis, presumably one of the many original victims of the shipwreck. By the 1890s, after Ter Meulen's death, the contract had been transferred to a British entrepreneur called Walter Kinipple. The idea now was to build an entire circular wall of sandbags around the wreck, pump out the water from within and salvage it in what would amount to dry dock conditions. It was a grand concept but proved a hopeless task. The wall was continually breached by the sea and the salvors achieved nothing. In 1910 the contract passed to a Charles Gardiner, a flamboyant businessman, who clearly had a strong sense of his own worth. He apparently charged the investing syndicate £6,800 for the benefit of his licence and information, a colossal sum of money in 1910. He deployed a very smart ship called the ss *Lyons* on which he lived with his entire family. The method he used was again one of suction and dredging but by the time war broke out only a handful of coins had been recovered.

After the ending of hostilities it was not long before the *Lutine* was again the focus of attention. A succession of companies using coal-grabbing techniques tried their luck without success. Then in 1933 came the most fantastic and ambitious concept yet, Frans Beckers's steel tower. It was the turn of the Germans. The basic concept was similar to the sand-bag idea, that is, to form a coffer-dam around the wreck and pump it dry, but the wall was to be constructed from Krupps-manufactured 16 mm armoured plates. The tower was hoisted into position on 21 July 1933. By the end of August it was completely bent and buckled. Beckers, however, was possessed of that essential quality of all salvors, namely endless optimism. A second, even stronger tower was constructed, which was put into position in the autumn of 1934, and which managed to survive the winter gales. However, the presence of the tower impeded rather than assisted dredging operations and by 1936 Beckers's funds had run out. Nothing of value had been salvaged, although large quantities of *Lutine* timber had been brought to the surface.

The world's obsession with the *Lutine*, however, did not fade away. One man's failure simply seemed to stimulate another's ambition. In 1938 the colossal industrial might of the Billiton Mining Company entered the fray. Billiton deployed a huge tin-dredger called the *Karimata*, 4,200 tons in burthen and 246 feet long. This was physical power on a completely different scale to anything that had been tried before. The *Karimata* demolished what was left of Beckers's second tower and then dredged an area approximately 200 yards long, 100 yards wide and over sixty feet

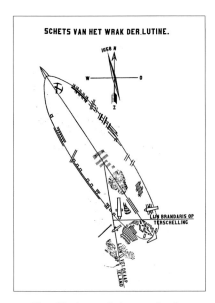

Plan of *Lutine* wreck site, 1913, showing where work had taken place so far

deep. One more gold bar was recovered twenty yards away, to the starboard of the wreck, evidence of the degree to which previous operations had scattered the original debris. The Billiton Mining Company made a large financial loss on the operation, but proudly recorded it as a technical success.

After the end of World War II interest in the *Lutine* subsided but it did not altogether die. In 1977 *The Sunday Times* carried several articles concerning the forming of a new consortium to salvage the *Lutine* treasure and, even today, there are internet sites suggesting that previous salvors have all been looking in the wrong place, and that the stern of the *Lutine* broke off during the sinking and sank in a different area altogether. According to Wijke Ruiter, for instance, 'modern archaeological research has showed that, within a few hours after the ship ran aground, the rear part of the hull broke off and drifted away, with wind and currents in south easterly direction and ended up at the more quiet south side of Vlieland, alone and forgotten. . . At this moment new excavations are in progress.' Quite how this is consistent with the rudder having been salvaged in the mid-nineteenth century and turned into a table still on display in the Lloyds building is not explained. One awaits with some anticipation further reports of progress.

So the question has to be asked why in the face of repeated failures have successive generations of salvors still dreamed of recovering the *Lutine* gold. Surely, one could reasonably argue, everything of value that was originally there has by now been brought to the surface. The problem is that the numbers do not add up. Official tallies of all the gold and silver recovered do not come to much more than £100,000. This is significantly less than even the lowest original estimate of the treasure on board of £140,000. It is vastly below the higher estimates that ranged from £300,000 to the extremely unlikely £1.6 million. The difference is perhaps explained by unauthorised pillaging down the centuries. But the *Lutine* is not an easy site to work and it would always have been

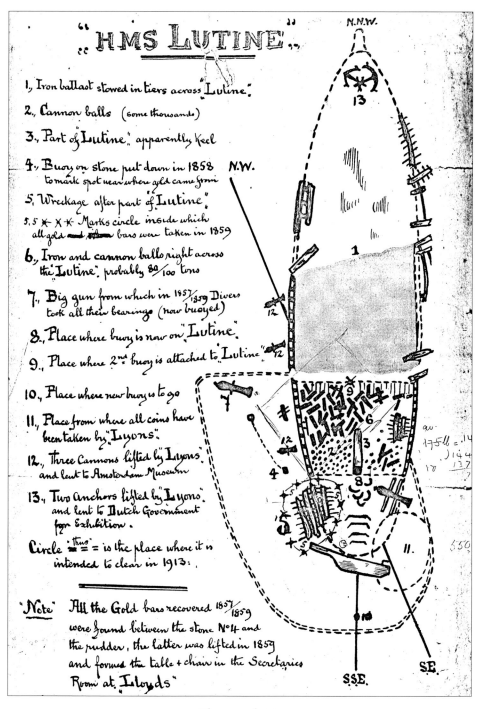

The survey of 1913.

The most famous relic, the ship's bell, has hung for two centuries in the Lloyds Underwriting Room, although the offices have been housed in four different buildings in that time.

difficult for the passing opportunist to obtain anything much of value. It is not very credible that £40,000 of gold and silver could have disappeared in this sporadic manner without someone noticing. There is also the convincing evidence of the recovered bars of gold and silver themselves. Each bar has its own individual number together with a series of letters. Taking the gold bars alone the Bank of England confirm that the numbers usually ran from one to one hundred. Detailed analysis of the bars salvaged down to 1900 revealed that there were nineteen different series of bars as a minimum sent on the *Lutine*. The Bank of England also confirmed that, while it would be unsafe to conclude that one hundred bars of each series would have been put on board the *Lutine,* it would be reasonable to believe that if say a number twenty and a number forty were found then the intervening numbers were also originally on board, that is, numbers twenty-one to thirty-nine. Using this logic only, we can infer that as by the year 1900 only a hundred gold bars had been recovered, then 289 still remained unaccounted for. Since 1900 only a few further gold bars have come to light. This leaves approximately £200,000 of gold bars alone still missing using original 1799 values. It is this calculation that has been the driving force behind the repeated searches. There is one further small anomaly relating to the *Lutine* story that in view of all the other anomalies seems somehow appropriate. The name inscribed on the famous *Lutine* bell hanging in Lloyds is not *Lutine* at all but *St Jean*.

The Wreck of the *Deutschland*

*T*HE WRECK OF THE *Deutschland* has been well known to countless generations of students of English literature by virtue of the poem of that name penned in the late nineteenth century by Gerard Manley Hopkins. Hopkins had read about the wreck in the pages of *The Times* newspaper and was deeply moved by the story. A number of the tragic ingredients caught his imagination. The stricken liner beached on a sandbank, the wildness of the snowstorm, emigrants seeking a new life, clinging to the rigging in their desperation, and, most crucially, the presence among the passengers of five young nuns calling out to their maker. The poem contains the memorable climactic lines,

> She to the black-about air, to the breaker, the thickly
> Falling flakes, to the throng that catches and quails
> Was calling 'O Christ, Christ, come quickly':

Hopkins uses the shipwreck as the springboard for a very personal meditation upon the nature of faith. It is quite possible that his attention was drawn to the story by his father, who had a professional interest in shipwrecks. He was a marine loss-adjuster and wrote one of the definitive nineteenth-century works on the subject, *A Manual of Marine Insurance*, as well as being something of a poet in his own right. The poem, 'The Wreck of the *Deutschland*' was not published until many years after Hopkins's own death. Its latter-day celebrity has made the ship famous, but few who have read the poem are aware that the wreck was a great cause célèbre at the time of its loss for reasons other than simply the presence of the five nuns.

The *Deutschland* was owned by the famous Norddeutscher Lloyd shipping line that had been founded in Bremen in 1857 by the enterprising H. H. Meir, together with his more low-key partner, Eduard Crusemann. Their aim was to exploit the burgeoning North Atlantic steamship trade that was seeing rapidly increasing volumes of traffic both in emigrants and goods. The line was called Lloyd, not because anyone of that name was a part of the company, but because Meir considered it would be a good idea to associate the company in people's minds with the redoubtable Lloyds of London. The 'Nord' (North) was a necessary part of the formula to distinguish it from the other Deutscher Lloyd shipping line already in existence based at Trieste on the Mediterranean. The company was highly successful and by the 1870s was competing to advantage against the other major North German shipping company, Hapag, based in Hamburg. Until the *Deutschland* disaster it was Norddeutscher Lloyd's proud boast that they had not lost a single life at sea.

From the old world to the new, an emigration poster of the period encouraging Europe's poor and huddled masses to try for a better life in the USA

The *Deutschland* was built, like so many others of the famous North Atlantic steamships, by Caird & Co. in Greenock, Scotland. It was the sixth ship that Caird had built for the company. It had two masts, a central funnel, a clipper-shaped bow, and a single-screw propeller. It was 2,898 tons in burthen, 328 feet long and forty feet broad. The shape of the stern was somewhat truncated in appearance, but it was a well-built ship, of iron construction, that provided the greater degree of comfort and style that the late nineteenth-century passenger was beginning to require. The main saloon was panelled with bird's eye maple and around the walls were paintings in oils commissioned from the German artist F. Hunten. This civilised setting was soon to become the scene of the most desperate carnage.

The *Deutschland* was fitted out to carry sixty first-class passengers, 120 in second class, 700 in steerage and it usually employed in addition around one hundred crew. The number of passengers, when it left Bremerhaven quayside on the afternoon of Saturday, 4 December 1875, was, most fortunately as it turned out, far fewer than this. There were only three in first class, twenty-four in second and ninety-seven in steerage. More passengers were due to embark in Southampton, the only port of call en route to New York, but their numbers would still

When the *Deutschland* was built in 1866 photography was in its infancy,
and this is one of the few early photographs of the ship.

have left the ship largely empty. The cargo holds were also only half full. The mid-1870s had
seen a temporary but sharp economic downturn in the transatlantic trade and Norddeutscher Lloyd
had been forced to lay up a number of their ships and lay off staff. Among the second-class passengers that were on board were the five Franciscan nuns, Barbara Hultenschmidt, Norberta Reinkober,
Aurea Badziura, Brigitta Damhorst and Henrica Fassbender. The nuns had all been working at the
convent orphanage in the small town of Salzkotten. They had been especially chosen by the head
of the orphanage, Mother Clara, to travel to Missouri to help with the Catholic teaching there. Part
of the reason for their departure was the growing religious persecution of Catholics in the newly
formed Germany of the Second Reich that had been created in 1871. The successful conclusion
of the Franco-Prussian war, from Germany's point of view, had led to the dominance of Bismarck
in German politics, and the implementation of his policy of *Kulturkampf* (literally, culture struggle). Bismarck was a fervent secularist and a believer in a strong centralised state and he had passed
new laws, called the Falk laws, that made it illegal for Catholics to teach. This meant that for the
small community of Franciscans at Salzkotten, much that was fundamental to their sense of voca-
tion was being undermined. Emigration was an obvious response. Like many of the their fellow
travellers on the *Deutschland* they were going to America to seek a new and better life.

The *Deutschland* had been launched in 1866 and so was already a well tried-and-tested ship. It had crossed the Atlantic on numerous occasions in both directions without mishap. The only occurrence of any note was the breaking of a propeller earlier in 1875 but on that occasion the ship had been towed to safety back in Southampton, a new propeller fitted and there were no ill consequences. The *Deutschland* also had a new captain, Edward Brickenstein, forty-five years old, the previous captain having been suddenly appointed to a more senior position inside the company just a few days before the *Deutschland* was due to leave. The surprise promotion had come as a direct result of an unexpected death. But Brickenstein was not a novice as a transatlantic captain. He had been a ship's master for sixteen years, eight of them with Norddeutscher Lloyd, and prior to the *Deutschland* he had been captain of the *Rhine*. He had had an unblemished career to date.

When the *Deutschland* departed from Germany at 3.30 p.m. on Saturday afternoon, 4 December, the weather was fine, but as it got dark it also grew misty. Negotiating a large ship out of a busy waterway was always difficult but doubly so in poor visibility. The *Deutschland* had two pilots on board who were responsible for this first stage of the voyage. They completed their task safely and once out into the open waters of the North Sea command was handed back to Brickenstein. By then the fog was so thick that Brickenstein decided it would be best to anchor up for the night. Both of the German pilots decided to stay on board for the trip to Southampton. Perhaps this was the usual procedure, rather than pick up a small boat to take them straight back up the river to Bremerhaven, or perhaps they just wanted to savour the delights of England for a few days. The English pilot, called Charles Harvey, who would have responsibility for guiding the *Deutschland* into Southampton, was also on board, suggesting that he must have recently stayed on for the voyage on another Norddeutscher liner going in the other direction.

By first light on the Sunday morning the weather had changed. The fog had lifted but it was not an unqualified improvement. A strong gale was now blowing from the north-east and there was a light scattering of snow. The *Deutschland* got under steam. The Borkum lightship was passed at 1.30 p.m. This was the last definite sighting made of any landmark before the *Deutschland* struck a sandbank at the entrance to the River Thames. At around 4 p.m. both Brickenstein and his first officer Lauenstein considered themselves to be about eighteen miles off the treacherous Terschelling Sands on the Dutch coast. They continued to steam in a south-westerly direction at twelve to thirteen knots. At 4 a.m. on the Monday morning the speed was reduced from twelve knots to about nine-and-a-half knots. The lead was being cast continually in order to ascertain the soundings they were in. The captain was on the bridge throughout the night and there were six lookout men at various points, but the snowstorm was now so thick no one could see anything. Shortly before 5 a.m. they sounded seventeen fathoms, a clear warning sign. A light was then noticed about three miles distant on the port bow. Brickenstein thought that it was the Hinder lightship off the Dutch coast. The next moment breakers were seen directly ahead. The order was given to go full speed astern. It was at this point, according to the later evidence of the captain, the first officer and the chief engineer, that the propeller broke. If the propeller broke before the vessel even hit the sand-bank, it was probably because they had struck some other underwater obstruction, possibly a previous wreck, or because the enormous pressure, resulting from suddenly throwing the ship into reverse, caused the metal to sheer off. An alternative explanation, put forward by an anonymous correspondent in *The Times* newspaper, was that the propeller sheered off when the ship first struck an outer lip of the sand bank, but this theory was not supported by the evidence of any of those involved. Whatever the cause, the failure of the propeller meant that the ship was left floundering helplessly, at the mercy of the wind and waves. In a very short space of time it had been driven by the wind and the prevailing currents on to the ridge of sand that lay ahead. They had struck not on the Hinder but on the Kentish Knock, the outermost of the sandbanks that hem in the entrance to the Thames, and a terrible graveyard for ships of all types and nationalities down the years. I have collected data on over one hundred ships that have come to grief on that single bank alone and there are no doubt several hundred more that have gone unrecorded. It is situated over twenty miles from the coast, is seven miles long and two miles wide, and part of it is dry at low water. It is a vicious trap lying in wait for the blinded, the ignorant and the unwary.

On striking the sand the *Deutschland* swung round with its port side exposed to the raging sea and the north-easterly gales. To be broached to in this manner was the worst possible situation to be in, for the huge waves broke directly over the entire length of the ship. It was also high tide, which meant that there was no chance that rising sea levels would lift the ship off the bank and allow it to float free. Not that there is an ideal time of the tide to strike a sandbank. If it is low tide and the hull is holed by the impact then as the tide rises the vessel runs the risk of floating off and then sinking through a sudden ingress of water. Brickenstein ordered rockets to be fired in the hope that someone would notice their distress and send boats to help. He also hoisted sail on the two masts in a vain attempt to shift the *Deutschland* off the bank. The attempt was ineffective and the

The *Deutschland* aground on the Kentish Knock sand with the decks awash.

sails were ripped to shreds. Brickenstein then attempted to lower one of the eight lifeboats with which the *Deutschland* was equipped. The quartermaster called Beck and two seamen got into it. To launch a small boat in such rough seas was extremely difficult. Twice it capsized but on both occasions the three crewmen managed to clamber back in. Then the rope attaching the boat to the ship gave way and Beck and his companions found themselves adrift without any supplies of any kind. This took place early on the Monday morning just an hour or so after striking. By the middle of the afternoon one of the three men was dead, probably as a result of the blow on the head he had received as the boat had been lowered as much as from exposure to the appalling weather conditions. By evening a second member of the tiny crew had died, this time definitely from exposure. Some how or other, though, Quartermaster Beck, who was at the tiller throughout, survived the ordeal and managed to beach his boat at Sheerness on the Tuesday morning and raise the alarm.

Meanwhile, on the *Deutschland*, Brickenstein had started the pumps going and was jettisoning cargo from the forehold. His idea was to lighten the head of the ship hoping that this would then enable him to swing it round, so that the bows of the vessel would be facing into the wind. This would considerably lessen the impact of the weather on the ship's structure and so decrease the chance of it breaking up on the sandbank. It was a sensible idea, but unfortunately the *Deutschland* refused to shift. Over the next few days the jettisoned cargo began to come ashore. A bundle of silks was taken up at Herne Bay and a large number of packages of gloves at Kingsgate. It is interesting that different items from the same ship, subject to the same weather and currents should end up in such different places. The variable drift is presumably dependant on exactly when the items went into the sea and the exact size and density of the various parcels of goods. One of the items to wash up some days later was a rather touching, if somewhat stiff, farewell note from one of the passengers clearly resigned to drowning. It read, 'We are ashore one hour, every minute terrific thumping. One boat and passengers already gone. D. J. Behring, Mrs Behring, Bremerhaven.' He then added as a kind of postscript, 'I believe we are lost. I depart in peace with my God, and without anxiety. Love to friends, children and mother-in-law. D. J. Behring.' A note in the bottle was obviously the nineteenth-century equivalent of the final mobile phone call. In the event Mr Behring survived but his wife did not.

To begin with morale among most of the passengers was reasonably high. A number of the men volunteered to help with the pumps and the throwing overboard of cargo. Food and drink were liberally distributed. Lifebelts were handed out in case the worst happened. As over 1,000 of them were carried there was no unseemly scramble. Hopes rose and fell when two ships, a steamer and a sailing brig, both approached, and then seemed to drift away without communicating. Even this disappointment was not entirely disheartening, however, because it reminded them that they were in a busy seaway and there had to be a good chance they would alert some other vessel, better-equipped for carrying out a rescue. When evening came they fired more rockets and this time there were answering flares from at least two lightships. It was further encouragement. However, the *Deutschland*, meanwhile, was taking a terrible battering. Its back was broken, the bows were under water and the stern was protruding into the air. Brickenstein, knowing that if the *Deutschland* came off the sandbank now it would fill with water and sink immediately, ordered anchors to be lowered to secure it in position. Even so it was increasingly obvious to everyone that as the tide rose again that night only a small part of the stern would be left above the sea, and even that area would have great waves constantly breaking over it.

Passengers and crew now took to the rigging, an unenviable situation with the wind screaming in their ears and the bitter cold freezing their hands. During the long night a number of them dropped off and fell into the sea, including Mr Benning the purser. Around 2 a.m. the captain ordered everyone on deck because even the aft saloon was by then under water. The five nuns apparently refused, preferring to remain where they were in the saloon. The behaviour of the nuns at this moment of crisis subsequently became a matter of considerable controversy. Some saw their refusal to leave as an example of high-minded resignation and collective solidarity. Others clearly considered their behaviour to have been hysterical and demoralising. A highly critical report carried by the *New York Times* ran, 'There were five nuns on board who, by their terror-stricken conduct, seem to have added greatly to the weirdness of the scene. They were deaf to all entreaties to leave the saloon, and when, almost by main force, the stewardess (whose conduct was plucky in the extreme) managed to get them onto the companion ladder, they sank down on the steps and stubbornly refused to go another step.' They seemed to have returned to the saloon again shortly, for somewhere in the dead of night, when the greater part of the crew and passengers were in the rigging, one was seen with her body half through the skylight, crying aloud in a voice heard above the storm, 'O my God, make it quick! Make it quick!' This is hardly the rapturous anticipation of union with God that Hopkins describes in his poem even if the final quoted words are almost identical. If the nuns were panicking they can hardly be blamed, for clearly the circumstances were truly horrific. Two other passengers hung themselves, another cut his wrists, and no doubt several others opted for being swept overboard rather than prolonging the agony. Some, however, showed throughout their ordeal considerable presence of mind and a determination to survive. One first-class passenger, William Leick from Cleveland, noticing that a number of his fellows had tied themselves to the rigging to stop them being washed away by the waves, went in search of some string as a prerequisite of survival. He found some round a bundle of bedding belonging to a steerage passenger. He asked if he may make use of it and on being refused he helped himself with the assistance of his knife. He reasoned correctly enough, no doubt, that the third-class passenger had

---

Overleaf:
A magnificent engraving from the *Illustrated London News* showing the tug *Liverpool* taking passengers off.

little chance of saving his bedding, and it was anyway less valuable than a life. The incident illustrates how rapidly normal concepts of ownership can break down in such extreme circumstances.

By daylight on the Tuesday the storm began to abate and the waves subside. At 10 a.m. help finally appeared in the form of a small paddle-steamer tug called the *Liverpool*, Captain John Carrington, out of Harwich. He moored a short distance away and lowered a small boat with instructions to bring off the women and children first. After three trips back and forth, and having established that there was three fathoms of water under the *Deutschland*'s port side, he felt confident enough to manoeuvre his ship right up against the wrecked German liner, to bring off the rest of the people and their baggage. The survivors were taken to Harwich where they were housed in the Great Eastern Hotel. A public collection was held which contributed more than £2 per survivor. The following day the *Liverpool* tug returned to collect the dead bodies. The *Essex Telegraph* made a point of describing in detail the exact situation in which the dead nuns were found. One of them, 'having apparently reclined her head upon her hands on the table had fallen so that she lay leaning over the stool, with her head resting on some wreckage'. The Victorian newspaper-reading public had it seemed a great appetite for the morbid detail. The same newspaper described the nuns again after they had been laid out in the mortuary. The nuns' dead bodies were on public exhibit a second time in the Roman Catholic Church in Leytonstone, Stratford, and by the time of their burial, their celebrity was such that thousands followed the cortege to the cemetery.

As soon as the German press got hold of the story of the sinking there was an outcry of nationalistic rage at what was regarded in Germany as a criminal act of negligence and cynicism on the part of the English. Without checking the facts it was generally assumed that the *Deutschland* had gone down close to the shore and all those on board could easily have been rescued if it had not been that the English preferred to wait for the ship to break up first, so that the salvaging pickings would be the greater. For those who knew of the circumstances of the sinking this was a quite scandalous and unjustified attack on the brave crew of the tug *Liverpool* that had gone out to assist at the first opportunity. The *Essex Telegraph* made a joke of it, headlining their response, 'Expected War between Germany and Harwich'. This show of joviality, however, was hardly likely to soothe outraged German sensibilities. The simmering animosity between the two nations, that the *Deutschland* incident dramatically reveals, did not bode well for future relations.

The accusations in the German press may have been ridiculous but there were some genuine questions that needed to be answered concerning the subsequent conduct of the salvage. Within two days of the sinking the crews of scores of small boats were swarming over the decks. *The Times* of 13 December recorded that 'the owner's agent and the third mate of the *Deutschland* went aboard on Wednesday, and found 50 or 60 men at work in the cabins and on deck, breaking open passengers luggage, fishing cargo up out of the hold, stripping the saloon and cabins, in short wrecking the ship.' The wreckers for their part claimed that 'they would take the plate, glasses, portmanteau

The looting of the *Deutschland*, also from the *Illustrated London News*.

& to the offices of the receiver of wreck.' But it does seem that not everything was handed over as it should have been. Again, according to *The Times*, 'Twenty bodies have been brought into Harwich by the steam tug. Mr Guy, the inspector of police here, tells me that, with one exception, not a single valuable was found on the persons of these unfortunate people, and it was clear that their pockets had been turned out and rifled. There were ring marks on the fingers of women, and of at least one gentleman. The rings themselves had disappeared. No suspicion whatever rests on the crew of the tug. The inference therefore is unavoidable, and it is one that must be painful to all Englishmen.' The *London Illustrated News* added to the general sense of unease with some graphic pictures of disreputable-looking wreckers at work dismantling the *Deutschland*. The pictures were drawn by their own artist who had gone on board the *Deutschland* the day after the rescue. 'Our artist, having been a witness to this proceeding on the second day named, gives his evidence in the form of a sketch, the perfect veracity of which may be relied upon.' The idea that the artist can always be relied upon to tell the truth is an interesting one. *The Times* also struck a very sanctimonious tone, which no doubt played well in Germany. 'While no salvaging smacks came near the *Deutschland* during the thirty hours in which her 200 passengers and crew were in such sore need of help, the steam tug *Liverpool* had hardly cleared from the wreck with the survivors, before two or three of those smacks came swooping down.' The author quite fails to mention that during the first thirty hours the weather was such it would have been extremely foolhardy for any smack to have approached the *Deutschland*. The remarks of the reporter from the *New York Herald*, who also went out to the wreck, were equally derogatory about the local fishermen, even if his comments were somewhat more folksy in style: 'Yes, sure enough, they were lying off the wreck, head to wind, cutters, schooners, and luggers, like a flock of vultures hovering around their prey.'

The amount of actual pillaging that went on was probably greatly exaggerated. By Thursday, 9

'Like a flock of vultures hovering around their prey': local small craft like this cutter were accused of pillaging the wreck.

December, Captain Heathcote of the Marine Salvage Association had taken control of the wreck. Justice Rothery, who conducted the Court of Enquiry into the loss certainly, considered the press reports to have been unreliable. In his summary he noted, 'the charge of wrecking and of pillage was fully withdrawn, both by the officers of the *Deutschland* and by the managing director of the company.'

A rather more productive line of questioning concerned the issue of why an important coastal port like Harwich did not have a lifeboat. It had possessed one earlier in the century but the institution had fallen into disuse. The reason for this was no doubt because the presence of a lifeboat did not suit certain local vested interests. Shipwreck had long been a useful source of supplementary income to the coastal population of this corner of Essex, and a publicly funded lifeboat was probably regarded as providing unwelcome competition. Also, it was pointed out, with some degree of justification, that when a shipwreck occurred a long way from land, as was the case with the *Deutschland*, the lifeboat would be dependant on a steam tug like the *Liverpool* to tow it out to the distressed ship. The scandal over the *Deutschland* sinking, however, was sufficient to prompt a sceptical local population into subscribing to a new lifeboat.

The conduct of the rescue and salvage operation was not the only issue that exercised the minds of the press and the public. There was also the question of why the accident had happened in the first place. The obvious explanation was that it was a result of extreme adverse weather conditions, an unfortunate act of God. But there was some debate about just how bad the weather was that night. Other ships had been at sea in the same general area on the Monday morning when the *Deutschland* struck the Kentish Knock. Also, it was evident from Brickenstein's own statement that it was not just a question of his being half-a-mile or so adrift in his calculations. The *Deutschland* was about fifty miles away from where the captain thought he was when he hit the sandbank. On 20 December Justice Rothery heard the case before the Admiralty Court. The enquiry continued for two weeks and was finally published in the February of 1876. It was found that the ship was in good order and that the lifesaving equipment was perfectly adequate and well maintained. The questions surrounding the propeller were examined in some detail. A diver had inspected the aft of the shipwreck on the seabed and his report made it clear that the shaft was intact but the propeller had sheered of, supporting the explanation that this had happened as a result of suddenly putting the ship into reverse. No criticism of Captain Brickenstein was made in this respect.

There was some considerable discussion about the steamship and the brig, both of which apparently noticed the *Deutschland* during the fateful Monday, but both of which had continued with apparent callousness on their course. It proved impossible to identify the steamer, but the crew of the Knock light vessel confirmed that the weather was so fierce, they did not think the anonymous ship could have done anything to assist those on board the *Deutschland*, except perhaps report the existence and whereabouts of the wreck at the nearest port. As it happened even if the unknown steamer had made such a report it would have made no difference to those on the *Deutschland*, because the situation of the wreck was already known about on shore from the sighting of distress rockets more than sixteen hours before a rescue attempt could be launched. As for the brig, the captain came forward at the enquiry and gave his evidence. His vessel was called the *Ino* and he explained how he was unable to render assistance because he had at the time 'as much as he could do to save himself'. His evidence was detailed and plausible and accepted by Justice Rothery. Rothery was also full of praise for the prompt action taken by Captain Carrington of the steam tug *Liverpool* and dismissive of all the fuss that had been made about the so-called wreckers and pillagers. He obviously regarded the press as little more than sensationalists and scandalmongers. Of the artist employed by the *Illustrated London News* he remarked, 'it is impossible to place any reliance upon a statement which is utterly unsupported by proof, and which is in direct opposition to all the evidence in the case.' Part of that evidence was supplied by the English pilot, Charles Harvey, who clearly felt that the press did not understand the difference between pillaging and legitimate 'salving', where the goods would later be handed in to the Receiver of Wreck. Rothery reserved his most stringent criticisms for Captain Brickenstein. He praised the captain's conduct after the ship had struck, supporting his decision not to launch any more lifeboats after the first one had got into immediate difficulties, and also the various efforts he had made to protect the structure of his vessel and the welfare of his crew and passengers. 'Throughout the whole of that day and the following night, and until the survivors were rescued by the steam tug, the master appears to have been always at his post, maintaining admirable discipline, taking every measure for the safety of those on board, and encouraging them by his example,' stated Rothery in his

Among the items recently
recovered from the wreck
are porcelain dolls' heads.
Mass-manufactured in
about a dozen sizes by the
German Kister company,
they were later attached to
a calico body, and sold
dressed in silk clothing.

Cutlery from the ship. The silver plating
has been eroded away but the company's
monogram is still visible.

More Kister porcelain products,
including figures, animals, a small vase
and a match holder with a strike area on
the back of the dog's kennel.

judgement. He was, however, not at all convinced by Captain Brickenstein's navigational abilities. In particular, Rothery did not understand why the clear disparity between the soundings the captain had actually obtained, and those laid down on the chart for the course that he had thought he was following, did not alert him to the fact that he was hopelessly adrift in his calculations much earlier on in the voyage. 'The Master was a good deal pressed, in the course of the enquiry, to point out where he found, on his supposed course, soundings corresponding to those which he had obtained, and which led him to think he was on his right course; but he was not able to do so.' Brickenstein defended himself by saying that the strong currents and the following gale had caused him to cover far more ground than he had anticipated from his dead reckoning. But these extraneous influences are exactly the kind of factors that a skilful seaman needs to take into account when calculating his position. It is difficult not to conclude that Brickenstein's unfamiliarity with his ship perhaps contributed to his fatal loss of judgement. Brickenstein did not accept Rothery's hostile verdict and a later enquiry held in Germany exonerated him of all guilt. However, despite this apparent clearing of his name, he was never to captain a ship again or work for Norddeutscher Lloyd.

It seems likely that the trauma of the *Deutschland* affair had put an end to his fondness for the seafaring life.

While the Court of Enquiry was taking place, efforts to salvage the *Deutschland*'s cargo were still busily going ahead. In *The Times* of 22 December it was noted that, 'The *Increase*, smack of Colchester, Glover master, landed here the undermentioned goods from the *Deutschland*, viz: 20 packages cotton goods, one bale herbs, 21 brass musical instruments, 61 china ornaments, 2 sofa cushions, 2 blocks, 4 dressing cases, fittings belonging to steam winch, one camp stool, one life belt, two pieces of carpet and one hawser.' The list gives an interesting insight into the nature of German exports to America at the time. But the salvage process soon ran into difficulties. The ship was rapidly becoming silted up. Even a week earlier the diver, John Fullager, had noted that 'the ship was now fast settling down into the sand' and Captain Glover reported: '*Deutschland* very much broken amidships, settling down at both ends on starboard bow and port quarter.' The *Increase* was the vessel most frequently mentioned in connection with the *Deutschland* during the following weeks, but conditions at the wreck continued to deteriorate making further salvage a very slow business. On 20 January 1876 it was reported that the *Increase* had landed 'five cases of merchandise and two casks' but 'lower hold sanded up; now very difficult to get cargo out; intends commencing forehold at the first favourable opportunity'. By 25 March reports published in *Lloyds List* had become even more gloomy: 'It is impossible to clear any more cargo from the *Deutschland*... unless the sand, with which she is fast filling, clears away.' Even so in April the *Increase* together with the *Snowdrop*, Captain Cook, landed 1,500 pairs of stays, twenty-five cases of wine, two cases of machinery and two casks of wine... Divers report that the vessel has listed to starboard forward and to port aft' – which suggests that its back must have been broken in two. In May a case of organ barrels was recovered and in June more wine, beer, wool and cotton goods, seeds and books. In August Swiss embroidery, Moroccan skins, cases of corsets and spirit lamps were all brought ashore. Reports of goods being landed become more and more sporadic, but the following year, 1877, salvors were still active. Some zinc and other metals were brought up as well as some cases of umbrellas, rolls of silk and essential oils. The divers were now having to cut away the iron work of the wreck in order to gain access to the holds, but the tenacity of the effort being made suggests that there were still rich pickings to be had. After the close of the 1877 season, however, the wreck appeared to have been abandoned for good.

There is something about famous shipwrecks, however, that suggests they are never quite forgotten. In 2002 the pages of *The Times* were again full of the recent rediscovery of the *Deutschland* wreck by a team of divers headed by Aaron Playle, a veteran of salvage projects in different parts of the world. Porcelain dolls, Meissen figurines, vases and other antique knicknacks were subsequently recovered. Somewhat amazingly, considering all the effort that took place at the time of loss and the two following years, it seems that there is still a vast treasure trove of fascinating artefacts down there.

The *Wilhelm Gustloff* and The Amber Room

O NE OF THE GRIMMEST EVENTS of World War II concerns the sinking of the German liner *Wilhelm Gustloff*. When it went down into the icy waters of the Baltic on 30 January 1945 approximately 7,000 people drowned. There were around 5,000 refugees on board, mostly women and children, as well as large numbers of injured soldiers, women auxiliaries and submarine officers and men. The exact number lost is not known because in the panic of evacuation the precise number that boarded was not recorded. Somewhat surprisingly, given the terrible circumstances of the sinking, there were nearly 1,000 survivors, but the *Gustloff* disaster still has the unenviable distinction of setting the record for the largest loss of life in a single maritime disaster.

The *Gustloff* had been built in 1937 by Blohm & Voss for the German National Socialist Government. It was designed as a cruise liner but not for the luxury end of the market. Its purpose

Wilhelm Gustloff in happier days: alongside the Tilbury landing stage in 1938.

was to provide cheap maritime holidays for worthy German workers. All its cabins were of a single uniform class in keeping with its socialist credentials. It was part of the 'strength through joy' recreational programme of the Nazis, and was named after the leader of the Nazi party in Switzerland who had been assassinated by a Jew. It was an enormous ship, 650 feet long with a 25,484 gross tonnage. Its incarnation as a cruise ship was short-lived. With the declaration of war it was converted into accommodation for the Second U-boat Training Division under Captain Wilhelm Zahn and stationed in the bay of Gdansk.

In the early weeks of 1945 the Russian Red Army was rapidly advancing on the German-controlled eastern Baltic ports. The situation within the German civilian and military population was chaotic. The arrival of the Russians was expected any day and rumours about the atrocities that would inevitably follow created a general atmosphere of terror and panic. Hardly surprisingly everyone was desperate to evacuate. On 22 January 1945 the *Gustloff* was prepared for sea and began to take on board passengers. It was situated in the small Polish port of Gotenhafen now known as Gdynia just to the west of Gdansk. Under the pressure of fear, discipline broke down. As soon as the gangplank was put into position the crowd surged forward and ugly scenes followed. Mothers were separated from their children in the crush and the less able were pushed aside by the strongest. There were far more people hoping to get on board than the ship could possibly accommodate. Among those who were privileged to embark were 373 young female naval auxiliaries. They were mainly housed in the former swimming pool area on E deck. Had they known what the immediate future held they may well have preferred to take their chance with those who remained behind.

The *Gustloff*, already packed with bodies along the corridors and in the hallways, did not depart immediately. There was much discussion among the evacuees as to the possible cause for the delay. Conditions on board were far from ideal and there was the constant danger of aerial attack. Everyone was anxious to leave Eastern Prussia and return to the relative safety of Germany. The delay, however, continued. Questions were asked but no one seemed to know what was going on. There were comings and goings, mysterious loadings, endless rumours. An entire week went past and still the *Gustloff* sat in the harbour apparently immobilised.

On Monday, 29 January 1945, a hospital train pulled in to Gotenhafen station and more injured soldiers were unloaded and carried onto the ship. The wounded were accommodated beneath a glass roof on the sun deck, although in the grey depths of a northern Polish winter there was precious little sun to be had. The recorded temperature was minus fourteen degrees centigrade. The following day, shortly after noon, four tugboats came along side the *Wilhelm Gustloff* and gradually manoeuvred it away from the quayside and towards the open sea. At the last moment more refugees came aboard from small boats that besieged the great ship. Mothers held babies in the air in a desperate attempt to gain sympathy and a boarding pass. The weather was miserable. A force-seven gale was blowing. Snow was coming down. There were small icebergs floating on the water.

Wilhelm Gustloff at sea.

The tugboats soon turned back towards Gdansk. From then on the *Gustloff* only had a small torpedo boat called the *Löwe* and a torpedo recovery vessel, the *TF19*, out in front for company. The
German Baltic navy was so hard-stretched that no proper escort could be provided for the *Gustloff*'s
defence. Another liner, the *Hansa*, also carrying refugees towards the west, departed from Gdansk
Bay at the same time as the *Gustloff*, but it very shortly developed engine trouble and had to turn
back. Around the same time the *TF19* dropped out because it was leaking so badly. That left just
the *Löwe* and the *Gustloff*.

A layer of snow froze hard over the open decks, making them treacherous to walk on. The crew
constantly had to hack thick encrustations of ice off the anti-aircraft guns to keep them operational.
As it grew dark, and the ship tossed more violently, large numbers of the passengers began to suffer from seasickness, which in the confined and cramped conditions must have been particularly
unpleasant. The euphoria of departure quickly turned into a mood of deep gloom. On the ship's
bridge there was increasing tension between Wilhelm Zahn, who was the military commander on
board, and Captain Petersen who was the master of the ship. Petersen was a former prisoner of war
in Britain who had been released on the basis that he was too old and broken down to be of any

further use to the German military machine. By this stage of the war, however, Germany was so desperate for naval officers, he had been appointed captain of the *Gustloff*. Petersen and Zahn did not get on and their personal antipathy led to some confusion of decision-making. Zahn was frustrated that the *Gustloff* could only achieve a speed of twelve knots when its top speed was supposed to be sixteen. At twelve knots the ship was vulnerable to submarine attack. He suggesting zigzagging, but Petersen preferred to head in a straight line through the danger area, reducing the amount of time the ship would be exposed to the enemy.

As it happened submarine attack was not considered to be the main danger to the retreating German forces at sea. Russian submarines up until this stage of the war had been largely ineffective and British submarines were not at this point active in the eastern Baltic. The greater danger was considered to be from mines or even aerial attack. Russian submarines had spent most of the war trapped by the German navy at Kronstadt. They were generally regarded as ill equipped and lacking in active-service experience. The Russian advance on Leningrad, however, had in part changed that situation. They might still be ill equipped, with poor torpedoes and hydrophones, but by the end of 1944 they were at least free to operate out of Finnish ports. The *S13*, a Russian submarine that was ironically based on a German design, previously supplied by Hitler when he and Stalin were allies, left Hanga Harbour in Turku on 11 January with the specific mission of intercepting the retreating German ships. Its captain was Alexander Marinesko. He very nearly missed the cruise because he had reported for duty three days late having been on an extended drinking and womanising binge. He badly needed to restore his reputation in the eyes of the Russian authorities.

By 26 January the *S13* was lying off Memel having so far failed to make contact with any potential enemy targets. It was at this point that the maverick Marinesko decided on his own initiative to head towards Gdansk Bay, where he suspected the pickings would be greater, even if the presence of enemy warships might also be more of a problem. His surmise was quickly proved to be correct. On the evening of the 30th he observed a large liner that he estimated at 20,000 tons. He decided to attack on the surface and from the shore side. Attacking on the surface meant that he would have the necessary speed to close on his target and his torpedoes were far more likely to hit their mark. Approaching from the shore side would give him the advantage of surprise as the enemy

A Soviet S-class submarine like *S13*.

The sole escort for the refugee-packed ship was the small torpedo boat *Löwe*. Sequestered from the Norwegian navy in 1940 and since employed training the Baltic U-boat flotillas, it was not really a frontline unit.

lookouts would be expecting their seaward side to be the more vulnerable. It was, however, a risky strategy. On the surface his submarine was far more likely to be spotted and fired on, and the shore side gave him only very limited depths of water to dive in, for after his torpedoes had struck he would need to rapidly get out of the enemy's way.

Shortly after 9 p.m., as the *Gustloff* laboured through heavy seas off the coast of Stolpmunde heading towards Bornholm Island, there was a sudden and enormous explosion. A torpedo had struck the bows deep below the waterline causing huge and immediate flooding of the forward holds. The ship lurched towards the starboard and pandemonium broke out. A number of those on board immediately threw themselves into the icy waters of the Baltic where they had no chance of surviving for more than a few minutes before succumbing to exposure. Then the ship slowly righted itself as the weight of water entering stabilised it. Renewed hope that the ship might yet continue to float was, however, short-lived. A second torpedo tore open the swimming pool area on E deck where nearly 400 young women had been quartered, killing most of them. For good measure a third torpedo was then fired amidships into the engine room. The *Gustloff*'s fate was sealed. The great ship began to sink bows first.

Marinesko's tactics had worked with devastating results. He was about to enter the history books as the submarine commander responsible for inflicting the greatest loss of life in a single sinking of the entire war. Somewhat ironically he had great difficulty in getting the sinking officially attributed to him. Shortly after the end of the war he fell out of favour with the Russian authorities and was transported to Stalin's gulag. It was not until the 1960s that he was rehabilitated and officially recognised as a Russian war hero. There has been much subsequent debate about the legal status of the sinking. It has been suggested that the *Gustloff* was a hospital ship, carrying wounded soldiers and refugees, and as such should not have been attacked. The argument is dubious. It is not clear whether the *Gustloff* sailed with the red cross on display – the last known photograph suggests not – but even if it did its status was far from straightforward. It was equipped with anti-aircraft guns and it was carrying submarine personnel for redeployment in the naval war. On both counts it was disqualified as being a hospital ship.

If the struggle to get on to the *Gustloff* in the first place had been fierce, the struggle now to get off it was still fiercer. Everyone simultaneously rushed for the top decks where the lifeboats were hung. There was no order, no command and no following of the principle of women and children first. The two requisites for survival were luck and fitness. Launching of the lifeboats, always a difficult business in rough seas and with an unruly mob pressing hard, was hampered further by the thick layer of ice that had formed over the lowering tackle. Only a few boats reached the water in an upright state. Many of those who had thought themselves lucky to gain a place soon found themselves upside down, feet caught in the ropes. Hardly surprisingly, a number of those who were possessed of guns turned them on themselves and their immediate family rather than participate any further in the hellish business of trying to get off the sinking ship. Others, however, continued to struggle until they could struggle no more. As the *Gustloff* plunged downwards large numbers of people could still be seen clinging desperately to the stern railings. The screams were awful and the occasional cries and shouts continued to reverberate from various corners of the sea for a good half hour or so after the ship foundered. Then all became silent. From start to finish the sinking had taken about seventy minutes.

Those who survived were mainly picked up by the German torpedo boat *T36*, commanded by Lieutenant Hering, and the torpedo boat *Löwe*, still faithfully in attendance. The *T36*, together with the German heavy cruiser *Admiral Hipper*, had both left East Prussian ports around the same time as the *Gustloff*. The *T36* arrived on the scene just as the *Gustloff* was finally going down. The *Hipper*, already full of refugees, and itself highly vulnerable because of its slow speed, arrived some time later and did not stop. Other ships in the area, however, that had picked up on the *Gustloff*'s desperate radio messages, also came to the rescue. The *Gotenland* and the *Gottingen*, the *M387* and the *M375*, the *TF19* and the *T52* all picked up survivors clinging to rafts, lifeboats or miscellaneous debris. The most extraordinary survivor was probably a small baby boy discovered still alive on a raft, some twelve hours after the sinking, huddled beneath a pile of corpses. All the other occupants were already dead. He was heard crying by Petty Officer Fisch of despatch boat *VP1703*. No one knew his identity, no parents came forward and so Petty Officer Fisch later adopted his near miraculous find. It is a small but uplifting incident in a story that is otherwise almost unremittingly gloomy. Strangely babies were something of a theme of the *Gustloff* sinking. Three of the young women who made it on to the *T36* gave birth during the remaining hours of darkness. It must have been a fairly traumatic entry into the world and further complicates the issue of exactly how many were rescued.

As always with calamities of this magnitude there are many conflicting versions of what actually happened. Lieutenant Hering of the *T36* was convinced that he detected the presence of a submarine and that two further torpedoes were fired at his ship while he was carrying out the rescue operation. It was this attack that prompted the *T36*'s immediate departure from the sinking area. Marinesko is adamant that no further torpedoes were fired and no other Russian submarine is listed as having been in the area at the time. It is one of those discrepancies that is unlikely to be resolved. The *T36* was anyway by this stage full to overflowing. A total of 550 survivors had been picked up. The *T36* headed for Sassnitz in modern day Mecklenburg, East Germany, where the rescued were transferred onto the Danish hospital ship *Prinz Olaf*.

The torpedo boat *T36* in Gothenhafen shortly before the evacuation.

It is not altogether surprising that since the *Gustloff* sinking certain legends have become attached to its final voyage and that several of them should have to do with treasure. Today there are many who believe that the wreck of the *Gustloff* contains a fabulous hoard of priceless looted Nazi artworks. The idea of treasure frequently becomes attached to famous shipwrecks. The *Titanic*, the *Lusitania* and the *Andrea Doria* are all cases in point. There is another strong reason, however, for thinking the *Gustloff* may contain valuables. It was one of the last ships to leave port in the face of a rapidly advancing enemy army. It stands to reason then, or so the argument goes, that those who were fleeing would cram any easily transportable high worth items into the ship's strong room. Similar rumours are attached to those British ships that were bombed and sank shortly after leaving Singapore just days before it fell to the Japanese and also those Japanese ships that met a similar fate having departed the Philippines as the Americans advanced.

The particular treasure story associated with the *Gustloff* is that it was carrying Catherine the Great's famous jewelled amber room when it disappeared beneath the icy waves of the Baltic. Further, as with all the best treasure stories, there is a curse attached to it. All those that seek to rediscover it are rumoured to die a premature and violent death. The history of the amber room is certainly fascinating. In 1716 Frederick, King of Prussia, presented Peter the Great, Tsar of all the Russias, with a room constructed entirely from amber. The total quantity of amber used weighed six tons. It was a copy of a similar room that Frederick already possessed himself. The present was both a masterpiece of Baroque art and a flamboyant gesture of friendship between the two enlightened European rulers. The beautifully rich-coloured amber had been originally mined by Prussian labourers in an area around the bleak town of Yantarny on the edge of the Baltic Sea, close by Koenigsberg, later named Kaliningrad by the Russians, and now part of the Russian Federation. Yantarny is one of those places that has never quite known whether it was German or Russian. It was, however, and still is, peculiarly rich in amber, producing fossils of the very highest quality. Peter the Great installed the room in his Winter Palace in St Petersburg where it was much admired by visiting dignitaries.

When Catherine, the great art connoisseur and collector, came to the Russian throne she had the room moved from St Petersburg to her summer residence at Tsarskoye Selo, now called Pushkin. She also set about improving and embellishing it. The new room was formed from 129 separate panels. The panels were studded with precious stones and set into the design were four Florentine mosaics constructed from marble and onyx. Dazzling mirrors with elaborately gilded carved wood frames created an illusion of infinite perspectives; 565 flickering candles completed the magical effect. Being inside Catherine's remodelled amber room must have been a little like being inside a jewelled casket, very impressive but perhaps not for the claustrophobic.

In 1941 Hitler's troops besieged St Petersburg, which by then had become Leningrad. The palace at Tsarskoye was also taken over. Many Russian artworks had already been evacuated eastwards but the amber room was too bulky to transport with ease and so the hastily dismantled panels had been hidden. The Germans did not take long to discover their whereabouts. Hitler gave orders for the panels to be packed up, transported to Koenigsberg and reassembled in the castle there. They had only been in their new home about three years when the fortunes of war were reversed. The Russian army was advancing and it was now the Germans' turn to dismantle the panels and pack them up. They were taken to the basement of the castle apparently ready for shipment and it is at that point that the trail goes cold. According to one theory they perished when the castle was bombed and burnt down. Another version has them being taken to an old abandoned salt mine near Göttingen, which has since become flooded. A third possibility, and the one most repeatedly advocated, although no positive proof has ever come to light concerning their loading, is that the panels were on board the *Wilhelm Gustloff*. The timing was certainly right but the

evidence has so far remained largely circumstantial. The packing of the panels is recorded as having been completed by 15 January. Dr Alfred Rohde who was responsible for the evacuation of the panels left a brief note stating that they would be sent to Wechselburg, near Rochlitz in Saxony. He did not state the mode of transportation.

Amazingly, in the year 2000, one of the four marble and onyx panels, especially constructed for Catherine, did turn up. It was discovered by German police specialising in the recovery of stolen art. They had been tipped off that a lawyer in Potsdam was trying to sell a rare war trophy for $2.5 million. It turned out that the lawyer was acting on behalf of a client who was the

A pre-war Soviet photograph of the Amber Room in all its glory.

son of one of the German officers who had originally escorted the shipment of the amber room from Tsarskoye to Koenigsberg.

In April 2001 the Germans handed the panel back to Vladimir Putin in a ceremony that strangely completes the circle begun by Frederick's gift of the amber room to Peter the Great some 300 years previously. The authenticity of the panel has been confirmed by Ivan Sautov director of the St Petersburg Palace Museum. Unfortunately, however, it provides no clue as to the present whereabouts of the remainder of the amber room. Photographs of the room in its Koenigsberg Castle incarnation reveal that it already had one panel missing when it was reconstructed there in 1942. How the German officer concerned came by his loot is not known exactly, but it was clearly acquired before the panels were installed in the castle. The Russians, however, regard it as an omen

Artist's impression of the wreck as it first settled on the bottom, by Martin Cahill.

that the rest of the fabled room may yet be discovered.

The possibility of excavating the *Wilhelm Gustloff* to determine once and for all whether the amber room is contained within its holds has often been mooted. The wreck lies in relatively shallow water, has already been found, and would technically be relatively easy to penetrate. However, there is a number of factors that militate against any such operation ever taking place, even disregarding the legendary curse. First, the *Gustloff* is regarded by many as being a permanent war grave and as it involved such a large loss of life this has to be a strong argument against any interference. Second, the *Gustloff* is an enormous ship and to search it exhaustively would take a huge expenditure of time and money, with always the strong possibility that the panels were never loaded in the first place. Even if the amber room was put on the *Gustloff*, it is perhaps best that it should remain on the seabed, a potent symbol both of the close friendship and the bitter enmity that has existed between two great northern nations, Germany and Russia.

Gazetteer

Active, 1803

Mentioned in *Lloyds List* as being lost on Nailand Rock, near Margate, nine of the crew drowning, on 10 January 1803. The *Active*, Captain Hornby, was a British West Indiaman, 350 tons gross burthen, laden with sugar and other Caribbean produce. It was at anchor in Margate Roads when it was driven ashore during a storm. Ten out of the nineteen people on board were saved. Later commentators have suggested that the *Active* had large quantities of gold on board when it wrecked, one mentioning a value of £200,000, but such a large quantity seems unlikely and none of the accounts contemporary with the sinking mention gold.

Admiral Gardner, 1809

The *Admiral Gardner* was an East India Company ship of 813 tons burthen, built at Blackwall and captained by William Eastfield. It was lost on the night of 24 January 1809. It was outward bound at the time of its wrecking, en route to Madras with a cargo of copper and iron ingots and a large quantity of copper

coin, the latter amounting to fifty-four tons in total. This coin had been especially minted by the East India Company for the Indian market. Towards evening on 24 January a strong gale got up from the south-west and the *Admiral Gardner* was anchored in fourteen fathoms of water just to the west of the South Foreland. During the night the anchors began to drag and the captain ordered the sheet anchor to be cut to try to save the ship. However, it was already too late and the *Admiral Gardner* very shortly was driven on to the South Sand Heads of the Goodwins. Boats came out and took all the crew off except one man who drowned. By this time the ship was already full of water to the level of the upper deck.

There was some salvage of the copper coin immediately after the loss of the ship by John and Edward Iggullen but a lot of coin was left behind. In 1979 dredgers brought up a quantity of copper cash and in 1984 the wreck was relocated by Richard Larn, Tom Henderson and others. More coin was recovered and the wreck was designated a historic wreck site. Since its rediscovery the wreck has been a source of much controversy concerning the methods used by some of the salvors and even whether or not it actually lies within territorial waters. The listed position is 51° 12′ 00″ N, 01° 30′ 56″ E.

Agatha, 1808

The *Agatha* was a German ship, based at the port of Lübeck. On 2 April 1808 it sailed from Libau in Prussia (modern Liepāja in Latvia) having been specially chartered by Lord Royston and his entourage, which included Colonel Pollen, to take them to Sweden. The port was surrounded by loose ice but the ship was able to sail through it without difficulty. Two days later, when they were in sight of the island of Öland, a strong gale began to blow. By 6 April the ship was leaking badly and, with the adverse weather continuing, it became clear that they would need to put into a nearby port as soon as possible. Eventually Memel was decided upon. There was some dispute between the mate and the captain when it came to sailing over Memel bar with the result that the ship was wrecked on the South Sand. Eventually boats from Memel rescued some of the passengers on board but not before both Colonel Pollen and Lord Royston had been washed overboard and drowned. Considerable property was lost with the ship.

Akerendam, 1725

The *Akerendam* was a Dutch VOC ship, Captain Nicolas de Roy, 850 tons burthen. It left Texel, Holland, carrying the usual outward-bound cargo of specie, in the company of the *Kockenge* and the *Gaasperendam*, on 19 January 1725. It was subsequently lost in a bay south-east of Kvalneset on the north coast of the island of Runde, Norway, on 8 March 1725. It was rediscovered in 1972 by amateur divers who recovered approximately 5,400 gold coins and 33,300 silver coins. Further recoveries were made the following year by archaeologists investigating the site. In total 57,000 coins were recovered, 6,625 of them gold. Over 400 different types of coin were discovered, including fifteen not previously catalogued.

Akersloot, 1640

The *Akersloot* was a Dutch VOC ship, 360 tons burthen, lost in the roads of Texel. It appears, however, to have been refloated as it is recorded as arriving in Batavia on 27 July 1640.

Albion, 1765

The English East India Company ship *Albion*, Captain Larkins, was en route from London to Madras when it drove on to the sands off the North Foreland on 15 January 1765. According to the *British Chronicle* all the money was saved almost immediately except for one chest. The total number of chests on board was sixty-three. The ship was also carrying a quantity of copper, lead and tin as well as the usual East India shipment of woollens, particularly broadcloths. The non-ferrous metals stowed in the lower holds of the ship proved much more difficult to salvage. As well as Company cargo there was also a lot of private cargo on board, in particular a number of chests of very valuable coral. Eight chests of coral were salvaged. There was a great problem with looting at the site of the wreck and the East India Company sent six sloops for the wreck's protection. Even this, however, did not seem to be sufficient to stop the pillaging for towards the end of March 1765 an Admiralty cutter was detailed to protect those working on the wreck. There is no evidence that the wreck has been rediscovered in recent times.

Alkmaar, 1625

The *Alkmaar* was a Dutch VOC ship, 800 tons burthen, lost on a sandbank outside the Texel on 6 January 1625. Its outward-bound cargo included specie.

Alma, 1856

The *Alma*, 75 tons, owned by Lord Alfred Paget, was his luxury yacht at a time when yachting had become very much the vogue for wealthy Victorian gentlemen. On the evening of Friday, 6 June, shortly before midnight, the yacht was in collision with the Belgian mail-packet called the *Diamond* en route to Ostend. It sank in the space of seven minutes. At the time the yacht was three or four miles off the South Foreland. Lord Paget and his crew were able to escape in the yacht's gig but a number of valuables went down with the vessel.

Almond River Loss, Roman

A superb Roman-period sculpture of a lioness was fished out of the River Almond to the west of Edinburgh in 1997, having been discovered by the local ferryman. The lioness is sculpted in the act of eating the head of a bearded man and would have been part of the funeral statuary of an important Roman officer or dignitary. It could have ended up in the river for a number of reasons other than shipwreck, such as being dropped during offloading or jettisoned by locals when the Romans left the area, but it could also lead the way to further finds. The lioness is in the possession of the National Museum of Scotland.

Amstelland, 1665

The *Amstelland* was a Dutch VOC ship wrecked at Terschelling on the coast of Holland on 25 October 1665. It was 142 feet long, 700 tons burthen, and belonged to the Amsterdam Chamber. The captain was Theunis Gijsbertsl. The cargo was largely salvaged at the time of loss.

Amsterdam, 1742

The *Amsterdam* was a Dutch VOC ship of 850 tons burthen, lost in the Shetlands during May 1742 when on a homeward voyage from Batavia with a cargo that included porcelain.

Amstelland, 1751

The *Amstelland* was a Dutch VOC ship, 850 tons burthen, lost on 18 September 1751 on the island of Sylt off the Danish Coast. It was outward bound with a cargo that included specie.

Andaman, 1953

The *Andaman* was a Swedish steel-constructed ship, gross tonnage 4,765 tons, owned by Svenska Ostasiatiska Kompaniet. On the night of 24 May1953, while en route from Göteborg to Calcutta with a general cargo, it collided in thick fog with MV *Fortune*. The *Andaman* sank soon afterwards in position 51°

08´ 21″ N, 01° 33´ 57″ E, approximately three miles south of the South Goodwin lightship. The crew were rescued by ss *Arthur Wright*. One box of gold and one bar of silver were salvaged at the time of loss. Further silver ingots remain unrecovered. The vessel lies at a depth of 164 feet. The bronze propeller weighing ten tons was salvaged in 1970 by Folkestone divers.

Anjelier, 1662
The *Anjelier* was a Dutch VOC ship, 440 tons burthen, wrecked on a homeward voyage at Terschelling on the Dutch coast.

Anna Catharina, 1735
The *Anna Catharina* was a Dutch VOC ship, belonging to the Zeeland Chamber, Captain Jacob de Prince. It was lost while in company with the *Vliegend Hert* on 3 February 1735. See chapter 9 on the *Vliegend Hert* for further details.

Anna Maria, 1764
The Dutch ship *Anna Maria*, Captain John Verboom, belonging to Rotterdam, en route from Hamburg to Bordeaux, struck on Haisborough Sand off Norfolk, came off and sank in deep water. The cargo included iron, copper, tin, lead, scythes and a bale of morocco leather, all of which was lost. The crew were saved in the boats.

Anne Lyon, 1623
The *Anne Lyon* was returning from a successful trading voyage in the West Indies with a rich cargo of Brazil wood, sugar, cinnamon and a large quantity of coin when it was wrecked near Sandwich on the east coast of Kent on 28 November 1623. The merchants Derrick Hoston, Abraham Ruytinck, Peter Mace, Samuel Vischer and Robert de la Bar all had an interest in the cargo. Money to the value of £8,000 to £9,000 was salvaged. There appears to have been some suggestion of potential corruption, instigated by Sir Henry Mainwaring, in order to defraud the merchants of their salvaged treasure.

Antiope, 1941
The *Antiope* was a British steel screwship built in 1930 by Napier & Miller of Glasgow, gross tonnage 4,545 tons, and owned by the New Egypt and Levant Shipping Company. It was bombed on 27 October 1941 when off the Norfolk coast while en route from London to New York. It sank at 53° 13´ N, 01° 08´ E. At the time of loss it was carrying a general cargo which included a large quantity of china, antique furniture, silverware, oil paintings, mother-of-pearl shells and glazed earthenware tiles.

Apollo, 1809
The sailing brig *Apollo*, Captain Riddall, was en route from London to Curaçao in the West Indies, when it was wrecked on the Goodwin Sands on 18 January

1809, just a week before the *Admiral Gardner* and the *Britannia* also came to grief in the same area. It is possible, though not certain, that the *Apollo* had a quantity of coin on board. A vessel which is thought to have been the *Apollo* was recently discovered by local divers upside down in twenty-two feet of water about half a mile distant from the site of the *Admiral Gardner*.

Ark Noah, 1621
This unusually-named ship of Hamburg, returning possibly from the Far East or the West Indies but more probably from Lisbon or Cadiz, with a cargo of cinnamon, pepper, sugar and a large quantity of specie was wrecked on the Goodwin Sands around 12 March 1621. £4,000 of specie was saved at the time of loss.

Baggage Ship, 1642
In February of 1642 hasty preparations were being made for the transportation of Queen Henrietta, wife to Charles I, and their daughter, Princess Mary, to Holland. Law and order in England was already breaking down in civil war. Charles had lost control of the best part of the navy, Admiral Pennington being one of the few officers that was still loyal to him. It was thought desirable for the Queen and her daughter to be removed from the country, not just for understandable reasons of security, but also because Princess Mary was betrothed to the Prince of Orange, and it was necessary that she should be presented at the Dutch court in the Hague.

Queen Henrietta's retinue progressed from Greenwich to Rochester, to Canterbury and finally to Dover. Deal had originally been suggested as the port of embarkation, but for some unexplained reason Dover was finally preferred. The destination was to be either Helvoet Sluys, Rotterdam or Flushing depending on the winds. The Queen was insisting on Helvoet but pilots were taken on board for all eventualities. The Queen and the Princess were to travel on the *Lion,* where Pennington was in charge. The Duchess of Richmond was to be accommodated on the *Entrance*, the *Mary Rose* was reserved for the Earl Marshal, Earl of Arundel, the Queen's servants were to go on the *Providence*, and Princess Mary's servants on the *Greyhound*. Accommodation also had to be found for six coaches and 120 horses. The *Tenth Whelp* was also to be part of this small fleet.

The crossing proved very rough and, just as they were approaching Helvoet, one of the baggage ships sprang a leak and sank before the Queen's eyes. On board was a considerable quantity of money as well as other valuables such as the silver chalices used by the Queen. The Duchess of Richmond, together with Lady Denbigh, Lady Roxburgh and Lady Kinalmeaky lost all their clothes. Lord Goring and Sir Thomas Hopton lost their money as well as their clothes. Elizabeth, Queen of Bohemia, who was at the Hague at the time of this misfortune, remarked in her usual laconic style in a letter to Sir Thomas Roe, 'all goes ill enough'. She clearly saw in the shipwreck just one more example of the general disintegration of the English state.

Bantam, 1697

The *Bantam* was a Dutch VOC ship lost at Vlissingen, Scheldemond, on the Dutch coast in December 1697, on the homeward journey from Batavia. The ship belonged to the Amsterdam Chamber and its captain was Pieter de Rande.

Barneveld, 1724

The *Barneveld* was a Dutch VOC ship, 1,008 tons burthen, Captain Gideon Kuiper, which was lost on 10 February 1724 between Grevelingen and Dunkirk. At the time it was outward bound to Batavia with specie.

Batavier V, 1916

The *Batavier V* was a Dutch steel screw steamship, 1,569 gross tons, built by Gourlay Bros & Co., Dundee, and owned by Wm H. Muller & Co. It was on a voyage from London to Rotterdam with a general cargo of rice, coffee, and 7,000 bales of cloth when it hit a magnetic mine on 16 May 1916 and sank shortly afterwards. It sank in a position half-a-mile east magnetic of the north buoy of the Inner Gabbard sandbank. As well as the general cargo, it was also carrying fourteen cases of gold valued at £90,000. The entirety of the gold was salvaged between 26 May and 1 June and the British Admiralty gave an award for the efficiency with which the operation was carried out to all those involved.

Bethlehem, 1741

The *Bethlehem* was a Dutch VOC ship, Captain Moens, lost on sandbanks off Odtens on 29 December 1741 while outward bound to Batavia with a cargo that included specie.

Blessing, 1633

The *Blessing* was a ferry boat carrying valuables belonging to King Charles I. See chapter 4 for further details.

Bona Confidentia, 1556

The Russian ship *Bona Confidentia* was part of the embassy to England and Spain from the Russian Tsar Ivan Vasilivich, Emperor of all the Russias. The cargo included presents and gifts. It was lost at Drontheim (Trondheim) in Norway, perishing on a rock according to Hakluyt.

Bonhomme Richard, 1779

The *Bonhomme Richard* was the American warship captained by Paul Jones. See chapter 11 for further details.

Brederode, 1658

The Dutch frigate *Brederode*, with bronze cannon and other artefacts, was lost near Helsingør, Denmark. It was first salvaged in 1909 and then again in 1950 and 1960. Artefacts from it can be seen in the Historisch Scheepvaart Museum, Amsterdam, Holland, and the Tøjhus Museum, Copenhagen, Denmark.

Bremen, 1916

The *Bremen* was one of eight unarmed merchant submarines built by the Germans to try to solve the problems brought about by the allied economic blockade. Its pressure hull was constructed by the Flensburger Schiffbau AG. It was sixty-five metres long with a gross registered tonnage of approximately 791 tons. The *Bremen* sailed from Kiel some time in late August 1916 en route to Norfolk, Virginia, USA. It was due to rendezvous with the *U53* off Newfoundland but it never arrived. The *Bremen* was never heard from again. At the time of its disappearance it was thought to be carrying a cargo of precious stones in the same manner that its sister vessel, the *Deutschland*, had transported precious stones on a previous voyage to Baltimore in June 1916. The *New York Times* reported in November 1916 that in view of the fate of the *Bremen* it was unlikely that bankers would risk the shipment of securities on such vessels in the future. The British 10th Cruiser Squadron was ordered to try to intercept the *Bremen* on its passage across the Atlantic and both the *Alsatian* and the *Mantua* reported ramming a heavy submerged object while patrolling south of Iceland. The British transport *Huntspill* reported sighting a submarine some 300 miles south of Iceland on 3 September steering south-west. Other theories claim that the *Bremen* was in fact lost in the North Sea.

Breslau, 1783

Sailing under a neutral flag the *Breslau* foundered close to Calais when returning from a voyage to the Far East. The cargo included tin and porcelain.

Britannia, 1809

The *Britannia*, East Indiaman, 1,200 tons burthen, en route from London to Madras, Captain Jonathan Birch, was wrecked on the South Goodwin Sands on the same day that the *Admiral Gardner* was also lost there. It was driven on to the sands during a south-westerly gale. It was carrying the usual cargo of woollen stuffs, mainly broadcloths, together with a quantity of lead ingots and copper coin. The *Britannia* was salvaged at the time of loss by John and Edward Iggullen and then rediscovered in 1979. As with the *Admiral Gardner* wreck it has subsequently been the cause of much controversy and dispute between underwater archaeologists and commercial divers.

Buitenzorg, 1759

The *Buitenzorg* was a Dutch VOC ship, 880 tons burthen, Captain Coenraad Dirk Volk, which was lost off Texel on 24 November 1759 when homeward bound from the Far East.

Burnholm, 1850

The Spanish ship *Burnholm* was lost off Heligoland in approximate position 54° 11′ N, 7° 53′ E. The gold on board was saved.

Buuren, 1729

The *Buuren* was a Dutch VOC ship which foundered on its departure in a gale of wind while in the Nooderhaaks near Texel. English divers recovered some of the cannon on board but the ship and its cargo were counted as lost.

Buza, c. 1300

The Norwegian ship *Buza* sank off the Faroes with the loss of fifty men and a valuable cargo.

Carlisle, 1696

British warship *Carlisle* sank with £150,000 of bullion and pieces-of-eight. See chapter 8 for further details.

Caroline, 1773

The American barque *Caroline* from Boston was wrecked on rocks at Naversgill on the western side of Fair Isle in the Shetlands in October 1773. The cargo was reported to include oak planks and logs, gold dust and silks. There are many local legends associating the wreck with a loss of gold including one which suggests a chest of gold floated from the wreck and went down at Hyuknigeo. If true it is the only known example of a chest of gold floating.

Cecilia, Ship of, 1248

Cecilia, daughter of King Hakon was returning home to Bergen after marrying King Harald in the Hebrides when her ship was lost in a roost (tidal current) south of the Shetlands. There were a large number of important dignitaries on board and there would have been many valuable artefacts and presents. The

wreckage was subsequently washed up on the shores of Shetland

City Of Birmingham, 1940

The *City of Birmingham* was a steel screw steamship that was sunk by mine while on a voyage from Beira to Hull. It carried 2,500 tons of copper most of which was salvaged by Sorima in the 1940s. It also carried a quantity of platinum. The wreck lies five-and-a-half miles, at 115 degrees, from Spurn Point.

Cimbria, 1883

The *Cimbria* was a German-flag transatlantic liner owned by the Hamburg-Amerika Line, 3,037 tons gross burthen, 329 feet long, and built by Caird & Co. in 1867. On the morning of 19 January 1883, in thick fog, it was in collision with the *Sultan* off Borkum Island. The *Sultan*'s bows were stoved in and the ship's captain, thinking that his ship was the more seriously damaged, did not stop to lend any assistance to the *Cimbria*. The *Cimbria*, however, was rapidly sinking and of the 402 passengers on board, most of them emigrants, only sixty-five were saved. Nearly all the women and children were drowned. At the time of loss the cargo on the *Cimbria* was valued at £100,000. A quantity of the porcelain on board, and other interesting artefacts, have recently been recovered by a German salvage company called Sea Explorer AG.

Claudia, 1809

The English cutter *Claudia*, 110 tons burthen, ten guns, was lost on rocks off the Naze of Norway on 20 January 1809. The commander of the *Claudia* at the time was Lieutenant Anthony Lord. The survivors remained on the rock for about fifteen hours. Lord described it as a small rock forty feet long and twenty feet wide. Towards evening boats came off from the shore but were unable to approach nearer than forty yards because of the strength of the surf. Worried that the boats would return without effecting contact Lord swam through the surf to one of the boats, after which they got a line to the shore and the rest of the men were hauled from the rock by that means. At his court martial Lord blamed the loss on the strong currents and the ice in the vicinity, and also the poor visibility because of the snow. Fourteen of the crew either drowned or perished with cold. The survivors were made prisoners of war. Previous to wrecking, the *Claudia* had captured a Danish privateer and it is probably for this reason that the wreck has been associated with the presence of gold coin. Eight of the cannon were salvaged.

Comet, 1827

The *Comet*, a Scottish packet ship belonging to the London & Edinburgh Shipping Company, struck a sunken wreck when sailing through the Haisborough Gat and sank in deep water in a little more than ten minutes. It was carrying a valuable cargo, all of which was lost.

Concordia, 1786
The *Concordia* was a large Danish East Indiaman, 900 tons burthen, Captain Kolle. It was outward bound from Denmark to Tranquebar, on the south-east coast of India, and centre of Denmark's Far Eastern trading empire. Among the passengers on board was the Governor of Tranquebar. The ship struck on a ridge of rocks at Helleness Point on the east side of the parish of Cunningsburgh in the Shetlands. Thirty-eight of those on board were immediately drowned including the governor, the captain and two women. Another man and a woman, inhabitants of Cunningsburgh, were also drowned while attempting to salvage parts of the wreck. A large amount of money and merchants' goods were lost with the ship. Some timbers from the *Concordia* were later sold at auction on the Shetlands.

Cornelia Petronella, 1783
The *Cornelia Petronella* was a Dutch sailing ship, Captain Meyndert, en route from London to Amsterdam when it was lost on the Gunfleet Sands in November 1783. A number of fishing smacks assisted in the salvage and eight cases of silver together with other goods were sent to Gravesend. The total volume of silver originally on board is not stated.

Curaçao, 1729
The *Curaçao* was a Dutch warship, 145 feet long, lost on the east coast of the Isle of Unst close to a rock called Ship Stack. It was built in Amsterdam in 1704 and carried forty-four guns. It was wrecked on 31 May 1729 during conditions of poor visibility. Most of the crew survived. It was relocated by Robert Stenuit in 1972 and a number of artefacts were recovered including silver spoons, ceramics, brass weights and ordnance. Some of the artefacts can be seen in the Shetlands County Museum, Lerwick.

Dannebroge, 1710
The *Dannebroge* was a Danish warship, Admiral Ivor Huitfeldt in command, and a crew of 550 men. It was fitted out with seventy-eight bronze cannon. On 4 October 1710 it sank during a battle with the Swedish navy in Køge Bay. All except nine of those on board were lost. Before sinking the *Dannebroge* had put up stout resistance but a fire broke out on the quarterdeck

and soon afterwards all three masts went by the board. The fire then reached the powder room and two massive explosions sank the ship. Some of the cannon were salvaged between 1711 and 1714 and further cannon were brought up between 1873 and 1875. The *Dannebroge* was rumoured to have on board 160,000 silver rigsdaler. During recent archaeological excavations in 1985, 500 silver coins were recovered together with the remains of the leather bags the money was stored in. Numerous other artefacts have been conserved in the Orlogsmuseum, Copenhagen.

Danish Ship, 1685
An unnamed Danish ship, outward bound from Copenhagen to Guinea with specie, lost near Göteborg, Sweden.

Danish Ship, 1760
A Danish West Indiaman, Captain Nils Groet, coming from St Thomas's and heading for Copenhagen, carrying a valuable cargo including specie, was lost near Bergen in Norway. All the crew were drowned.

Delft, 1797
A Dutch warship, the *Delft* of sixty-four guns sank after the battle of Camperdown on 11 October 1797 while in the tow of HMS *Veteran*. A valuable cargo was reported as having been lost and 200 men were drowned.

Delight, 1826
The *Delight*, Captain J. Smith, was a sailing smack owned by the Leith Shipping Company and was used regularly for passengers and cargo between London and Scotland. On 27 February 1826, while passing early in the morning through the Haisborough Gat, the ship apparently struck a sunken wreck and, making water, it beached on Haisborough Sand, came off and sank off Winterton. First reports claimed that there were 16,000 gold sovereigns on board, equivalent to a loss of £40,000, but this estimate was later revised downwards. The *Morning Chronicle* of 8 March stated, 'It was at first reported that specie to the amount of £40,000 was on board, but we now learn that the actual quantity of specie on board is only a tenth part of that amount and consisted of £3,000 in silver destined for the Bank of Scotland.' Messrs Bell and Deane attempted to salvage the wreck. The results of their operation are unclear.

Deutschland, 1875
The German liner *Deutschland* was lost off the Kent coast. See chapter 14 for further details.

Diamant, 1652
The *Diamant* was a Dutch VOC ship, belonging to the Amsterdam Chamber, 1,100 tons burthen, lost at Schouwen, Holland. Most of the cargo was salvaged at the time of loss.

Dolphin, 1747

An English East Indiaman, the *Dolphin*, Captain George Newton, was en route from London to Bombay carrying forty chests of silver specie as well as lead ingots. Its gross tonnage was 370 tons and it was equipped with twenty guns. It was never heard of again after leaving London but there have been suggestions that it was lost on the Goodwin Sands.

Dover, 1688

The *Dover* packet was wrecked near Calais with a quantity of gold on board in June 1688.

Downs Wreck, 1532

According to an entry in the Calendar of State Papers 'a treasure wreck' was lost in the Downs in the year 1532 but no name or details are provided.

Drakkar, 851

The *Drakkar* was a Viking longship lost in the River Thames.

Drottningen af Swerige, 1745

The *Drottningen af Swerige* (The Queen of Sweden), Captain Carl Treutiger, burthen 950 tons, was a Swedish East Indiaman equipped with thirty cannon, mainly iron. It was sailing from Göteborg to Canton in China, via Cadiz, and was in company with another Swedish East Indiaman called the *Stockholm*. It departed from Sweden on 9 January and on 12 January it ran into a fierce snowstorm. While making for Lerwick Harbour it struck a rock at the entrance to Bressay Sound and soon after sank. All those on board survived. There was extensive salvage at the time of loss mainly of the lead ingots that were carried. The *Drottningen* was not due to take on the bulk of its coin cargo until it reached Cadiz. It was rediscovered in 1979 by Jean Claude Joffre and more lead ingots were recovered together with wine bottles, pewter tableware, ship's pottery and small quantities of coin.

Drottningen, 1803

The *Drottningen* was a Swedish East Indiaman lost on the coast of Norway.

Duifje, 1730

The *Duifje* was a Dutch VOC ship belonging to the Amsterdam Chamber that was lost off the Texel while en route from Holland to China.

Dunbar Castle, 1940

The *Dunbar Castle*, Captain Causton, was built by Harland & Wolff in 1930, had a gross tonnage of 10,002 tons and was owned by the Union Castle Mail Steam Ship company. On 9 January 1940, en route from London to Beira, and sailing in convoy, it struck a mine two miles north-east of the North Goodwins. There were 150 crew and forty-eight passengers on board at the time. The vessel sank within thirty minutes. Nine people were killed including the captain. The remainder were rescued by the minesweeper HMS *Calvi* and a local coastal motor barge. The *Dunbar Castle* was carrying a general cargo including gin, spoons and a quantity of jewellery.

Dunwich Bank Wreck, c. 1596

See chapter 3 for further details.

Dutch Warship, 1639

An unnamed Dutch warship, Captain Soetendael, equipped with bronze cannon, was sunk by two Dunkirk frigates in an engagement during June 1639. It sank outside the Steebancq, north-west of the Walcheren. Half of the topmast was visible from the Walcheren.

Dutch Warship, 1652

A Dutch warship, part of Cornelius van Tromp's fleet, probably equipped with some bronze cannon, sank off the south end of Burra Island in the Orkneys in the summer of 1652.

Dutch Warship, 1683

A Dutch warship with Comte Styrum on board foundered in the North Sea while en route to Göteborg in Sweden. Valuables went down with the ship.

Eagle, 1703

The *Eagle* was a packet ship which, while en route to Holland during October 1703, was reported as foundering with a great quantity of guineas on board. All the crew and passengers, including an Italian count, were drowned. Other reports state that the *Eagle* did not sink but was captured by French privateers and taken into Ostend.

Earl of Hakon, Ship of, 1029

A Viking ship carrying the Earl of Hakon was lost in the Pentland Firth during a storm. All those on board at the time were drowned. The Earl was returning home after conducting negotiations with King Canute.

Earl of Holderness, 1764

This English East Indiaman of 499 tons and thirty guns, Captain Robert Brooke, was en route to Bencoolen (Bengkulu, Sumatra) and China when, on 11 January 1764, it struck the sands known as the Sandwich Flatts and was lost. Salvage work was carried out by a Captain Roxby using the *Robert & James*. The total value of the cargo carried was £36,929 including specie.

Edward Bonaventure, 1556

The *Edward Bonaventure*, an English ship, master John Buckland and grand pilot, Richard Chancelor, was wrecked while en route from Russia to London with a Russian embassy on board as well as the goods of a number of merchants. Jewels, rich clothes, presents, gold, silver and costly furs were all lost with the ship. It went ashore at Pettislego (Pitsligo) near Fraserburgh in eastern Scotland on 10 November 1556 during a storm. The ambassador survived the wrecking but the pilot, seven other Russians and a number of the crew were drowned. According to Hakluyt there was much embezzlement of the valuable cargo by local plunderers, 'whole masse and bodie of the goods laden in her was by the rude and ravenous people of the country thereunto adjoining, rifled, spoiled and carried away.' Queen Mary sent a special commission to Scotland to try to reclaim some of the pilfered goods but they only managed to obtain 'small trifling things of no value.' One of the items that went astray was 'a large and fair white Jerfawcon for the wilde Swanne, Crane, Goose, and other great Fowles, together with a drumme of silver, the hoopes gilt, used for a lure to call the sayd Hawke.'

Eendracht, 1665

The *Eendracht* was the flagship of the Dutch fleet at the battle of Lowestoft, 3 June 1665, under the command of Admiral Opdam, also known as Wassenaar. The ship was equipped with eighty-four bronze cannon and was the pride of the Dutch fleet. Although called the battle of Lowestoft the battle ranged widely over the southern part of the North Sea. The two fleets had made contact and begun manoeuvring two days before, in a position approximately forty miles south-east of Lowestoft. At dawn on 3 June Lord Sandwich in the *Royal Prince* recorded his position as '10 or 11 leagues from Southwold, E by S or ESE'. By 8 p.m. in the evening he calculated his position as twenty leagues east of Southwold in a depth of water of seventeen fathoms. The *Eendracht* had blown up between three and four in the afternoon when engaged by the Duke of York in the *Royal Charles* in an area most probably around fifteen leagues east of Southwold. Almost all those on board, including a large number of gentlemen volunteers, lost their lives. The *Oranjie*, a large Dutch East Indiaman converted to a warship, sank shortly after the blowing up of the *Eendracht* in the same general area. The battle was a great victory for the English. After the battle there was some suggestion that the English fleet should be split into various divisions and be despatched to different ports but Lord Sandwich and others were concerned that this might give the impression that English losses were greater than they actually were. In the end it was decided that the victorious fleet should sail as one body into the Downs.

Edenmore, 1909

The *Edenmore*, Captain Jones, was a British steel sailing ship, 1,726 gross tons, built in 1890 by Russell & Co., Glasgow, and owned by the Edenmore Shipping Company. It left Hamburg on 3 October en route to Sydney, Australia, with the usual general cargo of German manufacture at the time, including pianos and chinaware. Early on the morning of 7 October it was grounded on the south-east corner of Papa Stronsay in the Orkneys and was wrecked. Those on board were taken off by fishing boats. There was considerable salvage at the time of loss.

Egmont Wreck, 1733

A ship, associated with Lord Egmont, and carrying gold, was lost outside Harwich while en route to the Netherlands. One chest of gold was later salvaged by a Captain Philips.

Elbe, 1895

The German liner *Elbe*, 4,510 gross tons, was owned by the Norddeutscher Lloyd Company and built by Elder & Co. in 1881. It departed from Bremerhaven at 3 p.m. on 29 January en route to Southampton and then to New York. It was under the command of Captain von Gossel. There were 354 people on board including crew. A strong wind was blowing from the east-south-east but the weather was clear if bitterly cold. At 5.30 the following morning a small steamship called the *Craithie* was observed from the *Elbe* on a collision course. The liner sent up rockets to warn the other ship of its presence. It also had all its lights burning. However, the officers on the *Craithie* did not seem to notice. The *Elbe* was struck to the stern of the engine room on the port side by the bows of the oncoming steamer and sank in the space of twenty minutes. There was pandemonium on board not helped by the fact that the *Elbe*'s electric lights failed. Only one boat was got away from the sinking liner and this was mainly filled with crew members. 334 persons drowned. The *Craithie* continued on its way to Rotterdam apparently unaware of the disaster it had helped cause.

In recent years the wreck of the *Elbe*, situated about forty-seven miles south-west from the Haaks lightship, has been investigated by divers on a number of occasions. Part of the attraction has been the large quantities of porcelain with which the surrounding seabed is scattered. Less well known is the fact that among the passengers were the notorious Guttmann brothers. They were directors of a steam-mill company near Kaschan in Hungary and were fleeing Europe having defrauded the shareholders of some 300,000 florins. They were presumably carrying their ill-gotten gains with them when the *Elbe* sank.

English Ship, c. 1630

An English ship has recently been discovered at Bamble, on the south-west side of Oslo Fjord, carrying pewter and chinaware.

English Ship, 1679
An unnamed English ship was lost in October 1679 coming from Rotterdam in Holland 'laden with wines, brandy and other goods of a very great value besides gold'. It was wrecked near the Shipwash Sand.

Enighed, 1679
The *Enighed* was a Danish warship lost in the Kalmar Sound, Sweden, with valuable artefacts. It was salvaged in the early twentieth century and some of the artefacts are on display in the Naval Museum, Stockholm, Sweden.

Epirus, 1908
The *Epirus* with silver on board was lost in Flushing Roads on 20 January 1908.

Erfprins, 1758
The *Erfprins* was a Dutch VOC ship belonging to the Delft Chamber which was lost on 16 October 1758 near Calais. It was outward bound and its cargo included specie.

Eustace the Monk, Ships of, 1217
The notorious pirate, Eustace the Monk, lost several ships in a battle off the South Foreland, Kent, on 24 August 1217. The ships carried gold, silver, weaponry and silk vestments.

Evstafi, 1780
The *Evstafi* was a Russian warship, Captain Markov, built in 1773 at Archangel, and equipped with thirty-eight guns. It was en route from Archangel to Kronstadt when it struck on Griff Skerry and was wrecked. There were only five survivors. The wreck was extensively salvaged at the time of loss and the local inhabitants still remembered the event some 200 years later, the story having been handed down by oral tradition. The wreck was rediscovered by Robert Stenuit in 1972. Sections of pistols, sword hilts and a variety of coins were recovered.

Félicité, 1761
In January 1761 the 36-gun French war ship, *Félicité*, Captain Donnell, with 200 men on board, ran on shore near the village of Gravensande, three leagues

from the Hague in Holland and close by the Brill. At the time the *Félicité* was being attacked by Captain Elphinstone in HMS *Richmond*. England and France had been at war since 1756 in what was to become known as the Seven Years War. On board the *Félicité* was a cargo of 400 hogsheads of wine, 300 casks of brandy and other provisions, together with a large quantity of specie which according to some reports was ransom money from the *Dorothy and Esther*, a vessel previously captured by the *Félicité*. Other reports described the *Félicité* as an armed merchant ship bound for Martinico (Martinique), in which case the money may have been part of the usual outward-bound cargo. The English took what they could out of the *Félicité* before setting fire to the wreck. Contradictory reports suggest that the ship bilged before most of the cargo could be got out. There appears to have been some local plundering.

Fifa, 1148
The Viking longship *Fifa* lost in the Shetlands. See chapter 2 for further details.

Firth of Forth Wreck, 1589
An unnamed ship, supposedly carrying Anne of Denmark's dowry, was lost in the Firth of Forth in 1589. Anne of Denmark was the betrothed of James VI of Scotland, the future James I of England.

Firth of Tay Wrecks, 1651
There have been a number of reports that Cromwell's army under General Monck, after looting Dundee, and embarking on board ship, lost a number of those ships in the Firth of Tay. *The Times* in August 2002 carried an article which suggested that divers were getting close to rediscovering this treasure. The value put on the treasure in the article was £2.5 billion.

Flemish Bank Wrecks, c. 1696
A report dated August 1696 refers to two French capers fishing goods out of two Dutch East India ships cast away sometime previously on the Flemish Banks.

Flossi, Ship of, c. 1200
According to *Njal's Saga*, the Norwegian seaman Flossi set out from Norway in a ship that was overloaded and when the season was already late for sailing. It is stated that the ship was lost at Rull Rost in Westray Sound in the Orkneys. There were no survivors. The ship carried a valuable cargo including money.

Fluytschip, 1693
An unnamed Dutch fluytschip (flute) was lost near Yarmouth en route from Ostend to Leith with a large quantity of money on board.

Forgyllda Solen, 1673
The *Forgyllda Solen* was a Swedish merchant ship lost

at Tejn on the north coast of the island of Bornholm, Denmark. The cargo included silver coins. It was salvaged in 1969.

Fox, 1745

The *Fox*, Captain Beavor, was a sixth-rate man-of-war, 440 tons and twenty-four guns, built at Rotherhithe in 1740. On 14 November 1745 it was lost during a gale off Dunbar and all those on board, including a large number of Scottish rebel prisoners, were drowned. At the time the *Fox* was reputed to be carrying a large quantity of valuables seized from Scottish landowners. Divers from Dundee University may have discovered the remains of the *Fox* in the early 1980s but the wreck was not fully investigated or identified.

Foxe, 1614

The *Foxe*, thirty-four tons, was lost on the north coast of Kent between Queenborough and the Reculvers in January 1614. The vessel was returning from Flushing and on board was Sir Thomas Roe, one of James I's most important courtiers and diplomats. Valuables were lost with the ship.

Fredensborg, 1768

The *Fredensborg* was a ship of the Danish West India Company wrecked at Arendal in southern Norway with a cargo which included ivory and specie.

French Privateer, 1694

A French privateer struck on the sands close to the river at Berwick and was wrecked with the loss of all those on board except nine. A quantity of specie was lost with the ship.

French Warship, 1708

A French warship sailing from Dunkirk, part of the fleet that sailed with the Pretender to Scotland, was lost on the Nieuwport Sands, Holland. The fleet carried a large quantity of money.

Garland, 1653

A Dutch warship, apparently called the *Garland* (it does not sound very Dutch but a ship of this name was captured from the English in 1652) equipped with fifty

bronze cannon was lost during the battle of Scheveningen, eight leagues west-north-west of the Brill, on 31 July 1653. A letter, dated 1 August 1653, describing the loss was written on board the English naval ship *Society*.

Gelderland, 1607

The *Gelderland* was a Dutch VOC ship, 500 tons burthen, lost en route to the Far East with a cargo that included specie. On 19 July 1607 the *Gelderland* took refuge in the harbour of Vlissingen because of stormy weather.

General Barker, 1781

The *General Barker* was an English East India Company ship which left Madras in India in February 1780 with Sir Thomas Rumbold, Governor of Madras, on board with his wife, family and all their property, together with the usual Indian return cargo consisting largely of cottons. In April they put into St Augustine's Bay on the west coast of Madagascar and stayed there for six weeks. From St Helena they sailed in convoy arriving at Crookhaven in the south of Ireland around Christmas. At Crookhaven Sir Rumbold and his family disembarked but his property remained on the ship.

By 10 February 1781 the *General Barker* had finally arrived in the Downs. On the 12th, while they were still at anchor, the captain having gone on shore for some urgent supplies, a violent gale began to blow from the south-west. A number of the ships that were also at anchor collided in the storm, the *General Barker* coming athwart a 120-ton brig. The latter immediately sank and all on board drowned. Eventually the *General Barker* managed to clear the Downs, but not before striking the Break Sand. Luckily, they managed to wear the ship using a kedge anchor out of a quarterdeck port and came free. Early the following morning, in order to construct a makeshift tiller, they had to clear the great cabin of all of Rumbold's property which had been stowed there. According to contemporary accounts trunks full of valuable plate and money were thrown from the stern-quarter windows. This sounds somewhat exaggerated although the jettisoning of forty cages of valuable oriental birds was more probable. In all it was computed that £10,000 pounds' worth of valuable property went out of the windows. Shortly after 2 a.m. they were able to steer the ship, and between then and around 8.30 a.m. they made two knots an hour, at which time they saw the Kentish Knock Sand on the larboard bow. They tried to veer the ship to avoid it but it was already too late. They struck a second time. They now cut away the main mast but the ship began to make water rapidly and they had to man the pumps. The longboat was launched but immediately sank and the men in it were saved with some difficulty by means of ropes. Meanwhile, to compound their difficulties, the rudder came off. Eventually, at about 3.20 in the afternoon the flood tide lifted them clear of the bank and they came off into seven fathoms and then thirteen and twenty fathoms. In order to clear some space they killed all the animals on board including two Madagascan cows, a fine Arabian horse, a tiger, a hyena and the more usual sheep and goats, heaving their carcasses over the side. They also threw overboard chests, hammocks and bedding. The guns were left in place as too heavy to manoeuvre. At five in the afternoon they saw the buoy of the Long Sand Head. The water was rising at the rate of three feet an hour, they only had the foremast still standing, and their only means of steering the ship was by means of towing a heavy assemblage of wood from the stern. At 9 p.m. they decided they would have to heave the guns over despite the risks involved. By eleven o'clock in the evening they had jettisoned eighteen nine-pounders and two four-pounders keeping the remaining two nine-pounders and four four-pounders to make signals of distress with. At daylight on the 14th they made contact with a Danish ship from Christiansand on route to Ostende which agreed to stand by them after the drawing up of an appropriate salvage contract. However, towards evening the brig became concerned that they were drifting too close to the Flemish shoals and told those on the *General Barker* that unless they could immediately veer their ship they would have to abandon them. The problem was it was impossible to veer the *General Barker* by this stage. There was much imploring by the crew and passengers begging the brig to stay with them as being their only hope of survival but the brig still left them. During the next day they continued to struggle to keep the ship afloat and towards evening they saw lights on the land. On the morning of the 16th they saw the lights very close by and realised that the water was shoaling fast. They jettisoned four more cannon but to no avail. At 10.30 in the morning the ship struck at about two-and-a-half miles distant from the shore. The waves broke over the decks and the ship beat and swung stern towards the coast. A raft was constructed and about twenty men got on to it but most of them were washed off and drowned. Around three in the afternoon they lashed the invalids and old seamen, women and children to the poop, thinking that when the ship broke up the poop might wash safely to the beach. The ship in fact stayed together for another night and on the following day, which was the 17th, Dutch schoots came out and took off a number of those who were still surviving, just as the ship was finally breaking up. The wreck took place opposite Schevelling beach. Those who were rescued were immediately made prisoners of war and were transferred by dung carts to the town of Noordwyck, about six or seven miles distance. Somewhat remarkably only twenty-five of those on board had drowned.

George, 1692
The *George*, a West Indiaman, returning from Jamaica, with a cargo which included gold, sank in a storm near Sandwich at the beginning of January 1692.

Gloucester, 1682
The *Gloucester* was a third-rate English warship, built by Mr Graves at Limehouse, 755 tons burthen and armed with fifty-two cannon, mainly iron. It departed from Margate on 4 May 1682 with James, Duke of York, on board, together with a retinue of dignatories, including John Churchill, the future Duke of Marlborough, the Earl of Roxburgh, the Earl of Perth, the Earl of Middleton, Lord O'Brian, the Laird of Hopton and numerous others. Samuel Pepys, the famous diarist, had also been invited to accompany the Duke but he was travelling on an accompanying ship where, as he said in his correspondence, there was more room. There were seven ships in the fleet in total. The Duke was on his way to Scotland to fetch back to London his pregnant wife, Mary of Modena. On 5 May there was a violent argument between the pilot on board the *Gloucester*, James Aires, and Christopher Gunman, the master of the *Mary* yacht, as to the exact course they should be following to avoid running onto the Yarmouth sandbanks. In the event the Duke of York himself made the critical navigational decision to stand out to sea. The following morning at about 5 a.m., according to Sir John Berry's account (he was the captain of the *Gloucester)* the ship struck upon the west end of the Leman bank and beat along it for a short period, during which time the rudder broke off. It then came off the bank and sank down in deep water with just the top of the main mast showing. The Duke of York got safely off in a boat but nearly 200 people drowned including several of his closest associates. The Duke lost a number of his personal possessions although his strongbox was taken off and safely transhipped to the *Mary* yacht.

The sinking of the *Gloucester* was to become a cause célèbre for the next half-century. Supporters of the Stuart dynasty claimed that James had shown great presence of mind during the sinking and paid much attention to the fact that the sailors had supposedly cheered when he left the ship in safety, even though their own lives were still in great peril, and many of them were shortly to drown. James's enemies on the other hand claimed that it was James fussing about his strongbox that had caused the fatal delay in the launching of the boats and that when he himself went off all he had care of was his priests and his dogs.

Gokstad Burial Ship, *c.* 870
A Viking burial ship was discovered at Gokstad in Norway. The excavation has revealed superb wooden carvings.

Golden Lion, 1592
An English ship called the *Golden Lion* was lost on the

Goodwins in December 1592 with a cargo that included silver coin. It was partly salvaged at the time of loss by Richard Basset of Ramsgate.

Göteborg, 1745

The *Göteborg* was a Swedish East Indiaman returning from the Far East with porcelain, teas, silks and such which was lost off the Swedish coast. It was rediscovered in 1905. Some of its black oak timbers were used to make furniture. Artefacts from it can be seen in the Göteborg Historical Museum, Sweden.

Gottfried, 1822

The German ship *Gottfried* sank somewhere between Heligoland and Cuxhaven on the night of 11 March 1822. On board was a priceless collection of ancient Egyptian artefacts that had been collected by the famous Egyptologist, General Heinrich Minutoli. Some of the mummies on board floated to the shore and were later auctioned off. The ship itself has never been located.

Goude Leeuw, 1689

The Dutch West Indiaman *Goude Leeuw* was sunk by French corsairs. See chapter 7 for further details.

Gran Grifon, 1588

The *Gran Grifon*, Captain Juan Gomez de Medina, was one of the Spanish Armada ships and the flagship of the hulks in that fleet. It took a major part in the action both on 3 and 8 of August. It was, however, a poor sailer and was soon lagging the rest of the fleet as they battled there way up the North Sea into head winds. Battered by the dreadful storm that struck in mid-September they struggled on until the 27th when the water in the holds reached such a level it seemed impossible that the ship could survive for much longer. The crew tried to beach the *Grifon* on Fair Isle in the Shetlands, to the north of Scotland, where they were driven into Strombshellier Cave. They managed to get their treasure off but the vessel had ended up in such an awkward situation they were unable to procure any provisions. They were entirely reliant for food on the handful of families that lived on Fair Isle. There were 300 people who landed safely from the *Grifon* most of them soldiers, some of them taken from the *Barca de Hamburg* which had been abandoned some weeks beforehand. It was a month before the marooned were able to get a message to the mainland of Scotland and it was not until 6 December that they finally reached Anstruther on the Firth of Forth by which time about fifty of their number had died from starvation. Throughout their ordeal the men of the *Grifon* appear to have behaved well to the local inhabitants and been well received by them, partly, no doubt because of the Scots' age-old antipathy towards the English. The *Gran Grifon* was rediscovered in 1970.

Gudmund Ormsson, Ship of, c. 1300

The Norwegian ship of Gudmund Ormsson was lost off the Faroes with all its valuable cargo.

Guernsey Lily, 1799

The English transport *Guernsey Lily* was lost off Yarmouth. See chapter 12 for further details.

Gull Stream Wreck, c. 1400

A piece of ordnance cast in around 1370 was fished out of the Gull Stream, close by the Goodwin Sands, in 1775 by local fishermen. It was seven feet, ten inches long, breech-loading, and had been used as a swivel gun. The gun belonged originally to the crown of Portugal. No Portuguese wreck of that date in that same area has as yet been discovered. It is possible that the gun does not come from a wreck but was simply jettisoned.

Haan, 1640

The *Haan* was a Dutch warship, part of a small squadron of four that was sent to protect the incoming East India fleet. On 15 June 1640 it was surprised by a superior force of Spanish warships and in the ensuing battle in Bressay Sound, the *Haan* was sunk near Lerwick. The *Reiger*, another Dutch warship, was also sunk in a similar position. A third warship, the *Joanas*, was blown up at Tingwall. The fourth, the *Enkhuizen*, was captured by the Spanish. In dredging operations, carried out at Lerwick Harbour in 1922, four iron cannon were recovered which were thought to belong to the *Haan*, one of which was presented to the Prins Hendrik Museum in Rotterdam.

Haarlem Meer Wreck, 1629

On the evening of 7 January 1629 a large number of boats went out from the port of Amsterdam to view the triumphant return of the Dutch Admiral Piet Heyn with his captured fleet of Spanish galleons, worth four million ducats. In one of the boats was the King of Bohemia, his son and their retinue. In the dusk and crowded seas the boat collided with a bark laden with beer and immediately sank. Everyone in the boat was drowned except the king and two others. The accident took place three-quarters of a league from Amsterdam port.

Hampshire, 1916

The *Hampshire* was a British Navy armoured cruiser built in 1905 by Armstrong Whitworth. It displaced 10,850 tons, was 450 feet in length and had a top speed of twenty-two knots. On the evening of 5 June 1916, when in a position one-and-a-half miles offshore between the Brough of Birsay and Marwick Head on the north-west tip of Orkney Island, it blew up and rapidly sank after striking a mine. There were only twelve survivors out of a total of 662 men on board. The mine had been laid by Commander Kurt Beitzen in the German submarine *U75* about one week before. On board the *Hampshire* at the time was Lord Kitchener with a small group of seven officials and personal servants. He was on a vital mission to Tsar Nicholas of Russia in order to strengthen Russian support in the war. Russia had suffered a series of military defeats at the hands of the Germans during the previous year and it was felt in London that the Tsar's appetite for continuing hostilities was wavering. There was an urgent need to stiffen his resolve and discuss latest Russian demands for further supplies of munitions. Kitchener was not only a military man but was also a personal friend of the Tsar's and was therefore considered to be the ideal person for the task.

The death of Kitchener in the sinking was an enormous shock to the nation, many of whom still regarded him as a great military hero and the leading figurehead of the war, even though his position within government had already become somewhat marginalised. Lloyd George, who was to become Prime Minister before the end of the year, was particularly opposed to Kitchener because he had continued to refuse to agree to a policy of enforced conscription. There were many in London who saw the Russian mission as a useful way of getting Kitchener out of the way for a few months. Walter Hines Page, the American ambassador to Britain, wrote in his despatch on the evening of Kitchener's departure, 'there is a hope and a feeling that he may not come back'. In the event this was uncannily accurate. The sinking of the *Hampshire* was one of the worst naval disasters of the war and led to much subsequent scandal and rumour as to what exactly had gone wrong and who was to blame.

Kitchener left King's Cross station on the evening of 4 June and took the night train to Thurso. The following morning he crossed to Scapa Flow on the destroyer *Royal Oak*. He had lunch with Admiral Sir John Jellicoe, commander in chief of the Grand Fleet, on board the flagship *Iron Duke*. No doubt the conversation centred on the recent battle of Jutland that had taken place on 31 May. Jutland was far from a disaster for the British Navy but the loss of three battle cruisers, three armoured cruisers and several thousand men had been a great shock to British self-confidence. It is possible that the confusion caused by Jutland was a factor in the subsequent mistakes that were made

concerning the dispatch of the *Hampshire* and which contributed to its loss.

The *Hampshire* was scheduled to sail to Archangel along the west coast of Norway and far into the Arctic Circle before turning southwards past the Kola Peninsula and then into the White Sea. It was an extremely harsh and treacherous route even without the added hazard of enemy hostilities. However, the shorter sea-route to Russia through the Baltic Sea was not possible because it was controlled by the Germans.

During the afternoon of 5 June gale force winds began to blow from the north-east. It was suggested to Kitchener that he might delay his departure for twenty-four hours to allow the storm to subside. Kitchener rejected the advice. He was not the kind of man to put personal comfort before a sense of duty. The Admiralty then decided to reroute the *Hampshire* up the west coast of Orkney rather than follow the more usual route for warships up the east side. Part of the thinking behind this unfortunate decision was that, with the winds coming from the north-east, the land mass of the island would provide the ship with some protection. In the event the storm swung round and the winds began to batter from the north-west, exposing the *Hampshire* to the worst of the gales. Any local seaman could have informed the authorities that this circling motion was a common feature of cyclones in this area, but the Admiralty appeared to have acted in complete ignorance of local meteorological conditions. The gale posed no great threat to the safety of the *Hampshire* in itself. The armoured cruiser was still able to forge ahead at a speed of eighteen knots. However, the two destroyers, *Unity* and *Victor*, that had been assigned as escorts to the *Hampshire* were unable to keep up. The *Hampshire* reduced its speed to fifteen knots and headed closer to the shore where the water was a little calmer but the destroyers continued to fall yet further behind. At 6.30 p.m. Captain Herbert Savill on the *Hampshire* ordered his escorts to return to base on the assumption that if they could not keep up they were a liability rather than an asset. It was a reasonable decision but as it turned out it was also a most unfortunate one.

At approximately 7.40 p.m. there was a catastrophic explosion on board the *Hampshire* from the vicinity of the boiler room. The electric lights went out and a number of those working in the engine-room were scalded with boiling water. Within twenty minutes the *Hampshire* had sunk bows first. The terrible weather conditions and the speed of the sinking made it impossible to launch any of the lifeboats. Only three carley rafts got away, with about seventy men clinging desperately to the edge of each of them, their bodies largely submerged in the icy and rough seas. The rafts were desperately overcrowded but the overcrowding did not last long. One by one the men dropped off. Of those that did manage to reach land, many were so exhausted that they were unable to struggle up the cliffs. It later transpired that the British authorities, as soon as the disaster was communicated, ordered all the islanders to remain confined to their houses thereby cutting off a possible lifeline to those that had made it to shore, as well as bitterly alienating many of the locals. This insensitive decision reflected the near paranoia at the time among the British about German infiltration and Fenian plots on the outlying islands. It was two hours after the sinking before rescue ships were despatched from Scapa by which time it was far too late to do anything but pick up the corpses.

It seems possible that the British authorities were in part responsible for the *Hampshire* disaster in a more fundamental way. There had been a scandalous lack of security concerning the details of Kitchener's impending visit to Russia. His mission had been openly talked about throughout most of the capitals of Europe for over a week before his departure. This failure was compounded by a rogue signal picked up by the Germans at their listening station near Kiel. It purported to have been sent from a British destroyer to the Admiralty and claimed that the route to the west of the Orkneys had been cleared of mines and was now safe for transit. The Germans had not previously mined this route because it had customarily been used only by small merchant ships. They concluded from the intercepted signal, however, that it was about to be used for an important shipping movement and on 28 May *U75* under Commander Beitzen was despatched to lay its deadly load. The strangest thing about all this is that in British records there is no evidence of this intercepted signal ever having been sent, nor is there any evidence that the route was swept for mines on 26 May as claimed. On the contrary the Admiralty later publicly admitted that the route to the west had not been swept because the Germans had never previously mined it. One possible explanation of this conundrum is that British Naval Intelligence under the direction of Admiral Hall had sent the rogue signal in order to mislead the enemy into thinking that Kitchener would sail on the west side of Orkney rather than the more usual east side expecting that the east side would be the one that would be actually used. If this is the case then he had inadvertently scored the most calamitous own goal, for the authorities at Scapa do not seem to have been made aware of the deception that was being played.

The nation was stunned by news of Kitchener's death and for a number of years afterwards many simply refused to believe in it. There were constant rumours about how he had been seen coming ashore either on the Orkneys or in Norway. The faithful were convinced that he would return one day to lead his troops to victory and his image rapidly achieved a quasi-religious status. Parallel with this sanctification process there was much wild speculation about the cause of the *Hampshire*'s sinking. Some blamed it on Irish treachery. As the *Hampshire* had docked in

Belfast for a refit just a few months before its loss it was possible to elaborate theories of time bombs being attached to the inside of the hull during that period. Other explanations pointed to German stowaways detonating explosives. Fritz Dusquene and Ernst Carl both published books in Germany claiming credit for the sinking which naturally stimulated this line of thinking. There was also a general sense of unease that the Admiralty had behaved shabbily and were guilty of some kind of cover up.

In 1926, ten years after the *Hampshire*'s loss, the constant speculation forced the government to issue a white paper revealing the findings of an internal enquiry into the sinking. The white paper in fact failed to answer any of the major questions but the controversy did slowly die away. The next time the *Hampshire* was in the news it was in an entirely different context. The Berliner *Illustrierte Zeitung* in 1933 carried a report describing the salvage of £10,000 in gold bars from the *Hampshire*'s strongroom. The British and American press picked up on the story and very shortly there was such a furore that the Admiralty were forced to make a statement. In the usual way of such statements it was characteristically opaque. It claimed to know nothing of the salvage attempt, neither confirmed nor denied the presence of gold, but asserted that the *Hampshire* was the property of HM Government and that it should not be touched without permission.

Again the *Hampshire* legend was largely forgotten, this time until the early 1950s when a diver called Charles Courtney published a book called *Unlocking Adventure*. In it he claimed to have been part of the group who in 1933 had carried out the highly secretive salvage operation on the *Hampshire*. They had apparently recovered £60,000 of gold when the project had had to be aborted when one diver was killed and two others injured. Given the fierceness of the currents in the vicinity of Marwick Head this kind of accident is hardly surprising. According to Courtney there was gold to a value of two million pounds on board the *Hampshire* at the time of its loss. The gold was being sent to Russia to provide financial support to the Tsar. The most convincing part of Courtney's book is that he states that one of the financiers behind the salvage was Basil Zaharoff, the notorious arms dealer. It is known that Zaharoff had a keen interest in shipwreck salvage because he was also one of the backers of the highly successful recovery of gold from the *Egypt* in 1931. Interestingly Zaharoff and Lloyd George had been extremely close in 1917 when the arms dealer carried out a number of diplomatic missions for the then Prime Minister of a kind that were either too delicate or too nefarious to entrust to the usual channels. If anyone was ever in a good position to know exactly what was on the *Hampshire* it would have been Zaharoff. The puzzling thing is that it is evident from Cabinet Papers in the National Archives that in the first half of 1916 Russia sent ten million pounds' worth of gold from Vladivostock to Canada for the credit of the British Government as payment for arms and munitions supplied by Britain. Gold movements are frequently unpredictable and often illogical but it seems particularly confusing if at the same time that Russia was sending gold to Canada as a payment to Britain, Britain was sending gold to Russia. One possible explanation is that the gold on the *Hampshire*, if indeed there was any gold, was not British but privately owned Russian gold belonging to the Romanov family and urgently required in Russia because of the dire situation the Romanovs found themselves in by mid–1916. It is known that the Romanovs did repatriate much of their foreign owned wealth during this crisis period.

In the mid-1980s the *Hampshire* was again back in the news. A German underwater film-maker was accused by the British government of illicitly removing items from the wreck. This unauthorised operation did nothing to clear up the question of whether or not there still remained any gold on board. It did, however, make it clear that the damage to the *Hampshire*'s hull was consistent with a mine explosion and not an internal bomb, so putting an end once and for all to those who still believed the sinking was the result of saboteurs.

Healdton, 1917
The American tanker *Healdton*, owned by the Standard Oil Company (New Jersey), built in 1908 by the Greenock and Grangemouth Dockyard Company, 4,489 gross tonnage, was sunk by a German submarine on 21 March off Holland. According to an article in the *Sunday Examiner* for 7 April 1918 it had $3,000,000 on board at the time of loss.

Henrietta Yacht, 1673
The *Henrietta* yacht, Captain Thomas Guy, built at Woolwich in 1663, 104 tons burthen and equipped with eighteen bronze cannon, sank off Texel during the battle of Texel on 11 August 1673.

Hermonie, 1761
The *Hermonie* was a French frigate bound to Martinico (Martinique) from Dunkirk lost in the vicinity thereof in January 1761, with specie.

Hendrik, 1783
The German brig *Hendrik*, Captain La Frentz, en route from Hamburg to Oporto with a general cargo including copper ingots and other valuables, was wrecked on the Goodwins on 7 November 1783. The crew were rescued by the boats from Deal.

Hillegom, 1736
The *Hillegom* was a Dutch VOC ship, 1,150 tons burthen, belonging to the Amsterdam Chamber, Captain Jan Almees. It was lost in the Texel on 13 February 1736.

Hindostan, 1803
The *Hindostan*, an English East Indiaman, burthen 1,248 tons, Captain Edward Balston, departed London on 2 January 1803, en route to Madras (Chennai). It carried a valuable cargo including copper, lead and tin ingots, copper coin, and thirteen chests of privately shipped specie. On 9 January the pilot anchored off the Wedge Sand in the entrance to the River Thames. On Tuesday 11 January a strong easterly gale drove the ship onto the sands where by nightfall it had stuck fast. An attempt was made to launch the ship's boats but they were dashed against the ship's sides. The *Liberty* pilot sloop, hearing signals of distress, came to offer assistance and was at the scene of the wreck within two hours of the *Hindostan* striking. However, the weather was so fierce and the *Hindostan* was lying in such an awkward position, the *Liberty* could not approach closely enough to take the men off. In desperation some of the shipwrecked sailors hastily constructed rafts to try to reach the *Liberty* but they drifted off in the wrong direction, and although the *Liberty* tried to search for them they could not locate them. Faced with little alternative the majority of the crew who remained on board took refuge during the night in the ship's rigging. Some of them froze to death but early the following morning the majority were rescued by the *Liberty* pilot sloop with the assistance of the Margate hoy. During the following two weeks eleven of the thirteen chests of silver and a quantity of woollens were salvaged. After this the situation for further salvage at the wreck became far more difficult and it appears to have been abandoned. Between 1983 and 1985 a large number of artefacts were brought up from the wreck using a grab, a salvage technique much frowned upon by archaeologists. Some of the artefacts are now on display in the Powell-Cotton Museum in Kent.

Hjalp, 1148
The *Hjalp* was a Viking longship lost in the Shetlands. See chapter 2 for further details.

Hopewell, 1671
The *Hopewell*, Master John Pye, sank ten or twelve leagues east-south-east from the Spurn, in about fifteen fathoms of water so that the vane on the main top mast head was just visible. A number of valuables were lost with the ship.

Hoorn, 1637
The *Hoorn* was a Dutch VOC ship, 550 tons, belonging to the Hoorn Chamber, lost at Brouwershaven in January 1637.

Houghton, 1752
According to Sir Evan Cotton in his highly regarded and authoritative book *East Indiamen* the *Houghton* was wrecked off Margate in 1752 on its way home from China. The captain was Richard Walpole, son of Horatio Walpole, younger brother to Prime Minister

Robert Walpole. An East Indiaman from China of this date would almost certainly have carried an interesting porcelain cargo as well as the more usual tea and silks. *Lloyds List* carries no mention of the sinking which for a loss of this date is unusual.

Hoy, 1670
A Scottish hoy with a quantity of money on board was lost in 1670 on the 'rocks of Hull'. There were no survivors.

Hugh de Boves, Ship of, 1215
Sir Hugh de Boves was a Norman mercenary employed by King John in the latter's attempts to assert his authority over his disputing barons. In October 1215, shortly after the signing of the Magna Carta, Boves embarked a large force of troops, together with their families, at Calais. One version has de Boves' ship being cast away near Sandwich with a large quantity of money on board for the payment of his troops. Another chronicler claims that his drowned body was washed ashore near Yarmouth. One thing for certain is that his fleet suffered great losses in a storm during their crossing. So many bodies apparently washed up on the coast that the 'air was rendered pestilent'.

Invincible, 1801
The *Invincible* was an English warship, third rate, built in 1765 by Wells and Company at Deptford, with seventy-four guns and a gross tonnage of 1,631 tons. On 18 March 1801 at about 1 p.m. it sailed from Yarmouth. Rear Admiral Thomas Totty was the commander on board. It was en route to join the main English fleet under Sir Hyde Parker that was already off the Danish coast and was shortly to be involved in the battle of Copenhagen where Nelson famously disobeyed orders. The *Invincible* sailed through the Cockle Gat with the intention of then sailing through the Haisborough Gat and passing three leagues to the south of the Ridge Sand. At 2.30 p.m., travelling at nine knots with a strong ebb tide, the ship struck. The ship was 'tolerably quiet' until 5 p.m. when the wind began to freshen. The masts were at that point cut away after which the ship forged over the bank and began to float. It was, however, ungovernable because the rudder had broken off as a result of the impact with the sandbank. They anchored in seventeen fathoms of water and began to pump. By 8 p.m. there were only twenty-two inches of water in the ship and Admiral Totty was hopeful of saving it. Unfortunately, by 9 p.m. the flood tide began to flow strongly and the ship was again driven on to the bank and began striking violently. At 10 p.m. the ship came off the bank a second time. At midnight Admiral Totty gave the

order for the boys and the sick to be taken off, and he himself, together with his secretary and a bundle of government papers, also left the ship at this point. They transferred to the *Nancy* fishing smack which had been standing by since 7 p.m. Later in the night those remaining on board attempted to launch the *Invincible*'s boats but they were driven out into the North Sea by the strong tide that was flowing. At daylight the *Nancy*, which was still standing by, tried to approach under the stern of the *Invincible*, but again the tide proved too strong, and shortly afterwards the *Invincible* sank in thirteen fathoms. Around 400 of the 600 people on board drowned.

At the subsequent court martial the general opinion expressed was that the *Invincible* had struck on the Hammond's Knowl. This was the opinion expressed by the master of the *Nancy* smack, and as the smack was standing by for over twelve hours they would have had every opportunity for determining their position accurately. On the other hand, it is difficult to credit that the pilots on board the *Invincible*, who had had the benefit of both sight of land and the Newarp lightship, could have been quite so far out in their judgement as to hit Hammond's Knowl. According to Admiral Totty's evidence the pilots had informed him that they had intended to pass three leagues to the south of Ridge Sand. Either the pilots were lying, which seems unlikely as this intention must have been declared before the shipwreck occurred, or it seems probable that the *Invincible* in fact hit the south end of Ridge Bank. It is, of course, also possible that the Ridge was regarded by the master of the Nancy as being part of Hammond's Knowl at this time, for neither bank appears to have been individually charted for very many years previous to the sinking.

When the *Invincible* sank it was carrying military stores for the forthcoming engagement including bronze ordnance.

James Galley, 1694
The *James Galley*, Captain Soames, 436 tons burthen and equipped with thirty guns, ran on to the Long Sand six leagues off Margate and sank. All those on board were saved but the galley rapidly settled in the sands and a large number of valuables were lost. There were on board at the time a hundred officers and two hundred other passengers, all en route to Leith in Scotland. At the court martial the captain was fined £300 and the pilot sentenced to six years' imprisonment.

Jennet Perwyn, 1511
The *Jennet Perwyn*, a pinnace equipped with thirty guns, and part of Andrew Barton's Scottish fleet was sunk in a battle with Edward Howard off the Goodwin

Sands. The *Jennet Perwyn* had plundered English and Portuguese ships before sinking and so was thought to have a considerable quantity of valuables on board.

John, 1669

The *John* of London, returning from Guinea in West Africa, ran aground on the Goodwin Sands on 25 January 1669, and was abandoned by its crew, who left two young boys on board, one Irish and the other African. The ship caught fire and then drove four or five miles to the north of where it first struck. On board there was a cargo of canary wine and elephant's teeth together with 'two chests of gold dust and much other gold'. Seamen went out in boats and much of the ivory was later salvaged.

John Evangelist, 1576

The *John Evangelist*, master West, was lost on Shoebury Sands, off Foulness, on 6 October 1576, while en route from Lisbon to London with a valuable cargo including money. It was completely salvaged at the time of loss.

John the Baptist, 1710

The Russian warship *John the Baptist* was lost during the battle of Køge, near Helsinki, Finland, fought between Denmark and Sweden, when the Russians were allies of the Danes. In the nineteenth century various press reports associated the wreck with sunken treasure and there were several failed attempts at salvaging it.

Jönköping, 1916

The *Jönköping*, home port Gavle in Sweden, was a small wooden ketch sunk in the Baltic by a German U boat. When it went down it was carrying 6,000 bottles of Heidsieck & Co. champagne, as well as cognac and burgundy, all destined for the officers of the Russian army in Finland. It was discovered and salvaged in 1998 by Claes Bergvall. The champagne was said to be in excellent condition and was valued at more than £100 per bottle.

Kapelle, 1690

The *Kapelle* was a Dutch VOC ship, 136 feet in length, 641 tons, belonging to the Rotterdam Chamber, that was wrecked near the Shetlands.

Kennermerland, 1664

The Dutch VOC ship *Kennermerland*, belonging to the Amsterdam Chamber, 950 tons burthen, left Texel on 14 December 1664 in company with the *Rijnland*. Included in the cargo were 120,000 guilders in silver coin. The *Kennermerland* was wrecked on 20

December at Stoura Stack, Grunay, in the Out Skerries, Shetlands. There were no survivors from the 150 crew. The ship broke in two and the aft section drifted on to the isle of Bruray. Most of the treasure was salvaged at the time of loss under the direction of the Earl of Morton. The wreck was rediscovered in the 1970s and extensive further salvage took place including the recovery of a large number of silver coins. Some artefacts from the wreck are now exhibited in the museum at Lerwick.

King John's Jewels, 1216

Not, strictly speaking, a treasure ship, as no ship appears to have been involved, but certainly it was a loss involving both the North Sea and treasure. Accounts are greatly confused and, considering the enormous amount that has been written upon the subject, hard facts are few and far between. However, John's baggage train, including the crown jewels, apparently left Spalding in Lincolnshire to be taken by the short route across the Wash to King's Lynn in Norfolk, a journey which involved crossing the marshes by causeway. The baggage train was overwhelmed by an abnormally high tide and the jewels were lost as a result. King John does not appear to have been in company with his possessions at the time of the disaster. He is recorded as having died shortly afterwards on 18 October while at Newark Castle, which would place him still on the north side of the Wash. It seems reasonable that John may have had much of his valuables with him on this journey as he was at the time facing a general rebellion of English barons against his rule, the barons being in league with the French King Louis. There has been a suggestion that the jewels were later recovered towards the end of the fourteenth century by Robert Lord Tiptoft who became suddenly and inexplicably extremely wealthy. The supposed site of the treasure loss is at Sutton Bridge on the River Nene.

Koevorden, 1665

On 3 June 1665 during hostilities with the English in the Second Anglo-Dutch War, three Dutch warships, the *Koevorden*, vice admiral of the fleet, with sixty cannon, the *Prins Maurits* with fifty cannon, and the *Utrecht* with forty-four cannon, became entangled and were burnt by the English fireship *Fame*, Captain John Gethings. Lord Sandwich in the *Royal Prince* who observed this mêlée records his position a few hours later as being twenty leagues to the east of Southwold which would place these sinkings well over towards the Dutch coast rather than just off Lowestoft as some commentators have suggested. Shortly after this disaster, around 6 p.m., and so probably in a position around seventeen or eighteen leagues east of Southwold, three more Dutch warships were in collision, the *Merseveen*, seventy-eight cannon, the *Tergoes*, thirty-four cannon, and the *Swanenburg*, thirty cannon. They were subsequently burnt by a fireship under the command of Captain Gregory and sank shortly afterwards. Sandwich was of the opinion that this was an unnecessary and inhumane act on Captain Gregory's part for the ships had already surrendered and could have been taken over by prize crews. 'This cruel act was much detested by us as not beseeming christians.' He wanted Gregory to be court martialled. It may also be that he was concerned at the loss of potential prize money. (See the entry for the *Eendracht* for further details on the battle of Lowestoft.)

Koning William, 1696
The *Koning William* was a Dutch VOC ship lost on the Vlaamse Banken, Vlaanderen, Scheldemond, on 23 July 1696. It was 161 feet in length, 1,197 tons burthen, and belonged to the Amsterdam Chamber. Its captain was called Jan Hendrik Thin.

Krafsinn, c. 1300
The Norwegian ship *Krafsinn* was lost with valuables on the coast of Halogaland (Helgoland, Germany).

Kronan, 1676
The *Kronan* was a Swedish warship lost in the Baltic. See chapter 6 for further details.

Land van Schouwen, 1690
The *Land van Schouwen* was a Dutch VOC ship, 1,140 tons burthen, lost near the Shetlands on its homeward voyage from Batavia (Jakarta, Indonesia).

Lastdrager, 1653
The *Lastdrager* was a Dutch VOC ship, 640 tons burthen, which left Texel on 9 February 1653 en route to the Far East. During severe bad weather the *Lastdrager* began to leak and was finally forced ashore, at the Ness of Cullivoe, Bluemull Sound, Yell, Shetland Isles. The ship was carrying the usual outward-bound cargo which included a large quantity of silver coin. The survivors recovered two chests of silver from the wreckage and later the same year salvors made considerable further recoveries. Robert Stenuit rediscovered the wreck in the 1960s.

Laurel, 1657
The *Laurel*, Captain Francis Kirby, a third-rate man of war with fifty cannon, was lost on the Newarp Sands, eight miles offshore from Winterton. Nine of its cannon were made of bronze and the diver Robert Willis was instructed to recover them if it was found to be practicable. The results of his proposed salvage are not recorded. The men appear to have lost all their possessions. The ship's surgeon, Thomas Rooke, for instance, petitioned the Admiralty for £150 to cover the loss of his medicine chest, instruments, books, money and clothes.

Leith Packet, 1761
One of the London – Leith packets, which frequently transported specie and passengers, was lost en route to Leith around 20 October 1761 off the Norfolk coast. The captain was called Pitcairn. Some of the passengers were drowned but the cargo was largely salvaged at the time of loss.

Leith Road Box, 1765
In October 1765 a person going on board a ship called the *King George*, Captain Marshall, which was moored in Leith Roads, carrying a box of money, said to contain £1,000 in gold coin fell overboard. The man was immediately rescued but the box of coin was lost despite several attempts to fish it up during the following week.

Lelie, 1654
The *Lelie* was a Dutch VOC ship lost in the Roads of Texel on 12 January 1654. The wreck site was rediscovered in 1997 by Hans Eelman at a depth of seven meters. The cargo was largely salvaged at the time of the original loss.

Lesnoy, 1719
A large Russian warship built by Peter the Great bilged on an anchor and sank in Kronslot Harbour (Kronshtadt). Rear Admiral Gordon and Captain Batting were the commanders on board at the time, Peter the Great being very keen on employing English seamen for their expertise. The *Lesnoy* had much of value on board but most of it was saved and the ship was later weighed.

Liberty, 1650
The *Liberty*, forty-four guns, Captain Edward Hall, was a second-rate warship that ran on to a sandbank near Harwich and was wrecked. Most of the cannon on board were bronze and the diver Robert Willis was employed in their recovery. He was paid twenty shillings a hundredweight for the bronze guns that he recovered. Four in total appear to have been salvaged.

Liefde, 1711
The *Liefde* was a Dutch East Indiaman, 1,100 tons burthen, Captain Barend Meikens. The ship left Texel

for the Far East on 3 November 1711 and on the night of the 7th it miscalculated its position in conditions of bad visibility and was wrecked on the reef of Miouw in the Outer Skerries in Shetland. There was only one survivor. It was carrying a large cargo of specie, mainly silver coin but including some gold. As soon as the Dutch authorities heard of the loss they organised a salvage attempt but it was unsuccessful. Local wreck fishers had better luck. The wreck was relocated in 1965 and several thousand more coins were salvaged. In the opinion of some, the main part of the wreck has yet to be discovered. Some of the salvaged items are on display in the Lerwick Museum.

Lion, 1547
The *Lion* was a Scottish ship captured by the *Pauncy*, Captain Sir Andrew Dudley, before being lost off Harwich, some reports state in Harwich harbour, apparently through the negligence of the prize crew. The *Lion* was carrying valuable supplies including specie from France to Scotland at the time of its capture.

London, 1665
The *London*, a second-rate English warship, blew up when sailing from Chatham to the Hope, just to the west of the buoy of Nore. The Commander was Vice Admiral Sir John Lawson. The explosion resulted in most of those on board, approximately 300, losing their lives. Eighty bronze cannon were salvaged shortly after the loss.

Long Serpent, 1000
The *Long Serpent* was the ship of Olaf Trygvesson, the Norwegian warlord, which was sunk at the battle of Svolde off the coast of Rugen, northern Germany, while fighting against the Swedes and Danes. It was reputed to be 150 feet in length. Many valuables were lost with the ship.

Loosdrecht, 1736
The *Loosdrecht* was a Dutch VOC ship, belonging to the Amsterdam Chamber, 850 tons burthen, Captain Willem Vroom. It was lost on 19 February 1736 on the Goodwins while on its outward voyage to the Far East with a cargo that included specie. It was sailing in company with the *Meermond* and the *Zoals de Buis*.

Louisiana, 1868
The *Louisiana* was a German cargo ship, 1,300 tons gross, built at Bremerhaven in 1867. It sank during a storm on its maiden voyage to New York from Bremerhaven on 23 January 1868, 600 yards from the village of Fjaltring on the coast of Jutland, Denmark. Its cargo included lead and iron, as well as china dolls and toys which are now regarded as antiques. It was rediscovered in the 1990s and some of the recovered artefacts were exhibited at the Legoland Park.

Luchtenburg, 1727
The *Luchtenburg* was a Dutch VOC ship, belonging to the Amsterdam Chamber, 800 tons burthen, 180 crew, Captain Adriaan van Leeuwen. It was wrecked at Wielingen on 17 November 1727.

Lutine, 1799
The *Lutine* was a British warship lost off Holland. See chapter 13 for further details.

Lybska Svan, 1524
The *Lybska Svan* (Swan of Lubeck) was the flagship of Gustav Eriksson Vasa. The *Svan* was abandoned in a severely leaking condition somewhere to the south of Öland. Some of the bronze cannon from the *Svan* were salvaged at the time of loss and put on board another Swedish ship which sank between Djurshamn and Dalaro at a depth of twenty fathoms. In 1990 a Swedish archaeological team located a wreck in Namdo Fjord near Stockholm close by the Franska Stenarna Rocks which may be one or other of these two ships. Unfortunately two of the bronze cannon from the site have already been pillaged.

Maan, 1598
The *Maan* was a Dutch VOC ship which was lost on 23 March 1598 near Dover while on its outward voyage, with a cargo that included specie. It capsized while firing a salute.

Malaga Factor, 1679
The *Malaga Factor* was cast away in the Downs through stress of weather when outward bound with a considerable quantity of specie on board. There was no insurance upon ship or cargo.

Maloja, 1916
The *Maloja* was built in 1911 by Harland & Wolff for the Peninsular and Oriental Steam Navigation Company. It was a luxury liner 550 feet long with a gross tonnage of 12,431 tons and a top speed of nineteen knots. It left London for Bombay on 26 February 1916, Captain Irving in command. There were 456 crew and passengers on board. It carried a general cargo which included four boxes of gold, eighteen boxes of silver coin, a large quantity of bar silver and eight cases of bank notes. There were also diamonds on board, worth £10,536 at 1916 prices. At 10.30 a.m. on 27 February the *Maloja* hit a mine two miles south-west of Dover Pier. The order was given for the engines to be put into reverse to slow the ship but the rapid and severe list made it impossible to launch the boats and the ship sank very quickly in fifteen fathoms. 155 of the people on board were lost all of them passengers. In April 1916 the wreck was

surveyed by the Northern Salvage and Shipbreaking Company which reported that the vessel was lying on its starboard beam along a south-west/north-east axis, with its head to the south-west. Also in April 1916 Trinity House received instructions from the Admiralty to blow up the ship as it was considered a danger to navigation. Presumably dispersal was left until after the salvage of the valuables which took place in June and July of 1916. It must have been a difficult operation to carry out considering the hostilities. All the gold, silver and bank notes were recovered apart from one bar of silver. Twenty ingots of tin were also salvaged, original quantity unknown. There is no record of the diamonds being recovered.

Maria Juan, 1588

On 8 August with both the Spanish and English fleets having reached the southern North Sea during the battle of the Spanish Armada, the Biscayan ship *Maria Juan* was sunk through the quantity of shot in its hull. This sinking in relatively deep water was the only Spanish loss caused exclusively through enemy action. The chart of Robert Adams drawn shortly after the event shows the *Maria Juan* sinking in an area to the west of the West Hinder sandbank.

Mariusudin, c. 1300

The Norwegian ship *Mariusudin* sank near the Shetlands with all its crew drowned and a valuable cargo lost.

Mars, 1787

The *Mars*, Captain Farrington, was an English East Indiaman of 696 tons burthen. On the night of Saturday, 8 December 1787, returning to London from Canton in China, and having called at Mauritius and St Helena on the way, the ship was almost home when it got on to the sands seven miles from Margate and was wrecked. The *Mars* was sailing up the Queen's Channel when it approached too closely to Margate Sands. It is not often that log books survive shipwreck but the original log book for the *Mars* still exists among the India Office Records. It mentions that at 7 p.m. the water began to shoal. At half past seven they first touched the ground. They fired guns of distress and showed lights. By 11.00 p.m. the ship was stuck fast. The top gallant masts were struck and the booms were put over the starboard side of the ship to try and shore it up. A boat was then dispatched to Deal for another pilot, the first one presumably having been arrested at this stage. Captain Farrington also requested assistance from shore boats to lighten the ship. At 4 a.m. the following morning the *Mars* began to make water. The pumps were got going, the masts were cut down and the best bower anchor was heaved out. By 10.00 a.m. the ship's back was broken and it filled with water as the tide rose. They are the closing words. The log is a wonderful example of a meticulous and understated record of

events and suggests that Captain Farrington was a competent and unflappable seaman.

The pilot, William Johnson, who was in charge of the ship at the time of the disaster, blamed the seaman at the head of the ship, who was heaving the lead to establish the depth of water, for the accident. Apparently, he called out seven fathoms when he should have called out four, which caused the pilot to give the order to stand in nearer to the shore, which immediately brought them onto the sandbank. It seems like a rather desperate excuse and clearly one that Captain Farrington was not convinced by. The enquiry subsequently held by the East India Company considered that Mr Johnson was to blame for the loss and referred the matter to the court at Dover.

There was no loss of life but considerable loss of property. The *Mars* carried the usual Far Eastern cargo of spices, cottons and teas as well as 141 cases of Chinese porcelain. Captain Coggan, The East India Company's surveyor, was immediately dispatched to take charge of the situation. Salvage commenced straight away and large quantities of tea were brought ashore. The *Betsy* hoy, for instance, brought off 270 chests of tea. Much of the cargo that was saved, however, was so spoiled by sea water that it was of no value. The loss to the East India Company was variously computed at between £40,000 and £70,000. In addition there was considerable private cargo on board. Captain Farrington alone had shipped £12,000 of property. East India captains were at this time fond of purchasing high-quality porcelain for resale back in England and it is highly probable that at least some of Captain Farrington's investment had been made in this manner in which case these chests would have been additional to the 141 shipped on the Company's account. A number of the newspaper reports were also careful to make the point that the ordinary seamen were great sufferers by the loss of the *Mars* as well as the India Company and its investors. The sailors had not only lost their clothes and possessions but in the event of shipwreck they also forfeited their pay. There was a growing public sense at this time of the poor conditions for merchant seamen perhaps stimulated by the increasing number of mutinies that had lately taken place on Company ships.

During the two weeks after the wreck the small boats from Deal, Margate and other local ports were busy salvaging what they could of the cargo. Towards the end of the month, however, the ship was abandoned. *The Times* of 29 December records: 'The *Mars* East Indiaman is as last entirely left to the waves, everything being got out of her that was possible, though in so damaged a state as to be of little or no value.' The fate of the porcelain is unclear. Being relatively heavy it would have been stowed at the very bottom of the ship beneath the teas. The only definite reference to salvage of the porcelain is in a letter from one of the Igguldens which refers to twenty-two chests of china being landed, some of the packages broken. It is quite possible that the remainder was still inside the ship when it was abandoned. What state it would be in today is, of course, anyone's guess.

Mayflower, 1625
It is thought that the original *Mayflower* that took the Pilgrim Fathers to America may have been among several ships lost at Aldeburgh in 1625.

Meerman, 1761
The *Meerman*, Captain Evert Brisdom, a Dutch man-of-war of twenty-six guns, was lost on the Goodwins. At the time it was said to be carrying £28,000 in specie, the property of a London merchant.

Meermond, 1736
The *Meermond* was a Dutch VOC ship, belonging to the Amsterdam Chamber, 850 tons burthen, Captain Jacon Gosen Hoogstad. It was lost on the Goodwins on 19 February 1736 while sailing in company with the *Loosdrecht* and the *Zoals de Buis*.

Midloo, 1732
The *Midloo* was a Dutch VOC ship, belonging to the Amsterdam Chamber, 800 tons burthen, Captain Peter Tinnekens. It was wrecked on the Vlieland while homeward bound.

Moon, 1625
The English East India Company ship *Moon* was lost in Dover Roads with a cargo of pepper and other Far Eastern goods on 16 September 1625. Jacob Johnson, the famous diver, was responsible for the recovery of forty-three guns from the wreck.

Morris, 1623
The English East Indiaman *Morris*, 400 tons burthen, was lost on the Vlie near the Texel on 19 November 1628. The cargo that was lost included presents from the King of Bantam to Charles I. Among the latter was a gold-handled dagger and a lance part-plated with gold.

Nancy, 1795
The brig *Nancy*, Captain Roberts, from Swansea was laden with ordnance stores, consigned to Mr Raby, The Steelyard, Thames Street. The *Nancy* put into Ramsay in distress but sailed again and was lost in the Black Deep, about five leagues from the mouth of the River Thames, between the Sunk Sand and the Long Sand. A Mr Wells, who had been manager of the theatre at Waterford, had a considerable sum of money on board. His property, together with the ordnance, went to the bottom.

Neerlands Vrijheid, 1784
The *Neerlands Vrijheid* was a Dutch VOC ship, belonging to the Amsterdam Chamber, 566 tons burthen, Captain Frederik Floor. On 13 December 1784 it ran aground on the coast of England just one day after leaving the Texel and was wrecked.

Negotie, 1790
The *Negotie* was a Dutch VOC ship, belonging to the Amsterdam Chamber, 440 tons burthen, Captain Herman Driesman, that was lost on 27 November 1790 off Texel while outward bound with a cargo that included specie.

New Hazard, 1817
The *New Hazard*, Captain Andrews, possibly Dutch, although some reports state American, was sailing from Antwerp to Batavia (Jakarta, Indonesia), with a cargo that included a large quantity of specie. The vessel struck on the Galloper Sands on 1 July 1817 and later sank. All those on board were saved excepting the master.

Nieuwvijvervreugd, 1756
A Dutch East India Company ship, captain Marinus de Jonge, 1,150 tons burthen, thirty-two cannon, caught fire and exploded somewhere in the vicinity of the Shetlands. The return cargo would almost certainly have included porcelain as well as the usual silks and teas. The wreck has to date not been located.

Nijmegen, 1632
The *Nijmegen* was a Dutch VOC ship, belonging to the Amsterdam Chamber, Captain Dirk Adamsz, which was wrecked during August 1632 on the Borkumer Reef near Amelander Gat while homeward bound from Batavia (Jakarta, Indonesia).

Noordmunster, 1648
The *Noordmunster* was a Dutch VOC ship, belonging to the Zeeland chamber, lost at the Sluise Gat, Wielingen on the Scheldemond in November 1648.

Nottingham, 1743
The English East Indiaman *Nottingham*, Captain Thomas Brown, was en route to Bombay (Mumbai, India) when it was driven ashore during a gale from the north-east. It was wrecked near Broadstairs Pier. Its cargo included lead, iron and 1,230 elephant teeth weighing approximately fifteen tons. There was also a quantity of privately shipped silver on board. A large part of the cargo was subsequently salvaged.

Nyckeln, 1679
The Swedish warship *Nyckeln* was lost in the Kalmar Sound, Sweden, with a large number of valuable artefacts. It was salvaged in the nineteenth century and again in the early twentieth century. Some of the recovered artefacts are in the Naval Museum Stockholm, Sweden.

Oceanic, 1914

The *Oceanic* was a steel screw steamer, 17,274 gross tons, built by Harland & Wolff in 1899 for the Oceanic Steamship Navigation Company. On the outbreak of World War I it was requisitioned by the Royal Navy and converted to an armed merchant cruiser, with W. Slayter as Captain and H. Smith as Master. On 8 September 1914 it ran ashore on Hoevdi Rock just to the East of Foula Island in the Shetlands. Two days later the Liverpool and Glasgow Underwriters Association were requested to send the *Ranger* to the site for the purpose of immediate salvage but the order was cancelled on the 12th. The wreck has been associated with the presence of silver bullion on board but as the dispatch of the *Ranger* was cancelled this seems unlikely. In 1973 Alex Crawford carried out some salvage work on the wreck and a number of artefacts from it are now on display in the Shetland Counties Museum, Lerwick.

Olricca, 1683

The *Olricca* was a Danish ship lost on the island of Anholt, Denmark, with valuables.

Oostereem, 1783

The Dutch East Indiaman *Oostereem*, Captain Axel Land, was en route from Amsterdam to Batavia (Jakarta, Indonesia) when it was lost on the Goodwins. It departed from Texel on 17 January and was wrecked on the Heads on 21 January. It carried a considerable quantity of specie most of which was subsequently salvaged. It is probable that the *Osta Junis* referred to in the Reverend Treanor's book, *Heroes of the Goodwin Sands*, and which he describes as being 'treasure laden with money and other valuables to a great amount' and being wrecked on the Goodwins in the year 1783, was in fact the *Oostereem*.

Orkney, 1867

According to recent newspaper articles in Sweden, an American ship called *Orkney* sank somewhere to the east of Gotland with a large quantity of gold coin, the latter being the sum of $7.2 million due to the Tsar of Russia for the sale of Alaska to the USA. Although the sale of Alaska is well documented, and must represent one of the worst bargains (on Russia's part) that one nation has ever made with another at a time of peace, the suggestion that such a large sum was lost in transhipment seems, on the evidence available, unlikely.

Oseberg Burial Ship, *c*. 800

This elaborately carved Viking longboat, used as a burial ship, was excavated at Oseberg on the Oslo Fjord in 1904. Beautiful brooches and ornate examples of Viking weather vanes were among the many valuable artefacts unearthed at the site.

Ostend Wreck, 1586

A valuable wreck from Germany was lost on a sandbank off Ostend in October 1586. All the passengers were lost and the wreck was significant enough to be recorded in the newsletter of the famous Fugger bankers.

Ostend Ship, 1752

A ship belonging to the East India Company of Ostend en route from Göteborg to Amsterdam, laden with tea and porcelain, was wrecked near Oroust, a small distance from the island of Maarstrund.

Oude Zijpe, 1742

The *Oude Zijpe* was a Dutch VOC ship, belonging to the Enkhuizen Chamber, 650 tons burthen, Captain Joost Anker, wrecked on 22 September 1742 at Bloemendaal, Zandvoort, coast of Holland, during a storm, when homeward bound from the Far East. It was rediscovered in 1986.

Overhout, 1777

The *Overhout* was a Dutch VOC ship, belonging to the Amsterdam Chamber, Captain Pieter Angelvorst. It was wrecked on 31 August 1777 near Egmond aan Zee while homeward bound from the Far East.

Packet Boat, 1707

Early in December 1707 a packet boat from Ostend, with troops, passengers and valuables, sank through stress of bad weather and all but twelve were drowned. Four English gentlewomen of the family of Blunt, returning from a convent, were among those lost.

Pegasus, 1598

The *Pegasus* was one of the ships included in the Earl of Cumberland's twelfth voyage, which was a privateering expedition against the Spanish. It was returning from the West Indies after looting Puerto Rico when it ran on to the Goodwins and was lost.

Peggy, 1774
The *Peggy*, Captain Thomas Boswell, en route from London to Leith was lost near Berwick on 3 December 1774. Charles Spalding, the well-known diver, was on board with what was said to be a very valuable cargo. He salvaged his own cargo from the wreck of the *Peggy*. He was to die some years later when salvaging the silver dollars from the wreck of the *Belgioso*.

Phaeton, 1800
On 7 January 1800 a Swedish brig called the *Phaeton*, en route from Cayenne to Göteborg, with gold and other valuables, was wrecked near Fraserburgh on the east coast of Scotland.

Piero Quirino, ship of, 1431
A Venetian ship sailing from Candia to Flanders was lost in the North Sea in 1431 with a highly valuable cargo. The survivors ended up on the Isle of Saints in Norway.

Pijlswaart, 1690
The *Pijlswaart* was a ship of the Dutch VOC belonging to the Hoorn Chamber, 134 feet in length, 600 tons burthen and with twenty-five cannon. It was returning from the Far East with a cargo valued at 112,502 guilders when it sank. Privately shipped jewels as well as porcelain could well have been part of the cargo. It was lost in the vicinity of the Shetlands.

Pilot Boat No. 19, 1940
On 10 May 1940 news reached Britain that the German army had invaded Holland and Belgium. In response the Admiralty gave orders for immediate sorties across the North Sea to destroy key strategic installations on the Dutch coast. Neville Chamberlain resigned as Prime Minister later that same day. Lt Commander John Younghusband, in command of the destroyer HMS *Wild Swan*, stationed in Dover harbour, was one of those to receive urgent orders. He was to embark Special Party B and make immediately for the Hook of Holland. Special Party B was a small contingent of demolition experts under the leadership of Commander J. A. C. Hill.

Commander Younghusband had been advised that magnetic mines had been laid earlier that same day by the Germans at the entrance to the port of Hook. His ship, as it approached land, was also attacked by a squadron of bombers. However, with the assistance of a Dutch pilot boat (*No. 19*), whose captain knew where the mines had been laid, and by the device of approaching at twenty knots down the wrong side of the marker buoys, *Wild Swan* was able to get in to the quayside. Hill's team quickly set their demolition fuses throughout the port and prepared to move on to the more important targets of Rotterdam and Waalhaven airfield. The problem was that German troops were already everywhere, streets were blocked, the civil administration was in chaos and the

promised transport failed to show up. Faced with no obvious alternatives, Hill decided to commandeer the pilot boat. He was busy loading his explosives on board when a naval cipher came through to the *Wild Swan* from the British Admiralty. It involved a sudden change of priorities. 'Dutch foreign minister states that there is a large amount of gold at Rotterdam. Estimated weight 36 tons. It is essential to get gold away tonight. Make all arrangements in cooperation with local authorities. Gold to be loaded in merchant ships or *Wild Swan* as convenient.' After a brief discussion between Hill and Younghusband it was decided that Hill would take the pilot boat to Rotterdam, some miles further inland, load the gold, bring it back to the Hook and tranship there onto the *Wild Swan*, for onward shipment across the North Sea. *Wild Swan* itself would have been too obvious a target for German bombs to make the voyage to Rotterdam. The pilot boat was less conspicuous. On the downside, however, it had no degaussing equipment and so was vulnerable to magnetic mines.

Hill took three of his men with him and left for Rotterdam at 8.15 that same evening. He arrived in Rotterdam around midnight to discover that the southern and eastern sections of the town were already controlled by German troops. It was only with considerable difficulty that he made his way to the Netherlands Bank. Once there, with the assistance of the Dutch Marines, the gold was loaded into three vans and transported through narrow backstreets to the dockside at Leckhaven where the pilot boat was still waiting. There were 200 heavy boxes each containing four ingots. The only place this quantity of gold could be stowed on such a small boat was on the deck.

Meanwhile, on board *Wild Swan*, Commander Younghusband was being kept busy. Soon after Hill had departed for Rotterdam, a group of senior Dutch military officers under the command of Major General J. W. van Borschot had arrived seeking a safe passage to England. They were tired and hungry having set out from the Hague at 5 a.m. that morning. They were taken on to the destroyer and fed. Bombs were still dropping, but Younghusband's main concern now was that the *Wild Swan* might be boarded by the enemy and overrun. Increasing numbers of German paratroopers were constantly descending out of the skies with the assistance of night-time flares. To make boarding more difficult Younghusband moved his ship some twenty feet from the dockside. At 2.15 a.m. he received an urgent message from British Naval Command requesting him to contact the Consul General in Rotterdam with the order to direct all British and Norwegian shipping to depart immediately as the situation on the ground was rapidly deteriorating. Younghusband successfully passed on the order. On enquiring whether the Consul General knew anything about the whereabouts of Commander Hill and *Pilot Boat No. 19* the reply was that they had no information. A later telephone call, however, to the Harbour Master at Rotterdam told him that the gold was being loaded at that very moment.

At around dawn on 11 May destroyers *Wyvern, Hyperion* and *Havelock* arrived with more demolition parties to support those who were already in action. Commander Hill and the pilot boat had, however, failed to put in an appearance which was causing considerable concern to those on board *Wild Swan*. Their worst fears were confirmed when at 7.45 a.m. Commander Younghusband received a message from the Dutch military that, on its return journey to the Hook, *Pilot Boat No. 19* had hit a magnetic mine just off the eastern end of Rozenberg Island. There had been a devastating explosion. Commander Hill and his three assistants had been killed instantly. Out of the twenty-two Dutch crew only three survived, all of them seriously injured.

Shortly before dawn on 12 May *Wild Swan* was ordered to leave port and patrol along the Dutch coast between the Hook and Ymuiden. On departure they were again attacked by German bombers diving almost vertically out of the sky. Four bombs missed their target by as little as thirty feet but in swerving to avoid them the *Wild Swan* was grounded on a sandbank. It got off again almost immediately but the ship had been badly damaged and developed what Commander Younghusband termed in his report 'condenseritis'. This did not prevent *Wild Swan*, however, from giving valuable assistance to a Dutch troopship, *Princess Juliana*, which had been heavily bombed when just off the Hook. The *Wild Swan* took off thirty men trapped in the bows of the troopship shortly before it went down and fished another ten out of the water.

There are conflicting versions of what happened to the gold that sank so spectacularly and fatally off the eastern end of Rozenberg Island. According to some accounts the Germans discovered its whereabouts and salvaged part of it during the war leaving the famous Dutch salvage company Smit Tak to pick up the rest when hostilities ended. Enquiries with Smit Tak themselves, however, suggest a somewhat different scenario. The initial reaction of their senior management was one of amazement that anyone outside an exclusive circle of Dutch and English officials should know anything about the lost gold. However, they also confirmed that they had carried out a highly secretive salvage operation on *Pilot Boat No. 19* as almost their first job after the war had ended. It was also claimed that the Germans had not recovered anything of the gold having been entirely unaware of its presence throughout the duration of hostilities. There still remains some dispute as to whether or not all the gold bars, some 800 in total, were picked out of the mud.

Pinnace, 1697
Early in the morning of Friday, 25 June 1697, Captain Price, together with a Mr Morice of Canterbury, an Exeter merchant called Mr Drew and a fourth gentleman, left the *Centurion* frigate that was moored lower down the River Thames, and set out in the captain's pinnace towards the city. The pinnace was manned by a crew of eight sailors. The captain and the merchants were anxious to deposit 18,000 guineas in gold at the earliest opportunity and had it in the pinnace with them. Unfortunately, at 2 a.m., the seamen rowing through London Bridge against the tide ran upon a pier. The boat was split open, all those on board drowned and the gold was lost.

Prince Consort, 1867
The *Prince Consort*, Captain Robert Parrott, was a British iron screw steamship, 623 gross tons, owned by Webster & Co. of Aberdeen and built by J. & G. Thomson of Govan, Glasgow, in 1858. On 10 May 1867 the vessel left Granton for Aberdeen with mail, sixty passengers and a general cargo. Conditions were foggy and at 5 a.m. the following day the ship went ashore on Hasman Rocks, close by Alton Rocks, Aberdeen. A number of valuables were lost, one passenger alone abandoning £300 of gold coin. There was no loss of life.

Princess, 1692
The *Princess* was a Dutch packet boat en route to Holland from Harwich in August 1692 when it disappeared presumed sunk. It was carrying specie.

Prinz Adalbert, 1915
The *Prinz Adalbert*, Captain W. Bunnemann, was a 9,050-ton German armoured cruiser built at Kiel in 1901. In June 1915 the Germans bombarded and later captured the important port of Libau (Liepājā, Latvia) from the Russians. On 23 October 1915, the *Prinz Adalbert*, after undergoing repairs at Libau, was steaming westwards in the company of two destroyers, when it was hit by a torpedo fired from the British submarine *E8* commanded by Lieutenant Commander F. H. H. Goodhart. The *Prinz Adalbert* sank very quickly and all except three men out of a crew of over 500 were lost. Since its sinking there have been persistent rumours that the *Adalbert* was carrying gold in its strongroom when it went down. The basis for these rumours is unclear.

Prophet Samuell, 1692
A richly laden West Indiaman, with a cargo that included some specie, sank at the buoy of the Nore in the gales of January 1692.

Pudding Pan Shoal Wreck, *c.* 200
Roman wreck with porcelain in Thames Estuary, see chapter 1 for further details.

Queen Charlotte, 1827

The *Queen Charlotte*, Captain Nicholson, was one of the Leith smacks that ran between London and Edinburgh. On 26 October 1827 coming from Leith she was in collision with the *Sylvan*. The two ships were off Lowestoft at the time and the *Queen Charlotte* sank very quickly in a depth of seventeen fathoms. The crew and passengers were saved. A quantity of valuables were lost with the vessel.

Raadhuis Van Enkhuizen, 1721

The *Raadhuis* was a Dutch VOC ship, 578 tons burthen, lost on 22 December 1721 on the Dutch coast when outward-bound with specie.

Red Lion, 1592

The *Red Lion* was an English ship with a very valuable cargo, including considerable treasure, which was lost on the Goodwins around 17 December 1592. The *Golden Lion* and the *St Peter* were also lost on the Goodwins around the same time. All three are thought to have been very richly laden. The *Red Lion* was partly salvaged by Richard Basset of Ramsgate at the time of loss.

Reigersbroek, 1738

The *Reigersbroek* was a Dutch VOC ship, belonging to the Zeeland Chamber, 600 tons burthen, Captain Elias Moeninx. It was wrecked in July 1738 on its homeward bound voyage from Ceylon (Sri Lanka), smashing against the Westkapelle Dijk, Zeeland.

Renate Leonhardt, 1917

The *Renate Leonhardt* was a German cargo ship sunk off Texel, Holland, on 23 August 1917 by British torpedo boats. The *Renate* had departed from Rotterdam en route to northern Germany in the middle of July 1917, but had stranded near Bergen aan Zee on 16 July 16. It then went into Ijmuiden for repairs and, commencing its voyage for the second time, it was torpedoed and sunk close to Den Helder. The world in general subsequently heard very little

about the *Renate* until 1953 when an article appeared in the respectable shipping and commercial publication called *Fairplay* describing a proposal to salvage 454 cases of gold, supposedly shipped on the *Renate*, weighing a total of seventeen tons. The evidence for the gold was almost entirely hearsay. A stoker, who had deserted the ship in Ijmuiden, because he had a bad feeling about it, claimed to have been told about the presence of the gold by the second engineer. Also a fisherman called de Vries had apparently boarded the *Renate* after its initial stranding and been told by a young woman that there was gold on board. This same young woman was apparently one of those who was to be drowned in the later torpedoing. In 1953 a prospectus was put before the Dutch public, seeking out investors to subscribe funds for the raising of the gold. The would-be salvors had designed a caisson, similar to that used on the *Lutine* wreck, to be hoisted over the *Renate* and lowered down. The clinching piece of evidence supplied by the would-be salvors in their prospectus was provided by a water diviner, who claimed to have a definite reading signifying a large quantity of gold being present when taken by boat over the wreck. It seems the credulity of investors, when a 10,000 per cent return on their original stake is dangled before them, is almost limitless. There is no evidence that any gold was ever salvaged or even that the caisson was ever put into position, although the gold story did continue to resurface in the press several times during the 1950s. The *Renate* was carrying 1,600 tons of coconut butter.

Renswoude, 1703

The *Renswoude* was a Dutch VOC ship belong to the Amsterdam Chamber, 588 tons burthen, Captain Lendert de Haan. It was lost on 13 December 1703, outward bound on its maiden voyage, at Ameland on the Dutch coast

Resolution, 1666

The *Resolution* was a third-rate English warship, Captain Willoughby Hannam, 885 tons burthen, built at Ratcliffe on the Thames, and equipped with fifty-eight guns, all of them bronze. It was burnt in the vicinity of the Thames Estuary at the St James' Day battle of 25 July 1666 during the second Anglo-Dutch War.

Rijnenburg, 1713

The *Rijnenburg* was a Dutch VOC ship, belonging to the Amsterdam Chamber, Captain David Brouwer, 618 tons and twenty-five guns. It departed from Texel on 9 March, outward bound en route to Batavia (Jakarta, Indonesia), and on 15 March it struck on a reef off Mu Ness, Unst. It carried the usual cargo of silver coin, much of which was salvaged soon after the loss. There was a subsequent dispute between the Earl of Morton, who had the right to wreck in the Shetlands, and the

Dutch East India Company, over what should be a reasonable payment for his expenses and share of the salvaged goods.

Riksapplet, 1676
The Swedish warship *Riksapplet* sank in 1676 close by Dalaro, south-east of Stockholm. Some bronze cannon were salvaged in the 1920s

Riksnyckeln, 1628
The Swedish warship *Riksnyckeln* was wrecked during a storm in September 1628 off Viksten Island, close to the Stockholm archipelago, with the loss of nineteen lives. It was returning from Gdansk to Sweden. The ship had been built in 1617 at Vastervik and carried about twenty-six bronze cannon. Four cannon were raised at the time of loss. In 1920 it was rediscovered by fisherman and four more cannon were raised and sold. In the late 1960s there was an archaeological excavation and four further bronze cannon were located and raised including one superb piece, manufactured in Danzig in 1525, with the macabre inscription, 'I am Evil Grete, inexhaustible, XII sisters were cast in Danzig in 1525.' (Translation courtesy of Bengt Grisell, Royal Institute of Technology, Sweden.)

Rob, 1640
The *Rob* was a Dutch VOC ship lost during a storm in the roads of Texel on 5 January 1640. It was rediscovered by Hans Eelman in 1985 and a number of artefacts have been recovered.

Robert and John, 1701
The *Robert and John* was a rich ship from Guinea, which belonged to the Royal African Company, which was wrecked on the Goodwin Sands in October 1701, while carrying the usual return cargo, including gold and ivory.

Roman Ships, 55 BC
Some of Caesar's invasion fleet in 55 BC are thought to have sunk off Walmer Castle. None of them have ever been located.

Rooswijk, 1740
The *Rooswijk* was a Dutch VOC ship, belonging to the Amsterdam Chamber, 850 tons burthen, Captain Daniel Rousiers. It was en route from the Texel to Batavia (Jakarta, Indonesia) when on 9 January it wrecked on the Goodwins. It carried the usual outward-bound cargo including specie.

Royal Adelaide, 1850
The *Royal Adelaide*, Captain J. Batty, was a side-wheel paddle steamer, gross tonnage 450 tons, owned by the Dublin Steam Packet Company. It left Cork on 27 March en route to London with a crew of twenty-four and a cargo of horses and cattle. It called at Plymouth where it took on twelve passengers. On the evening of

30 March during a severe gale the *Royal Adelaide* was seen by a passing barque, stranded on Tongue Sand off Margate firing signals of distress. The pilot on board the barque later stated that the weather was so bad that he was unable to render help but that it also sent up signals to alert those on shore. However, the weather conditions continued to be poor so that it was nearly another forty-eight hours before help arrived, by which time the *Royal Adelaide* had broken in two and sunk and all on board had drowned. Subsequently there has been much speculation that the *Royal Adelaide* was carrying a cargo of gold when it sank, some commentators mentioning sums as large as £300,000. *Lloyds List* mentioned gold but also reported that the divers that were sent down were unable to find anything. The disaster prompted the Margate boatmen to purchase a lifeboat.

Royal James, 1672
The English warship *Royal James* was lost during the battle of Solebay off Southwold. See chapter 5 for further details.

Royal Prince, 1666
The *Royal Prince* was a first-rate English warship that had originally been built by Phineas Pett at Woolwich in 1610 and had subsequently been entirely rebuilt twice, in 1641 and 1663, by Phineas's son and grandson respectively. In its final incarnation it was 1,432 tons burthen and equipped with ninety-two bronze guns. On 1 June 1666 George Monck, Duke of Albemarle, in command of the English fleet, was heading back towards the Thames to join with a few badly needed extra ships that were waiting there, when he sighted the Dutch fleet under Admiral de Ruyter and chose to give battle straightaway, against the advice of his subordinate commanders. The Dutch had an advantage at this stage of eighty-four ships against fifty-six. A large part of the English fleet had already been previously detached, under the command of Prince Rupert, in order to waylay the French fleet, which was thought to be approaching up the Channel to join with the Dutch. The Dutch and the French were on this occasion allies. Two days of extremely bloody encounters followed with both fleets ranging across the North Sea between the North Foreland and the Flemish sand banks. During the night of 2 June, the wind, which had been blowing from the south-west, changed to the east, and Albemarle, having lost the advantage of the wind, chose to head back towards the English coast. The winds, however, were very light and from eight on the Saturday evening until eight on the Sunday morning the English fleet, which now consisted of only thirteen ships, the remainder having scattered widely, only made two miles an hour. At midday on the Sunday the master on board the *Royal Prince*, George Fairbrother, made an observation on the sun and was concerned that on their present course they ran the risk of ending up on the Galloper

Sands. He suggested altering course to west-by-north and discussed the matter with Admiral Sir George Ayscue who was on board the *Prince* and was Admiral of the White Squadron. Ayscue was sufficiently alarmed that he immediately went in a boat across to the *Royal Charles* where a consultation was held. George Monck who was on board the *Charles*, and who was in overall command, was insistent that they should remain on a WSW course. He had sighted another fleet in that direction, thought it might be Prince Rupert returning from the Channel, and was understandably anxious to link up with him at the earliest opportunity. He also had a pilot from Deal on board who assured him that they would be safe on their present course.

The fleet that they had sighted to the south-west was indeed that of Prince Rupert. The rumour about the French fleet having entered the Channel turned out to be based on false intelligence. The French were not even at sea. But George Fairbrother had also been correct. Between George Monck and Prince Rupert was the dangerous Galloper Sandbank. At around 5 p.m. on the Sunday afternoon four of the English first-rate warships struck. The *Royal Charles* was the first to hit, rapidly followed by the *Royal Prince*, the *Royal Katherine* and the *Royal Oak*. They were all sailing in line about a cable's length between them. The disaster could have been worse than it was. With the Dutch fleet following close behind they could all four have been sitting ducks. As it was only the *Prince* remained stuck fast, the others coming off very quickly. The tide was a quarter flood. Later reports identified the *Prince* as having struck the tail of the Galloper Sands.

The Dutch quickly took possession of the *Royal Prince*. At the court martial that was held afterwards there was some heated discussion about why those on board the *Prince* did not put up more resistance. Sir Joseph Jordan and Sir Thomas Tiddeman when examined said, 'they thought the flag struck too soon, upon a fright, without any resistance.' However, the surviving officers claimed that it was impossible to do anything other than surrender. Large numbers of men had taken to the boats, the ship had heeled over making it impossible to fire the guns, and the rest of the English fleet had already sailed on into the distance. Sir George Ayscue, when asked by some of his men to surrender, had apparently replied, 'do what you will,' though in other versions he is said to have denied all knowledge of the lowering of the flag. The man who actually struck was identified only as 'a waterman living at Lambeth, a yellow haired man.'

Once in possession, the Dutch hastily removed the easily portable valuables such as Sir George Ayscue's silverware, then abandoned the ship and set fire to it. The pillaged tableware, including biscuit boxes, sugar bowls and candle sticks, has survived and can be seen today in the Scheepvaartmuseum in Amsterdam. Interestingly, some of the items still have Ayscue's coat of arms, while others have the coat of arms of Isaac

Sweers, one of Dutch officers involved in the capture of the *Prince*. Ayscue was taken prisoner and kept for some years in a Dutch gaol. Usually prisoners of war at this time were quickly exchanged but the Dutch were keen to hang on to Ayscue regarding him as something of a trophy. The English press claimed he was kept in a cage and generally humiliated but there is, in fact, no evidence for such ill-treatment.

Royal Transport, 1714
The *Royal Transport*, Captain Hutchinson, was a Russian warship, wrecked with valuables on the coast of Sweden near Maarstrand.

Russian Ship, 1721
An unnamed Russian warship, fifty-four guns, Captain Michecoff, was wrecked on the island of Osel coming from Holland. Valuables were lost with the ship.

Russian Warship, 1721
An unnamed Russian warship lost off Helsingfors in 1721 was believed to contain gold according to various reports in the *New York Times* in 1935.

Russian Frigate, 1760
An unnamed Russian frigate with valuables was lost at the beginning of December 1760 between Drondheim (Trondheim) and Bergen on the Norwegian coast. Only fourteen men were saved out of a crew of 140.

St George, 1811
The *St George* was a second-rate British warship, 1,950 gross tons, and equipped with ninety-eight cannon. It was built at Portsmouth in 1785 and was very similar in structure to Nelson's ship *Victory*. When Nelson served on the *St George* at the battle of Copenhagen, however, he described the ship as being 'in a truly wretched state ... the water comes in at all parts and there is not a dry place or a window that does not let in wind enough to man a mill.' It probably was not in a much better state in 1811 when it was the flagship of Rear Admiral Reynolds, who was in charge of a convoy of 130 merchant ships from Sweden, carrying the usual supplies from the Baltic which were vital to the fitting out of the Navy, namely wood,

iron, tar and copper. The convoy left Hano Bay near Matvik in Sweden on 9 November 1811. It ran into a storm in the vicinity of Bornholm Island and the *St George* received some severe damage, particularly to the stern area and the rudder. It made it back into Göteborg Harbour where temporary repairs were carried out. It was in Göteborg that Sergeant William Galey of the Royal Marines wrote a letter to his wife that was later to be published in the pages of the *Naval Chronicle*. In it he described what he called the 'perfect hurricane' that they had come through with great vividness and he closes in a light hearted if also slightly apprehensive mood. 'We shall sail for England with the first fair wind. We have a fine ship to drag us along – the new *Cressy* – so that when we arrive to England the people may say – "Here comes old St George like a child in leading string." I resign myself, however, to the Almighty Disposer of all things, and doubt not that we shall arrive safe in England soon after your receipt of this.'

On 17 December the *St George*, with those of the convoy that still survived, again departed Sweden. Off Jutland they again ran into severe gales with fierce winds from the north-west. The *St George* in its damaged state laboured badly. The *Cressy* and the *Defence* were ordered to stay in company while the rest of the fleet stood out to sea and headed straight for England. The situation on board continued to deteriorate and on 23 December the *St George* drove ashore and was very soon swamped by huge waves that washed most of those on board to their death. Out of 865 people on board only twelve survived. The *Defence* was also wrecked two miles further to the north. Again the death toll was horrific. Only six survived out of approximately 560 on board. It was one of the worst human disasters in the history of the Royal Navy. Of the three separated ships only HMS *Cressy* managed to claw its way out to sea again. Nor was that the worst of it. HMS *Hero* was also wrecked in the same storm though some way further south, at the Texel in Holland. Again the death toll was enormous, only eight surviving out of 550. In total around two thousand sailors had been lost on that single voyage.

As soon as the storm had abated the business of salvage started. One eighteen-pounder gun still on its wooden gun carriage was washed ashore, which demonstrated the extraordinary violence and power of the storm. Other guns were pulled out of shallow water, but the *St George* had ended up in such a remote position that the salvaged cannon were just abandoned on the beach. The wrecks quickly became forgotten. In 1876 there was a brief foray by some divers using helmets and some ordnance was brought up, together with the bell from the *St George*. It now hangs in a local church. In 1904 there was a renewed and more serious effort. The motivation behind both attempts was the recovery of £500,000 of gold that the *St George* was supposed to have been carrying when it went down. There were further salvage sorties during World War II and again in 1970, but no treasure was discovered. It is difficult to think why the *St George* should have been carrying such a large quantity of gold. There was probably some ship's money aboard but it is unlikely to have amounted to very much.

In 1980 heavy storms exposed what remained of the wreck and it was decided by the Danish authorities to excavate it before it was further destroyed by the forces of nature. The wreck was carefully mapped and then over the following six years a fascinating collection of artefacts was recovered. These included numerous humble items that provide an insight into the life of an ordinary mariner of the period, such as the stack of unused shoes, regulation issue, which did not distinguish between the left and the right foot. The shoe came to fit the man through wear rather than design. More poignant perhaps were the numerous wooden tags with names inscribed such as Blow, Birch and Lucas. The tags would have been attached to their bags that held their few belongings. The bags and the belongings have disintegrated leaving only the names behind. There were also numerous more glamorous items recovered that had belonged to the officer class, such as a cutlass with a gilded lion's head made by Prosser of Charing Cross, London, an extensive collection of bottles for port, champagne, claret and gin, and a very distinguished tobacco pipe made from porcelain and brass. There was also treasure of a kind though not quite in the form originally anticipated by generations of previous salvors. A number of the officers had acquired considerable amounts of prize money in previous engagements and some of this money had clearly been used to buy luxury items, mainly of Swedish origin, such as a beautiful chandelier that has been magnificently restored to its original condition and a pair of black porphyry stone vases, the latter valued at around £100,000 at the time of excavation. The recovered artefacts can be seen at the Thorsminde Museum, which is close to the place of the original wreck.

San Agustin, 1639

The *San Agustin* was a large Spanish warship carrying fifty-nine bronze cannon, the Vice Admiral of a Spanish treasure fleet heading for the Spanish Netherlands with 3 million escudos in money for the army. In a sea battle with the Dutch, in which the English were caught in the middle, and which was largely fought out in the vicinity of the South Foreland, a number of Spanish ships were sunk. The *San Agustin* ran ashore on 21 October 1639, between Walmer Castle and the village of Kingsdowne and sank three or four days later. Most of the treasure had been transhipped before the sea battle began. Other ships lost were the *El Pingue*, sunk in the Downs, the *Orfeo*, lost on the Goodwins, the *Santo Cristo de Burgos* lost on the French coast, and the *San Carlos* and the *San Juan Bautista*, place of loss not specified.

San Felipe, 1588

The *San Felipe*, forty bronze guns, commanded by Don Francisco de Toledo, captain, Juan Pozas de Santiso, was by 8 August in the southern North Sea, stranded at the end of the Spanish line of battle. Early on in the day it ran out of cannon shot and was immediately surrounded by numerous English ships that poured cannon fire into it at close range. The Spanish tried to grapple but the English avoided boarding, preferring to inflict damage with gunfire. At around 7 p.m. the *San Felipe* signalled for help. The *Doncello* hulk approached and took off the men but both the commander and the captain refused to leave. They drifted in company with the *San Mateo* onto the shoals of Nieuport.

San Juan Bautista, 1803

This ship was a sixty-ton Spanish brigantine. It sank in the Downs on the 25th December 1803, after crashing into a larger English ship. It was not possible to save anything of its valuable cargo, which included some specie.

San Lorenzo, 1588

On the night of 7 August the Spanish armada was at anchor in Calais Roads after three days of skirmishing with the English fleet. The Spanish Admiral in overall command, Medina Sidonia, was hoping that a meeting could be effected there between the fleet, and the Duke of Parma's invasion troops, the latter at present still in Flanders. France was neutral in this conflict and although the mayor of Calais did not exactly welcome the Spanish fleet in its roads he was happy to supply them with fresh provisions. Calais was not a very favourable port being subject to cross currents and surrounded by sandbanks as well as open to the winds, but Medina Sidonia was planning for Parma to embark his troops on small boats and make his way the thirty miles down the coast from Dunkirk to rendezvous with him, so that the battle fleet, still largely intact, could then escort the troop ships across the Channel. Unfortunately for Sidonia's plans the English sent in fireships that night which caused panic among the Spanish. As it happened none of the fireships found their targets but the Spanish fleet, taken by surprise, scattered widely and in the sudden pandemonium that followed, the giant galleas *San Lorenzo* was in a collision and lost its rudder.

At dawn the following day, Lord Howard, the English Admiral, observing the stricken galleas, was intent on capturing it. Don Hugo attempted to ground his ship in the shallows where the English could not approach close enough to fire upon it with their ships' cannon. Unfortunately for the Spanish the galleas beached at such an angle that it was unable to deploy its own guns in self-defence. This left the English free to send in boarding parties in boats. A fierce small-arms battle followed which lasted some hours until Don Hugo was killed, at which the Spanish fled

ashore. Just when the English thought they had possession of the galleas, however, the French opened fire on them from the ramparts of Calais and so the English were forced to abandon their hard won prize to the French.

San Luis, 1615

In 1615 the *San Luis*, the flagship of Diego Brochero, one of four galleons escorting fifteen merchant ships, with troops on board for Flanders, was lost entering Dunkirk. It carried a considerable quantity of money.

San Mateo, 1588

By 8 August 1588 the Spanish Armada had reached the southern part of the North Sea between the Goodwins and the sandbanks off Belgium. The battle between the English and the Spanish was probably at its fiercest on this day. The *San Mateo* with thirty-four bronze guns went to the assistance of the *San Felipe* which was on the leeward or eastward wing of the Spanish fleet and in difficulties, surrounded by English ships pouring shot into it. The *San Mateo* itself became equally embroiled and soon ran out of shot. After this it drifted helplessly towards the Flemish Banks off Nieuport in Belgium. Medina Sidonia, the Spanish admiral in command, sent a pinnace to take off the men but the captain of the *San Mateo*, Don Diego de Pimentel, refused to leave his ship, asking only for a diver and a pilot to be sent him. The latter never arrived and the *San Mateo* drifted onto the Nieuport Sands and wrecked. The Museum of Lakenhal in Leiden has a remarkable fragment of a pennant taken from the wrecked *San Mateo* which shows a crucified Christ.

Sankt Mikael, 1747

The *Sankt Mikael*, a galliot about eighty feet long, was probably Russian-owned, but was captained by a Dutchman called Carl Amiel. It sank off Borsto Island, Finland, in 1747 while on a voyage from Amsterdam to St Petersburg, Russia. It was discovered by amateur divers in 1954 and a large number of valuable artefacts were recovered including gold jewellery and other items, all destined for the wealthy Russian market, and so carried as trade goods not personal possessions.

Santa Teresa, 1639

A very large Portuguese ship, nearly 2,000 tons burthen, built in Lisbon by Bento Francisco and part of the Spanish treasure fleet which was heading for Holland when it was intercepted by the Dutch. The Spanish put into the Downs and sought protection from the English but Charles I prevaricated and in the end his navy under Admiral Pennington stood by and observed helplessly as the Dutch attacked in English waters. The *Santa Teresa* blew up and sank in deep water off the South Foreland on 21 October 1639. Over 800 men were on board at the time and all perished. The ship had on board sixty bronze cannon plus other valuables.

Scarborough Wreck, 1314

A very valuable ship was driven ashore during a storm near Scarborough in September 1314. Gold florins, jewels and silver in bar form were included in the cargo. All those on board were drowned and some of the bodies washed ashore at Ryxton. There was some pillaging of silver.

Schiedam, 1625

The *Schiedam* was a Dutch VOC ship lost in the Roads of Texel.

Sedgemore, 1689

The *Sedgemore*, Captain David Lloyd, was a fourth-rate Royal Navy ship, having fifty cannon on board. On 2 January 1689 the ship was anchored off Dover having taken on supplies. A strong wind beginning to get up, the pilot on board persuaded the officer in charge, Lieutenant Thomas Bulkeley, to weigh anchor. The captain at the time was on shore. Unfortunately, with the wind increasing and dense snow making visibility poor, the ship drove onto the coast in St Margaret's Bay, near Dover, and was wrecked. It has been suggested that a very large quantity of bullion was on board when the *Sedgemore* wrecked, but the source for the rumours is vague. It seems likely that if there was any treasure it would have been salvaged.

Sir Theophilus Biddulph, Wreck of, 1663

In August of 1663 a ship with Sir Theophilus Biddulph on board was lost in the Downs with valuables.

Snape Wreck, c. 600

The Snape wreck is a Viking burial ship, similar to the Sutton Hoo find, and excavated in the 1860s by Septimus Davidson. The Snape Ring, onyx set in gold, comes from this site.

Soe Roderum, 1775

On 12 January 1775 a large Danish ship called the *Soe Roderum* (the Corsair), Captain Neils Mochrum, 500 tons burthen and carrying forty cannon put into the Bay of Sandwich in the southern Shetlands for shelter from a storm. It was en route from Copenhagen to St Croix or Santa Cruz in the West Indies. On 16 January the storm worsened, the *Soe Roderum*'s anchors gave way, and the ship was driven onto the lee shore near the church and close by the house of the local laird called John Bruce. The crew on board, who in one report are stated as numbering thirty, were all saved with the active help of the local inhabitants, who risked their own lives in the rescue. One version of what happened claims that twelve local people were drowned in attempting a rescue. The cargo, which was very valuable, and which included tea, porcelain and silks, was almost entirely lost. The supercargo on board, who was responsible for the shipment and eventual sale of the cargo, was called Peter Tutein. The

cargo carried had clearly originated in the Far East and, as was quite common in this period, after being brought to Europe, was being shipped onwards to a colonial outpost in a different part of the world. According to local legend part of the tea carried was thrown up onto the sand in large heaps like seaweed and the local people, not familiar with tea, boiled some of it, threw away the water and ate the leaves. In the same storm a dogger of 200 tons from Archangel and another of sixty tons from Amsterdam were also wrecked in the Shetlands. The captain and the crew of the *Soe Roderum* returned to Copenhagen in a ship called the *Dolphin* with what few items they had managed to salvage from the wreck. News of the disaster was brought to the mainland by Captain Bruntholm of the *Lovely Jean* who arrived at Aberdeen on 1 February.

Another Danish West India ship, the *Christian den Syvende*, Captain West Bohn, was also lost in the Shetlands the following year, on 1 December 1776, this time in the Voe of Symbister, Whalsay. The ship and cargo were totally lost. The captain, twenty-one seamen and six passengers were rescued. It seems highly probable that the *Christian* would have carried a similar cargo to the *Soe Roderum*, including tea, silks and porcelain. John Bruce Stewart was closely involved in the rescue of those on board the *Christian* and in their subsequent care and a grateful Captain Bohn later presented him with 'a very fine set of table china' which was intercepted by local customs as a result of a personal dispute between John Bruce Stewart and the local customs officer.

Solen, 1621

The *Solen* was a Swedish warship lost during a battle between Sweden and Prussia in 1627 that took place in Gdansk Bay, Poland. It contained a large number of bronze cannon, valuable artefacts and specie. It was relocated and salvaged between 1969 and 1980 and some of the recovered artefacts are in the Gdansk Maritime Museum, Poland including a superbly carved knight's head.

Somali, 1941

The *Somali* was a steel screw steamer, 6,809 gross tons, built by Harland & Wolff in 1930 for the Peninsular & Oriental Steamship Company. It was en route from London to Hong Kong via Methil when it was bombed by German aircraft and badly damaged. It was then taken in tow by a tug called *Sea Giant* but exploded catastrophically before reaching port. It sank one mile east of Snoop Head, Sunderland. Its cargo included eighty boxes of liquid gold, 1,616 carats of precious stones and 1,000 tons of lead soldiers. There have been recent attempts at salvage.

Sophia Magdelena, 1801

The Swedish East Indiaman, *Sophia Magdelena*, Captain Hanson, from China with a cargo which included 7,000 chests of tea as well as valuable porcelain, went ashore near Kingsdown on the South Foreland on 28 November 1801. The salvaged cargo was sold by public auction at Deal on 21 December, the remains of the ship itself fetching £307. This would imply that all the porcelain would have been salvaged. The brig *Anacreon* and the *Eugenie* sloop-of-war gave assistance.

Sosevig Wrecks, 1678
A group of Swedish wrecks were lost at Sosevig on the coast of Bornholm, Denmark. They carried gold specie, part of the payroll for the Swedish army. Nineteen ships sank in total. They were salvaged in 1978.

Spanderswoud, 1758
The *Spansderswoud* was a Dutch VOC ship, belonging to the Chamber of Amsterdam, 850 tons burthen, Captain Nicholas Pietersz. It was burnt in the roads of Texel while homeward bound.

Spanish Ship, 1690
A Spanish ship, name unknown, sank near Calais with a large quantity of silver ingots on board.

Spanish Ship, 1692
A Spanish ship, name unknown, sank at Kvitsoy near Stavanger in Norway. It was carrying silver at the time of loss. It has been recently excavated.

Speedwell, 1624
The *Speedwell*, Captain Chudleigh, en route from Flushing to London was lost off Flushing. Count Mansfeldt lost a large amount of money and other property.

Stadt Haarlem, 1676
The *Stadt Haarlem* was a Dutch galliot en route from Terschelling in Holland to Stavanger in Norway. It sank near Kvitsoy and has recently been excavated by the Norsk Sjøfartsmuseum, in conjunction with the Stavanger Sjøfartsmuseum. An interesting collection of clay pipes and ceramics as well as other artefacts has been salvaged.

Stirling Castle, 1703
The *Stirling Castle*, Captain John Johnson, a third-rate man-of-war, was lost on the Goodwin Sands during the great storm of November 1703. The *Restoration*, the *Mary* and the *Northumberland*, all Royal Navy ships, were also lost in the same area on the same night, that is, 26/27 November. Over 1,000 men were drowned from the four ships. In the 1970s the sands receded and the wreck of the *Stirling Castle* re-emerged into daylight after nearly 300 years of being covered. The ship was not carrying a treasure cargo at the time of loss but a large number of fascinating personal items as well as ship's fittings have

subsequently been recovered. The sands have now once again engulfed the remains. It is a protected historic wreck site.

Stockholm, 1745
The *Stockholm*, Captain Mathias Estbergen, was a Swedish East Indiaman, 900 tons burthen, armed with twenty-eight cannon, mainly iron. It was on a voyage from Göteborg in Sweden to Canton in China when on 12 January 1745 it wrecked during a snow storm near Braefield, Clumlie, Dunrossness, in the south of the Shetlands. All those on board were saved. The cargo included Bordeaux wines, lead ingots and navigational instruments as well as silver ingots and a considerable quantity of private trade. At the time of loss the *Stockholm* was sailing in company with another Swedish East Indiaman called the *Drottningen af Swerige* which was also lost. Both ships were scheduled to call in at Cadiz where they would pick up the bulk of their coin cargo. It was the normal system at this period for Swedish East Indiamen not to take on their coin cargo until they reached Cadiz. The wreck was extensively salvaged at the time of its loss. It has recently been rediscovered and designated an historic wreck site.

Sun, 1644
A Danish East India ship, the *Sun*, Captain Rytter, went ashore in the Downs when returning from the Far East. Details of the cargo carried are scanty but it may well have included gold and jewels.

Sutton Hoo, 625
Viking longboat excavated at Sutton Hoo on the river Debden in Suffolk in the 1930s was to reveal an amazing hoard of treasures. The wood of the vessel itself had entirely disappeared and even the bones of whatever bodies had been interred there were also gone, not through grave robbing but through decomposition as a result of the acidity of the soil. The boat, however, had left a ghostly and exact impression of its original structure in the sand. The original ship was over ninety feet long with a beam of sixteen feet amidships and it has been estimated that the stem and stern posts would have risen to a height of thirteen feet above the keel. The jewellery reveals an exotic mixture of influences, including German, Roman and Middle Eastern, suggesting that this quiet part of Suffolk was once part of a vibrant international trading community.

Svecia, 1740
The *Svecia* was a Swedish East India Company ship that had been built in Stockholm in 1736. It had a burthen of 600 tons, a length of 127 feet, was equipped with twenty-eight cannon and carried a crew of around 150 men. It sailed from Bengal with a cargo of silks, cottons, saltpetre and a special wood used in the dying process. The return voyage was a difficult

one over forty men dying en route. It was probably because of poor supplies and exhaustion that the *Svecia* called in at the island of St Thomas off the west coast of Africa. It was nearing the end of its long and tortuous journey that had originated in Japan, when it struck the hidden reef between Sanday Island and North Ronaldsay known as the Reefdyke. Details are scanty but it appears that when the ship hit there was a breakdown of discipline among the crew. Thirty-one of them seized the ship's boat and were fortunate enough to end up on Fair Isle about forty miles distant. Meanwhile, the captain, with some of his senior officers and merchants, hastily constructed a raft, and chests and other treasured items were loaded on to it, probably the perquisites of private trade. That raft was driven northwards by the tide and was dashed to pieces off Kirk Taing. All those on board drowned and all the possessions were lost. Another raft with thirteen men on it reached shore safely.

Some of the cargo from the ship later washed up on nearby beaches but the bulk of it remained unrecovered. The following year a salvage expedition was organised and a London diver called Evans came north with his boat called the *Dolphin*. The tides and currents, however, were too strong for him to work at the site of the wreck with any success. Attempts at further salvage were soon abandoned.

In 1975 the wreck was rediscovered by Rex Cowan, Terry Hiron, Peter Macbride and others and was carefully excavated over the next seven or eight years. In the 1980s divers from the Royal Navy were brought in to assist with the operation. A large and disparate collection of artefacts have been brought to the surface, including cowrie shells, navigational instruments, a wide variety of different textile remnants, pieces of dyewood, a few coins, ship's pottery and so on. Some of them can be seen in the Malmö Museum in Sweden and other items went to the Register House in Edinburgh.

Ter Nisse, 1720
The *Ter Nisse* was a Dutch VOC ship, 810 tons burthen, belonging to the Amsterdam Chamber, Captain Thielman Sterling. It was lost on 4 January 1720 near Eijerland, Texel.

Thomas Arundell Wreck, 1596
See chapter 3 for further details.

Tidore, 1683
The *Tidore* was a Dutch VOC ship, belonging to the Zeeland Chamber, 160 feet long, 1,094 tons burthen. On 27 September 1683 it was lost at Ameland on the return voyage with a cargo valued at 645,273 florins.

Tobias Leidsman, 1688
The *Tobias Leidsman* was a Dutch VOC ship, belonging to the Amsterdam Chamber. It was equipped with thirty cannon and sailed from the Vlie Island on 26 November 1688 en route to the Far East. It carried a cargo of silver specie. On 29 November it was wrecked at Hanglip in the Shetlands.

Tostig's Ships, 1066
In June of 1066 Tostig, son of Godwin, and the rebellious younger brother of King Harold, lost some of his fleet in the river Humber, having previously plundered the Isle of Wight of goods and money.

Tubantia, 1916
The *Tubantia* was built on Clydeside by the famous Scottish shipbuilding company of Alexander Stephen & Sons Ltd. It was 560 feet long with a gross tonnage of 14,053 tons and at a cost of approximately £300,000 was one of the most luxurious liners of the period. It was commissioned by the Dutch company Koninklijke Hollandsche Lloyd, based in Amsterdam, and it was launched on 15 November 1913 less than a year before the outbreak of World War I. It was intended to serve on the European South American run and was sumptuously fitted out. In particular it made extensive use of the great new ultra-modern power source – electricity. Electric lights and electric ventilation systems had been introduced on board ships several years beforehand but the *Tubantia* took the machine-age to a whole new level of inventiveness. Electric radiators were fitted in the cabins, electric dishwashers made life easier for the stewards, electric ironing machines and washing machines were deployed in the laundry room, and automated electric gadgets such as cigar lighters, equestrian exercisers, and even boot polishers were provided for the amusement of the well-heeled passengers. The most ostentatious demonstration, however, of electrical power was the giant illuminated sign hung between the two funnels which spelled out the name *Tubantia* and which could be seen at a great distance.

On Wednesday, 15 March 1916, the *Tubantia* set out from Amsterdam on its regular voyage to Buenos Aires in Argentina. Holland was neutral and so Dutch ships were theoretically permitted to sail the oceans without fear of attack from either of the belligerents. The ship, however, was almost empty of passengers. The elegant Verandah Café with its art-deco style of furnishings was deserted. The *Tubantia* had the capacity to carry 1,520 passengers but on board there were only eighty-seven in addition to the 294 crew members. Two years of war had caused a world depression in trade.

When about four miles east-north-east of the North Hinder lightship, and about fifty miles off the Dutch coast, the *Tubantia* was rocked by a sudden and violent explosion on its starboard side. It rapidly began sinking. The crew and passengers were all saved by three other vessels that were fortunately in the area, namely the *Breda*, the *Krakatau* and *La Campine*.

An immediate and vituperative slanging match broke out between the German and British press over who was to blame for this flagrant breach of neutrality. The Germans claimed that the sinking was the result of the *Tubantia* hitting a British mine. The British counter-claimed, saying that the loss was the result of a torpedo fired from a German submarine. At the inquiry into the sinking which followed most of the Dutch crew seemed to think that they had been hit by a torpedo which caused the German press to shift their argument. If a torpedo had been involved then it must have come from a British submarine not a German one. The problem the British press had in laying the blame on the Germans was to put forward a convincing motive for the sinking. There were nineteen German passengers on board. From a logical point of view there was no obvious reason why the Germans would wish to sink the *Tubantia* with some of their own citizens. This meant the only alternative explanation was incompetence. But it was difficult to believe that a German submarine could have mistaken the *Tubantia* for an enemy ship when its name was so brilliantly displayed in electric lights for all to see.

It was then ingeniously suggested by the British that the *Tubantia* was carrying a large quantity of valuable German securities that were desperately required in South America. The Germans, knowing that the British would confiscate them if they decided to search the ship, which they would almost certainly do, decided to sink them first, so that the securities could then be legitimately reissued in South America. Such a tortuous explanation may have been ingenious but it was a little too elaborate to be plausible. It may, however, have had something to do with the later association between the *Tubantia* and a valuable cargo of gold.

Meanwhile, a stray lifeboat from the *Tubantia* had been picked up with fragments of bronze metal in it. It was suggested that the metal may have come from a torpedo and as the Germans were the only ones to use bronze in their torpedo bodies the finger again seemed to point clearly in their direction. The Dutch vessel owners sent down divers to examine the wreckage. They came back with the definite opinion that the damage had been caused by a torpedo not a mine. In the face of the growing evidence against them the German authorities now offered compensation of £300,000. The Dutch, however, turned the offer

down on the basis that the *Tubantia* when sunk had been worth much more than its original building cost. The argument dragged on with the Germans eventually settling the matter in 1922 for an enormous £830,000.

All may have ended there if it were not for the fact that shortly after the conclusion of the compensation package a British company led by Major Sippe DSO began a salvage operation to recover what was claimed to be two million pounds' worth of German gold twenty-mark coins that had been on board at the time of loss. Major Sippe's original intention had been to keep his salvage operation entirely secret but in July 1923 a rival salvage enterprise headed by Count Landi also started work on the *Tubantia* with a view to recovering the alleged gold cargo. Major Sippe immediately went to the courts to seek an injunction. The case that followed was to become a landmark in salvage law because it established the principle of salvor in possession. As the Major's divers had found the wreck and commenced operations, and had every intention of continuing work on it, for which purpose he had buoyed it, he had the right to do so without fear of others muscling their way in.

Having seen off Count Landi, Major Sippe returned to the business of locating the *Tubantia*'s gold. This proved rather more difficult than winning the court case. The gold was reputedly stowed in hold number four, packed in wooden casks that had been listed on the manifest as containing butter. Operations, however, were extremely difficult. Large amounts of miscellaneous cargo had to be removed before hold number four could be properly penetrated. To make matters worse the currents were so strong it was only possible for the divers to work at times of slack water. At the commencement of the 1925 season and after already spending £100,000 on the project, Major Sippe brought in Captain Damant to provide an expert opinion. Damant had previously been involved in the highly successful, if painstaking, salvage of the gold on the *Laurentic*. His report on the *Tubantia* included the following: 'It is possible to reach the cargo in number 4 hold by crawling aft under certain overhanging plates and through a moderate sized aperture, and I have done so in company with Clear [one of Sippe's divers] and afterwards a second time alone. One finds oneself resting on soft mud through which can be felt various items of cargo; towards the forepart of the hold is undisturbed cargo rising above the mud.

'The space is constricted and the darkness absolute, for the movements of one's body fill the water with suspended mud through which no light, however powerful, could shine effectively. Thus, it is impossible for divers to accomplish useful work there. The roof of the hold is torn and probably quite unstable.'

This must have made dispiriting reading for Major Sippe. Damant concluded that Sippe's divers had made reasonable progress given the difficult circumstances. However, he considered that Major Sippe's basic concept of penetrating the *Tubantia* through its side was mistaken because it risked the almost certain collapse of the entire deck structure downwards. The only safe way to proceed was to dismantle the wreck from the top. He calculated that this would take a minimum of a further three year's work and that Major Sippe's present salvage ship was not large enough to support the weight of lifting gear that was required. Hardly surprisingly Major Sippe gave up the task. Numerous other entrepreneurs, however, were prepared to follow, including, pre-eminently, a Captain Wilson in the 1930s who deployed an iron-man diving suit.

No one to date has ever recovered any gold which does make one wonder what evidence Major Sippe possessed for gold being on board in the first place. A *Tubantia* cargo manifest, located in a Paris archive, refers to a standard if somewhat light Dutch export cargo which included such items as 2,000 crates of Dutch gin. Mention is made of ten casks of butter. It is not out of the question that this could be gold. Certainly, the British Admiralty was in the habit of sending gold around the world at this same period of World War I, listing it under such unlikely terms as 'boxes of nails' for reasons of security. However, it would be quite impossible to pack £2 million of gold at 1922 prices in only ten casks. Interestingly the Paris manifest does also make reference to the *Tubantia* carrying a large quantity of cut diamonds. Hardly surprisingly Mr Sippe's divers do not appear to have laid their hands on them during their operations. They would not be easy to find amid so much wreckage.

U534, 1945

The German submarine, *U534*, Captain Herbert Nollau, was one of the last German vessels to leave Germany before the allies took final control. Admiral Doenitz had already given the order for most of the U-boats to be scuttled. The *U534* was, however, detailed to go to Norway, still under German occupation, and it was rumoured to have been loaded with gold, drugs, secret documents and high-ranking German officials, all fleeing the allied invasion. It never made its destination, sinking close to the island of Anholt, Denmark, as a result of bombs dropped from an RAF Liberator aircraft. In October 1993 it was located and raised but none of the expected treasures were discovered.

Umgeni, 1917

The *Umgeni* was a British merchant ship, 2,662 gross tons, owned by Bullard King & Co. It left the Clyde, en route to Lagos in West Africa, with a cargo that included twelve boxes of silver coin, and was never

seen again. One report referred to it as having sunk north of the Shetlands but this seems widely at odds with its supposed route and it was more probably sunk north of Ireland.

Unicorn, 1567

The *Unicorn* was lost as a result of striking on a rock near the northern entrance to Bressay Sound. The rock has subsequently become known as Unicorn Rock. At the time of loss the *Unicorn* was in pursuit of the Earl of Bothwell in a ship called the *Pelikan*. On board the *Unicorn* was the Laird of Grange. The *Unicorn* is unlikely to be of much intrinsic value but would be of great historic interest. It has never been located so far as is known.

Valk, 1791

The *Valk* was a Dutch VOC ship, belonging to the Amsterdam Chamber, 600 tons burthen, Captain George Hebries. On 27 February 1791 it was wrecked on the banks of Yarmouth while outward bound.

Vasa, 1628

The *Vasa* was a 1,279-ton, Swedish warship, 170 feet long, equipped with bronze cannon and built in 1627. The vessel departed from Stockholm harbour on 10 August 1628 only to sink almost immediately as a result of being constructed in a top-heavy manner. Many of the cannon were salvaged in the years soon after the sinking. In 1961 the hull of the vessel was raised and was found to be in such a sound state that it floated without repairs. It has since been conserved and is now on permanent exhibition in the Vasa Museum in Stockholm.

Vejby Cog, 1380

The ship known as the Vejby cog, around forty feet long, was discovered by two teenagers in 1976 off the North Sjaelland coast at Vejby, thirty miles north-west of Copenhagen in only seven feet of water. A pewter plate and over one hundred fourteenth-century, English gold nobles (coins) were found at the site. The ship was identified as originally coming from the Gdansk area owing to the fact that two coins of that region were recovered from beneath the mast step, a common practice among shipbuilders, who put the coins there for luck.

Ven Island Wreck, 1658
A valuable wreck was lost off Ven Island, Denmark in 1658. It was heavily plundered in the 1950s but some of the artefacts can be seen in the Handel-og Sjøfartsmuseet, Kronborg, Denmark and the Orlogsmuseet, Copenhagen, Denmark.

Vigsø Wreck, *c.* 1400
In 1974 two remarkably beautiful bronze hand-washing ewers in the form of riders on horseback were discovered through dredging among the sand dunes at Vigsø in Denmark. It was thought that the ewers must have been relics of a shipwreck but no trace of the ship was found, probably because it had completely decomposed.

Viking Ship, 1323
A Viking ship was lost on the west coast of Norway in approximate position 65.50° North with the Lord Bishop Elect on board and a large quantity of money.

Vine, 1693
The *Vine*, an English packet boat en route from Holland to Harwich in early July 1693, with a valuable cargo including specie, met in her passage two French privateers. A battle followed which lasted six hours and eventually the packet boat sank. The Earl of Suffolk was among the passengers who drowned. Captain Stephens survived and arrived back in England on 22 July.

Vliegend Hert, 1735
The *Vliegend Hert* was a Dutch VOC ship. See chapter 9 for further details.

Vrouw Maria, 1771
The Dutch merchant ship *Vrouw Maria* was lost in the Baltic. See chapter 10 for further details.

Walcheren, 1667
The *Walcheren* was a Dutch VOC ship, belonging to the Zeeland Chamber, 170 feet long, 840 tons burthen, which during September 1667 was wrecked near the

Faroe Islands. It was on the return voyage from Batavia (Jakarta, Indonesia) to Holland and the cargo probably included porcelain and jewels.

Wapen Van Alkmaar, 1690
The *Wapen van Alkmaar* was a Dutch VOC ship, 160 feet long, 892 tons burthen, lost near the Shetlands while on a homeward voyage with a valuable cargo.

Wapen Van Amsterdam, 1613
The *Wapen van Amsterdam* was a Dutch VOC ship that was lost while entering into the Wad through the Amelander Gat.

Wapen Van Amsterdam, 1667
The *Wapen van Amsterdam* was a Dutch VOC ship lost on 19 September 1667 while on a return voyage from the Far East. The cargo included porcelain, jewels and a large quantity of gold. It was extensively searched for during the 1980s and 1990s but has not been located.

Wapen Van Vlissingen, 1670
The *Wapen van Vlissingen* was a Dutch VOC ship, 145 feet in length, 725 tons burthen, belonging to the Zeeland Chamber. It was lost on 26 November 1670 on the Goodwin Sands.

Watervliet, 1742
The *Watervliet* was a Dutch VOC ship, belonging to the Enkhuizen Chamber, Captain Gerbrand Swaag. It was lost on 5 May off Calais while outward bound with a cargo that included specie.

Weerestein, 1711
The *Weerestein* was a Dutch VOC ship, belonging to the Amsterdam Chamber, 240 tons burthen, Captain Jan Krijnebak. It departed from the Texel on 3 November 1711 and was lost soon after in the Shetlands on its outward-bound voyage.

Welsh Prince, 1941
The *Welsh Prince*, Captain H. M. Butlin, was a steel screw steamship, 5,148 gross tonnage, owned by the Prince Line. It was en route from London to New York, part of convoy F.N.71, when it was mined and broken in two. It sank in position 53° 23´ 40″ N, 0° 58´ 55″ E, or 110 degrees, 5 cables from no. 59 buoy, Spurn Head. All the crew were taken off safely. At the time of its loss it carried a large quantity of valuable silverware and antiques. Typical items on the manifest are a Coalport Swansea dinner service, about 1820, bought from Mr Roberts of the High Street, Camberley, in 1939 for thirty-one pounds, ten shillings, or a fine Derby sporting jug being shipped by Harold Davis of St James' London, valued at thirty-five pounds. The shipment also included large quantities of antique swords and pistols.

Wendela, 1737
The *Wendela* was a Danish East India Company ship that was wrecked at Fetlar in the Shetland Islands. It carried a large quantity of silver coin and at the time of loss it was regarded as one of the richest ships ever to be wrecked in the Shetlands. The famous eighteenth-century diver Jacob Rowe was involved in the subsequent salvage effort and in the years following the loss over three-quarters of the silver was brought up. Robert Stenuit rediscovered the wreck in 1972 and a large number of coins from different European mints were salvaged. It is thought that the diversity of coinage aboard most probably reflected the weakness of the Danish currency at the time of loss.

Wilhelm Gustloff, 1945
The German passenger ship *Wilhelm Gustloff* was lost in the Baltic. See chapter 15 for further details.

Woestduin, 1779
The *Woestduin* was a Dutch VOC ship, belonging to the Amsterdam Chamber, 1,150 tons burthen, captain Gerrit Berg. It was wrecked on 24 July 1779 off Zeeland between Norderrassen and Deurloo, on its homeward voyage with a cargo that would most probably have included porcelain.

Wolf Rock Wreck, 1335
One of the best and most valuable ships of the English fleet was lost on 1 July 1335 after striking Wolf Rock at the entrance to the Firth of Forth.

Wrangels Palais, 1687
The *Wrangels Palais* was originally built as a Swedish merchant ship but was taken into the Swedish Navy in 1669 and later captured by the Danes in 1677. On 23 July 1687 it was wrecked at Tapped Lamba Stack, in the Out Skerries in the Shetlands during thick fog. The captain was Jacon Roelack. At the time of loss it was convoying a Danish fleet of merchantmen on route to Iceland that were under threat from marauding Turkish privateers. It was rediscovered in 1990 and two bronze cannon were recovered. The remaining complement of iron cannon have been left at the site.

Yarmouth Wreck, 1607
A very valuable Scottish ship is recorded as coming ashore near Great Yarmouth in May 1607. Included in the cargo was a large quantity of silver coin.

Yarmouth Wreck, 1652
An unnamed ship with troops and pay money, en route to Scotland from London, was lost on the

Yarmouth Sands in 1652. Richard Pettock, commander of the *Hare* ketch was involved in the subsequent salvage of some of the specie.

Young Catherine, 1760
The *Young Catherine*, Captain Methuen, en route from Rotterdam to London, was lost on the Gunfleet Sand. Fifteen of the passengers and two of the crew were drowned. According to the *London Evening Post* there was on board at the time of loss 'a large quantity of silver for the East India Company, several bales of silk, and other rich goods, which are entirely lost'. Other reports mentioned 30,000 pieces of eight. There were extensive efforts at salvage afterwards but none of the cargo appears to have been recovered.

Zeepard, 1665
The *Zeepard* was a Dutch VOC ship, belonging to the Zeeland Chamber, lost on 28 October 1665 to the west of the Shetlands with a cargo that included specie.

Zeerobbe, 1640
The *Zeerobbe* was a Dutch East Indiaman that was leased to the Admiralty as a warship and formed part of Admiral Tromp's fleet. It would have been equipped with brass cannon. It sank in the Texel in 1640. The remains were relocated in 1988.

Zoe, 1857
The *Zoe* was a luxury yacht belonging to Lord Yarborough, 'most magnificently fitted up'. On the night of 24 May 1857 Lord Yarborough, aged 47, was aboard, partying with friends, including the Honourable W. Monson and Dr Duigan, RN, when the wind fell and the yacht drifted on to the Haisborough Sandbank and was wrecked. All those on board escaped in the yacht's boat. The yacht itself, however, with all its valuable contents was completely lost. The Yarborough family home was at Appuldurcombe, Brocklesby, Lincolnshire.

Zorg, 1795
The *Zorg* was a Dutch VOC ship, 142 feet long, 900 tons burthen, lost on its homeward voyage on 4 November 1795 close to Calais.

Zutphen, 1651
The *Zutphen* was a Dutch VOC ship, belonging to the Amsterdam Chamber, 550 tons burthen, lost on the Vlaamse Banken in the Scheldemond, on 6 May 1651.

Sources and Bibliography

ARCHIVES & MUSEUMS:
Algemeen Rijksarchief, Den Haag
Archives Generales du Royaume, Brussels
Archives Nationales, Paris
Bank of England Archives, London
Bibliotheca Pepysiana, Cambridge
Bibliotheque Nationale, Paris
Bodleian Library, Oxford
British Library, London
British Library, Newspaper Library, Colindale, London
Cambridge University Library
Cleveland County Archives
Department of Transport Marine Library Glasgow
   City Archives
Glasgow University Archives
National Maritime Museum Library, Greenwich
Guildhall Library (Lloyds Collection) London
House of Lords Record Office, London
Hydrographic Office, Taunton
Imperial War Museum, London
India Office Records, British Library, London
Koninklijke Bibliotheek, Den Haag,
Liverpool University Archives, Liverpool
Lloyds Register of Shipping, London
Merseyside Maritime Museum, Liverpool
Norfolk Record Office, Norwich
Powell, Cotton Museum, Kent
Public Record Office, Kew, London
Scottish Record Office, Edinburgh
Strathclyde Regional Archives, Glasgow
Trinity House Corporation, London
Tyne & Wear Archives, Newcastle

PERIODICALS AND NEWSPAPERS:
Annual Register
Archaeologia
Archaeological Journal
Antiquaries Journal
Bremen Handelsblatt
British Chronicle
Canterbury Journal
Diver
Domestick Intelligence
Flying Post
Gazette d'Amsterdam
Gazette de France
General Evening Post
Gentleman's Magazine
Hollandtse Mercurius
Impartial Protestant Mercury
International Journal of Nautical Archaeology
Journal of Commerce
Journal of Modern History
Journal of the Royal Asiatic Society
Kentish Chronicle
Kentish Gazette
Lloyd's List
Lloyd's Evening Post
Lloyd's Registers of Shipping
London Chronicle
London Evening Post
London Gazette
Maidstone Journal
Mariner's Mirror
Mercure Gallant
Morning Chronicle
Nautical Magazine
National Geographic
Naval Chronicle
Naval Review
Norfolk Chronicle
Norwich Mercury
Post Boy
Post Man
Proceedings of the Society of Antiquaries
Public Ledger
Public Advertiser
Sea Breezes
Sherborne & Yeovil Mercury
St James Chronicle
Subaqua Magazine
Times
United Services Magazine
Whitehall Evening Post

Sources and Bibliography

PRINTED BOOKS:

Ahlstrom, Christian: *Looking for Leads* (1997 Helsinki)

Ahlstrom, Christian: *Sjunkna Skepp* (1979 Stockholm)

Aitzema, L.van : *Vereenigde Nederlanden 1687-1692* (1698 Amsterdam)

Anderson, R.C.: *Journals and Narratives of the Third Dutch War* (1946 London)

Anderson, R.C.: *Naval Wars in the Baltic 1522-1850* (1910 London)

Allin, Sir Thomas: *The Journals*, 2 vols (1939 London)

Anderson, Joseph: *Orkneyinga Saga* (1873 London)

Askwith, W.H.: *History of Officers of Regiment of Artillery* (1900 London)

Atkinson, C.T.: *The Anglo Dutch Wars* (1908 Cambridge)

Balfour, J: *Annals of Scotland*

Bang-Andersen, A.: *The North Sea: a highway of economic and cultural exchange* (1985 Stavanger)

Benham, Harvey: *Once upon a Tide* (1971 London)

Benham, Harvey: *The Salvagers* (1980 Essex)

Bevan, John: *The Infernal Diver* (1996 London)

Boudriot J.: *John Paul Jones and the Bonhomme Richard* (1987 Paris)

Bound, Mensun: *Excavating Ships of War* (1998 Oswestry)

Bound, Mensun: *The Archaeology of Ships of War* (1995 Oswestry)

Bille, Clara: *De Tempel der Kunst of het Kabinet van den Heer Braamcamp* (1961 Amsterdam)

Blomefield, Francis: *History of Norfolk*, 11 vols (1805-10 London)

Bradford J.C.(ed): *Guide to the Microfilm edition of the Papers of John Paul Jones* (Cambridge 1986)

Brandt, Gerard: *Vie de Michel de Reuter* (1698 Amsterdam)

Brenton, E.: *The Naval History of Great Britain*, 5 vols (1823-5 London)

British Vessels Lost at Sea 1939-1945 (1976 Cambridge)

British Vessels Lost at Sea 1914-1918 (1919 London)

Brøgger, A.W.: *The Viking Ships* (1953 Oslo)

Bromley, J.S.: *Corsairs and Navies* (1987 London)

Bruijn, J.R., Gaastra, F.S., Schoffer, I.: *Dutch Asiatic Shipping in the 17th and 18th Centuries*, 3 vols (1979 Den Haag.)

Bruijn, J.R. and Gaastra, Femme S.: *Ships Sailors and Spices* (1993 Den Haag)

Burchett, J.: *Memoirs of Transactions at Sea ... 1688-1697* (1703 London)

Burnet, Gilbert: *History of his Own Times* (1850 London)

Calendar of State Papers, Domestic (various volumes)

Calendar of State Papers, Venetian (various volumes)

Calendar of State Papers, Far East & Colonial (various volumes)

Campbell, John: *Lives of the Admirals*, 4 vols (1742 London)

Charnock J.: *Biographia Navalis*, 6 vols (1794 London)

Chaudhuri, K.N.: *The English East India Company* (1965 London)

Chaudhuri, K.N.: *The Trading World of Asia and the English East India Company* (1978 Cambridge)

Clarke, J.: *The Life of James II*, 2 vols (1816 London)

Clowes, W.L.: *The Royal Navy*, 7 vols (1897-1903 London)

Colenbrander, H.T.: *Bescheiden uit vreemde archiven...* (1919 Den Haag)

Colledge, J.J.: *Ships of the Royal Navy*, 2 vols (1969 Newton Abbot)

Collins, Greenville: *Great Britain's Coasting Pilot* (1693 London)

Comfort, Nicholas: *The Lost City of Dunwich* (1994 Suffolk)

Cooper E.R.: *A Suffolk Coast Garland* (1928 London)

Crowhurst, P.: *The French War on Trade* (1989 Aldershot)

Dam, P. van: *Beschryvinge van de Oostindische Compagnie* (1976 Den Haag)

Davis, Robert H.: *Deep Diving and Submarine Operations*, 2 vols (1935 Tolworth)

Delgado, James P.: *British Museum Encyclopaedia of Underwater and Maritime Archaeology* (1997 London)

Dobson, Christopher; Miller, John; Payne, Ronald: *The Cruellest Night* (London 1979)

Drechsel, Edwin: *North German Lloyd Bremen, 1857-1970*, 2 vols (1994-5 Vancouver)

Duncan, Archibald: *The Mariner's Chronicle*, 6 vols (1805-1812 London)

Ehrman, J.: *The Navy in the War of William III* (1953 Cambridge)

Entick, John: *A New Naval History* (1757 London)

Evelyn, J.: *The Diary of John Evelyn* (1955 Oxford)

Ferguson, D.M.: *Shipwrecks of North East Scotland* (1991 Aberdeen)

Fernandez-Armesto, Felipe: *The Spanish Armada* (1989 Oxford)

Forbin, C.: *Memoires*, 2 vols (1730 Amsterdam)

Fortescue, J.W.: *History of the Army* (1899 London)

Fox, Frank: *Great Ships* (1980 London)

Franzen, A.: *HMS Kronan* (1981 Stockholm)

Gardner, Thomas: *A historical Account of Dunwich* (1754 London)

Geyl, Peter: *Netherlands in the Seventeenth Century*, 2 vols (1964 London)

Glamann, Kristof: *The Danish East India Company* (1970 Paris)

Gosset, W.P.: *The Lost Ships of the Royal Navy 1793-1900* (1986 London)

Greene, Kevin: *The Archaeology of the Roman Economy* (1986 London)

Grocott, Terence: *Shipwrecks of the Revolutionary and Napoleonic Eras* (1997 London)

Guerin, L.: *L'Histoire Maritime de France*, 6 vols (1859-63 Paris)

Hakluyt, R.: *The Principal Navigations, Voyages and Discoveries of the English Nation* 1903 Glasgow)

Harris, F.R.: *Life of Edward Montagu* (1912 London)

Harris, G.G.: *The Trinity House of Deptford 1514-1660* (1969 London)

Hayes Derek R.: *Wreck of the Invincible* (1985 Ludham)

Haythornthwaite, P.J.: *Weapons and Equipment of the Napoleonic Wars* (1979 Poole)

Hepper, David: *British Warship Losses in the Age of Sail, 1650-1859* (1994 Sussex)

Historical Manuscripts Commission, MSS Hatfield House

Historical Manuscripts Commission, MSS Duke of Rutland

Historical Manuscripts Commission, MSS Duke of Leeds

Historical Manuscripts Commission, MSS Finch

Historical Manuscripts Commission, MSS Bath

Historical Manuscripts Commission, MSS Dartmouth

Historical Manuscripts Commission, MSS Buccleuch and Queensbury

Historical Manuscripts Commission, MSS Le Fleming

Historical Manuscripts Commission, MSS Ormonde

Historical Manuscripts Commission, MSS Downshire

Historical Manuscripts Commission, MSS Hastings

Historical Manuscripts Commission, MSS Portland

Hocking, Charles: *Dictionary of Disasters at Sea During the Age of Steam*, 2 vols (1969 London)

Huntress, K.: *Checklist of Narratives of Shipwrecks and Disasters at Sea* (1979 Iowa)

James, William: *The Naval History of Great Britain*, 6 vols (1878 London)

Jarvis S.: *East Anglia Shipwrecks* (1990 Berkshire)

Jonge, de J.C.: *Geschedenis Nederlandische Zeewezen*, 5 vols (1860 Haarlem)

Kent, H.S.: *War and Trade in Northern Seas in the Eighteenth Century* (1972 Cambridge)

Koven R. de: *The Life and Letters of John Paul Jones* (nd London)

Lamb,H. & Frydendahl K.: *Historic Storms of the North Sea* (1991 Cambridge)

Larn, Richard & Bridget: *The Shipwreck Index of the British Isles*, 5 vols (1995-2000 London)

Laughton, J.K.: *Studies in Naval History* (1887 London)

Lavery, Brian: *The Arming and Fitting of English Ships of War 1600-1815* (1987 London)

Lediard, T.: *Naval History of England*, 2 vols (1735 London)

Lewis, A.R.: *The Northern Seas* (1958 Princeton)

Macready, Sarah and Thompson F.H. (eds): *Cross-Channel Trade Between Gaul and Britain in the Pre-Roman Iron Age* (1984 London)

Malo, Henri: *Les Corsaires Dunkerquois et Jean Bart*, 2 vols (1912-13 Paris)

Marcus, G.J.: *The Conquest of the North Atlantic* (1980 Woodbridge)

Martin, Frederick: *The History of Lloyds and of Marine Insurance in Great Britain* (1876 London)

McCormick, Donald: *The Mystery of Lord Kitchener's Death* (1959 London)

McDonald, K.: *The Treasure Divers* (1977 London)

Molen, S.J. van der: *The Lutine Treasure* (1970 London)

Morrison, I.: *The North Sea Earls* (1973 London)

Murray, Howard: *A King's Treasure Lost* (1999 Fife)

Norman, C.B.: *The Corsairs of France* (1887 London)

Ollard, R.: *Man of War: Sir Robert Holmes and the Restoration Navy* (1969 London)

Padfield, Peter: *Tide of Empires* (1982 London)

Parker, G.: *The Armada of Flanders and the Spanish Road* (1972 Cambridge)

Pepys, Samuel: *Samuel Pepys's Naval Minutes* (1926 London)

Pickford, Nigel: *Atlas of Shipwreck & Treasure* (1994 London)

Pickford, Nigel: *Lost Treasure Ships of the Twentieth Century* (1999 London)

Plat Taylor, Joan du and Cleere, Henry (eds): *Roman Shipping and Trade*, The Council for British Archaeology (1978)

Potter, T.W, and Johns, Catherine: *Roman Britain* (1992 London)

Powell, J.R.: *The Navy in the English Civil War* (1962 London)

Powley, Edward B.: *The Naval Side of King William's War* (1972 London)

Richmond, H.W.: *The Navy in the War of 1739-1748*, 3 vols (1920 Cambridge)

Robinson, M.S.: *Van de Velde, A catalogue of the Paintings of the Older and the Younger*, 2 vols (1990 London)

Roden, Hans: *Treasure Seekers*, translated by Frances Hogarth-Gaute (1966 London)

Rodger, N.A.M.: *Safeguard of the Sea* (1997 London)

Ronciere, Charles de la: *Histoire de la Marine* (1899 Paris)

Ronning, Bjorn R.: *Akerendam, The Story of the Runde Treasure* (1979 Oslo)

Rule, Margaret and Monaghan, Jason: *A Gallo-Roman Trading Vessel from Guernsey* (1993 Guernsey)

Schaefer, Thomas J.: *Battle of Flamborough Head* (1989 New York)

Schomberg, Isaac: *Naval Chronology* (1802 London)

Seller, J.: *The English Pilot* (1692 London)

Sourches, Marquis de: *Memoires* (1882 Paris)

Spalding, J: *History of the Troubles and Memorable Transactions of Scotland, 1624-1645*, 2 vols (Aberdeen 1792)

Starr, Chester G.: *The Roman Imperial Navy* (1941 New York)

Stow, John: *Chronicles of England* (1580 London)

Stradling, R.A.: *The Armada of Flanders* (1992 Cambridge)

Street, Sean: *The Wreck of the Deutschland* (1992 London)

Suckling, Alfred: *Antiquities of the County of Suffolk*, 2 vols (1846 London)

Sue, Eugene: *Histoire de la Marine Française*, 4 vols (1845 Paris)

Temple, C.R.: *East Coast Shipwrecks* (1974 Norwich)

Tennent, A.J.: *British Merchant Ships Sunk by U Boat in the 1914-18 War* (1990 Gwent)

Urquhart, James: *John Paul Jones bicentennial* (1982 Dumfries)

Walsh, J.E.: *Night on Fire* (1978 London)

Watkins, J.: *Memoir of the Duke of York* (1827 London)

Wiborg, Susanne & Klaus: *1847-1997, 150 years of Hapag Lloyd* (1997 Hamburg)

Wood, A.C.: *A History of the Levant Company* (1935 Oxford)

Index